School as a Journey

The Eight-Year Odyssey
of a Waldorf Teacher and His Class

Torin M. Finser

 Anthroposophic Press

The essay in the appendix "Educating for Creative Thinking: The Waldorf Approach" appeared previously in *Revision*, vol. 15.2, pp. 71–78, Fall 1992. It is reprinted with permission of the Helen Dwight Reid Educational Foundation, published by Heldref Publications, 1319 18th Street, N.W. Washington, D.C. 20086–1802. Copyright 1993.

Published in the United States by Anthroposophic Press
RR4, Box 94-A1, Hudson, New York 12534

Library of Congress Cataloging-in-Publication Data

Finser, Torin M., 1956–
    School as a journey: the eight-year odyssey of a Waldorf teacher
and his class / Torin M. Finser.
        p. cm.
    ISBN 0-88010-389-2 (paper)
    1. Waldorf method of education—Case studies.
2. Finser, Torin M., 1956– .   3. Teachers—United States—
Biography.   I. Title.
LB1029.W34F55   1994   94–35018
371.3'9—dc20   CIP

10 9 8 7 6 5 4 3 2 1

Contents

Acknowledgments

It is with deep appreciation that I recognize and thank the following individuals and organizations for their support and timely help with this book:

Christopher Bamford for suggesting the project, Dr. Judy Borrelli-Caldwell for her encouragement, vision, and thorough editing of the early drafts, Jill Fox for her proofreading and faithful assistance, Jeanne Bergen for her editing of the final copy, Patricia Moreell for her efforts towards the designation of this book as a 75th anniversary publication, Dave Alsop for the support of the Waldorf Schools Association of North America, The Waldorf Schools Fund, The New England Waldorf Teacher Training Council, my colleagues here at Antioch New England Graduate School, especially Dr. Heidi Watts, David Sobel, and Jim Craiglow.

This volume would not have been possible without the students and colleagues of the Great Barrington Rudolf Steiner School, who helped shape the experiences reflected in the following pages.

To children, parents, and teachers

seeking change in education

Preface

This book tells a personal story. It describes some of the events, highlights, struggles, changes, frustrations, and achievements of the journey with my class at the Great Barrington Rudolf Steiner School from 1982 to 1990. Although this narrative is based upon classroom experiences, the children's names have been changed to protect their privacy (however, I suspect some will enjoy decoding the fictitious names I have given them!)

The chapters that follow contain only a small sampling of my experiences over a period of eight years with the same group of children. The winnowing process was not easy, yet the passage of time, both in terms of my teaching and in regard to my own childhood in Waldorf schools, helped me clarify which aspects might be shared.

My hope is that, by participating in a personal account such as this one, readers—whether parent or prospective parent, teacher, or administrator—will be encouraged to reexamine existing practices of teaching, reflect on their personal philosophies of education, and explore alternatives for educating children. This book is an introduction in every sense of the word. Those who wish to do further reading are invited to explore some of the many resources offered by the Anthroposophic Press. Many works are listed in the footnotes.

This personal narrative cannot possibly represent all the dimensions of the Waldorf curriculum and the stages of child development as seen from the Waldorf point of view, or of Anthroposophy, the spiritual orientation that underlies it. In several instances, entire subjects have been omitted or are mentioned only briefly. The events and experiences that have been included are meant to illustrate particular aspects of Waldorf education, leaving room for the active imagination and interpretation of the reflective reader.

The pages that follow are also intended to stimulate a process of personal and professional renewal. This goal has guided me in the selection of the material and my choice of narrative style. My hope is that this book will point toward the remarkable healing potential of Waldorf education, both for today's children and for those teachers fortunate enough to journey with them.

1. Once Upon A Time

*T*here is a timeless quality about all beginnings, and so it is with this story. It was a cold, clear winter evening in early December, 1981. I found myself walking the field behind my home in Hillsdale, New York. The impressions of the day— mainly interactions with my eighth-grade students—reverberated in me as I walked; but what stood out above everything else was a brief visit I had made to the kindergarten that morning: I recalled the warm, rustic room (which had once been a barn), the simple wooden toys and beautiful fabrics, and especially the eager faces of the children looking up at me as they sat around the snack table. I saw joy, wonder, and excitement in those faces. Time stood still as I looked from one to another. I left the room feeling that the impressions had nourished me in a full and satisfying way.

Now in the snow-covered fields, I recalled images from those moments in the kindergarten. Who were these children? Where were they coming from, and where were they going? I had already taught foreign languages as a special-subject teacher and grades six through eight as a class teacher. Now I was considering the position of first-grade teacher, and the unforeseeable responsibilities connected with taking that group of kindergarten children through the grades. Could I really make an eight-year commitment? What about the children's deeper, hidden connections with one another and with me? Would we be able to work together?

As I pondered these questions, I remembered that Rudolf Steiner had spoken of the "imponderables" that can awaken and guide the inner life of the teacher.[1] I walked and pondered my imponderables, knowing that I could not hope for "answers" in the traditional sense. Yet I was yearning for a picture, some image to help carry me into my future teaching—something to sustain and enliven me through the years ahead.

I happened to lift my gaze from the snow to the clear night sky above. What splendor! There, right above me, arched a great expanse of starlit heavens. Through a frame of trees and a solitary cloud sparkled an especially bright cluster of stars. At that moment I was not at all concerned with which constellation I was seeing. The remarkable fact was that the stars in that group were sparkling at me! Where had I seen them before? The children! Yes, these stars reminded me of the children who had been smiling at me earlier that day, the children with whom I was meant to work—this was my constellation. This was my class! I had found them, and they had found me.

My feelings of joy and enthusiasm settled into reverence and deep respect as I retraced my steps homeward.[2] More was at work than I could understand. My decision to take a new group of children, this time for a full eight years, had been made with the help of stargazing. Yet in another sense I felt the decision was only partially mine. Perhaps that is the difference between making a "career decision" and responding to a vocation, or "calling."

It was not until some years later that I realized yet another aspect of this calling: the children who were to become my class had been born six years earlier (for the most part within a few months of one another), just at the time I had decided to begin my Waldorf teacher training. No wonder those stars had sparkled so brightly on that December night!

Before welcoming the first-grade children on opening day of the new school year, I needed to supplement my inner picture of them by consciously building relationships with their parents. To do this I made a series of home visits.

I had the luxury of spacing these out over the summer months. Consequently, they were relaxed, informal occasions. Yet they proved invaluable in terms of connecting with the children in the context of their own homes.

I was able to see each child's room, toys, decorations, and sibling interactions. I observed family dynamics, which helped form a personalized picture of the entering first-grader. Children at age six want to express what they experience of the world, and they rejoice when their teacher takes an interest in the small things that matter so much to them both in and out of school.

My first visit was to Doug's home. He was playing ball with his older brother when I arrived. When Doug saw me, his vigorous play changed to a shy, respectful greeting. This image impressed me deeply. In later years, I always felt I had recourse to the "gentleman" within the rowdy athlete. Once inside Doug's house, I had a warm, hospitable conversation with his parents. I also visited his room, which at the time was strewn with playing cards from a mysterious new game that Doug had invented himself.

Susan lived in a big, white, newly redecorated house. My strongest memory of this visit was the way in which her mother described how Susan had loved to sing as a young child. In addition to all the other information about her early years—the parents' separation, her sister, and so on—the emphasis on Susan's musicality helped me in the years to come. With her big eyes, her wide-awake consciousness, and her many, many questions, she gave me a special task: to become a "music" teacher in a larger sense. I wanted to help her find inner harmony and security.

Abbie disappeared soon after I arrived at her country home on a hill. Her mother seemed relieved to be able to have a long, uninterrupted conversation with me. As we sat at the kitchen table, we talked about Abbie's birth, her early years, and her role as the youngest of three exceptionally bright children. In the back of my mind the question kept lurking: Where is Abbie? Because this family homestead seemed a safe place for a child to play, I dismissed my anxiety and refocused on our adult conversation. As I was leaving, Abbie reemerged. She had brought me a present. While her mother had been so conveniently engaged, Abbie had pulled up every carrot in the garden as a present for her teacher. We were overwhelmed.

The "carrot connection" theory of child development was reinforced during my visit to Mary's. She was chronologically young for the entering class. Although she would not be six until October, she had lost several teeth—for most Waldorf teachers a better indication of maturity than calendar months and days.[3] Should she remain in kindergarten another year, or enter first grade? Her doctor had noticed an especially rich imaginative life and felt she was ready to be challenged by first-grade work. The clincher for me, however, was when I heard that Mary had wandered into the neighbors' yard and —you guessed it! She too had pulled up some prized carrots. I began to think that Piaget may have missed something. Mary, Abbie, and Peter Rabbit did not.

The above are four glimpses into the twenty-three home visits I made that summer. These visits set a precedent for teamwork. The parents had much to tell me. The education of their children was a joint undertaking, one that in this day and age cannot be fully successful without the cooperation of all the adults concerned. In the early years, the children were often "charmed" by the curriculum and the activities of the classroom, but as this effect lessened in the middle-school years, the foundation prepared through parent-teacher teamwork proved to be essential. In the end, the quality of the relationship is what holds people together. Education is about relationships, yet so often the dynamic is skewed too far in favor of institutions, or just the relationship between teachers and children. I encourage teachers and parents to give themselves permission to work together. I also found it to be more fun that way.

The first day of school was anticipated by many—and perhaps dreaded by a few. It was the journey's beginning.

I later learned (from her mother) that Margaret had left home that morning with the serious intent of going to school to learn how to read. This determination and clarity were typical of Margaret throughout the years that followed. However, as she came into the kitchen after her first day at school she declared: "I haven't learned how to read yet!" If we had not taught Margaret how to read, what had we done that day?

The classroom had been thoroughly prepared for the first-graders' arrival. Their wooden desks had been sanded and polished; name cards, painted with watercolors, adorned the front of each desk. A coat hook similarly identified awaited each child as well. Hardy geraniums (a staple in many classrooms) had been placed on the window shelves. Crystals, sand dollars, and other natural treasures were temptingly displayed in small clusters in special corners. The room was bright and festive, with freshly painted red walls, a new rug, and a blackboard drawing of sun, moon, and twinkling stars. There were even twenty-three drinking mugs awaiting twenty-three potentially thirsty children.

The flutter in my stomach was probably shared by most of my students that first morning. How would it go? Would the children be engaged and happy? How in the world could I hope to weave twenty-three separate individuals into a group called a "class"?

As they arrived with their parents, I stood at the door, greeted each one with a handshake and words of welcome, and led them, one by one, to their special places in the room. Without conscious intent, the welcoming took on a sort of ceremonial quality. Bidding the parents good-bye went well; I remember only one case of tears. Soon all the children were seated at their desks, wondering, "What's next?"

In passing, I gave Anthony a compliment: "I see you already know how to sit tall in your chair." (He was sitting ramrod straight, chair pulled up tight, hands folded in front of him on his desk.) No sooner had the words left my mouth than twenty-two other little chairs were swiftly pulled up, and twenty-three sets of hands appeared on the desks. Such is the potential of positive feedback, not to mention the six-year-old's desire to please and capacity for imitation.

Because a young child becomes one with the surrounding environment, it is especially important that our classrooms be beautiful; the teacher's speech and gestures should also be worthy of imitation.[4] The marvelous fact that young children copy everything in their surroundings can become a tremendous teaching tool if used responsibly.

After exploring our new classroom that first day, we all went to the auditorium for an opening assembly. Following our singing together as a school, each teacher rose to welcome his or her class. Since the Waldorf class teacher usually stays with a group for eight consecutive years, the teachers would welcome their old students back and hint at the new adventures in learning that lay ahead in the coming year. Children in the upper levels could look back, through the words of each teacher, on the journey they had already traveled. Opening day in a Waldorf school thus offers a moment to look ahead with anticipation and curiosity, and one to look back through the memories of past years. Past and future converge in the present, and the big picture is fleetingly visible.

My words of greeting to the first grade were brief, since I knew that the enormity of their new situation—with all those "big kids" seated behind them—would sweep over almost anything I said. So I described my walk in the fields that winter night and ended by saying, simply, "I want to be your teacher." They looked up at me as I finished, and I knew that many were thinking "Yes," in response.

Back in the classroom we had a brief lesson; we practiced drawing a straight line and a curved line. This launched what became a series of form drawings in those first few days—

drawings that used lines to form and shape space. On the first day we simply practiced drawing a straight line and a curved line, by walking them on the floor, drawing them with a wet sponge on the board, and forming them with an imaginary crayon in the air. Finally, after much practice, we drew them on pieces of paper:[5]

I C

It was interesting to observe how the children made those first lines—the building blocks of all writing. Some did it as I had indicated, from the top down; others started at the bottom and worked to the top. The gesture of writing has to do with finding a place on this earth and in the physical body that is given us in this life. Those who wrote their lines from the bottom up later showed other signs of a rather tentative "settling in," whereas the majority who wrote from the top down were strongly present, as signified also in their more decisive walking. I saw all these little things as indications of the beckoning mystery that each child presented. Every clue was helpful in gaining a sense for the child. The main thing, however, was the search for knowledge itself, the teacher's yearning to know and understand his students at a deeper level.

We had an early snack and then recess that first day—we all needed it. The informal conversation over our first meal together helped break the ice of newness and strangeness, and the recess games united us as a group. We played together often. I really believe that recess is as important as any class work. In first grade we played variations on hide-and-seek— like Fox and Squirrel—in the woods, jump rope, and hopscotch; in the later grades, Kick the Can, Steal the Bacon, Capture the Flag, kickball, basketball, volleyball, and running games not only developed large motor skills but helped to build camaraderie as well. In the first grade, it was the imaginative games, such as Fox and Squirrel, that the children most enjoyed. My class was a group that liked to run, and there were some very fast runners indeed. The cooperation and interaction needed in some of those recess games did marvelous things for our group dynamics. Even in free play, I felt that in terms of deeper, latent issues, much was being worked out on the playing field that I could not possibly have resolved in the classroom.[6] As a beginning teacher I had only fragments of insight to work with, so the best I could do at times was simply to create a space for the children to learn and grow, respecting their sense for what was needed socially. However, for the sake of safety, as well as for my own exercise, I always maintained a presence on the playground. Just one turn at being the fox was enough to get my blood flowing vigorously for the day! Recess was always an active time for all of us.

School was out at noon that first day, and families arrived with younger siblings for a school potluck. It was helpful to chat with parents, give and get feedback, and look toward future expectations. Once reunited with their parents, many of my students reverted to more informal, less disciplined behavior, and the potluck picnics each year were sometimes stressful for me. My consciousness was divided between the conversations I was having with parents and the various escapades of the children as they disappeared into the nearby woods. It took a few years for me to settle the "who's in charge" question and come to an inner orientation for the in-between times. Simply put, I had to be the authority figure.[7] The parents did not seem to mind.

I can't remember ever being as tired as I was after that first day of teaching first grade, nor sleeping better than I did that night. Indeed, my bedtime grew progressively earlier with each day that passed. My vital forces were so engaged in working with the children—as they acquired new capacities for learning and continued the building process of their own physical bodies—that I needed extra replenishment through sleep each night.[8]

Before describing some of the aspects of our first-grade year, I want to outline the morning main-lesson routine so as to frame the content of later lessons.

In the morning when the children arrived, I greeted each one with a handshake and took a moment to share personal news and conversation. This helped me become aware of individual concerns and issues before I worked with the group as a whole. Then I would sing a few notes of the theme "time to begin" as they settled into their seats, ready for the roll call. If they needed a few extra moments, I often played a "settling-in tune" on a pentatonic recorder, then sang the name of each child, and he or she would answer back. At first I used just one note, but soon experimented with pentatonic intervals. The children became adept at echoing the notes and in this way practiced their listening skills. Rudolf Steiner indicated that the mood of the fifth, the pentatonic scale, is especially appropriate for young children, as it belongs to a time in human history when humanity experienced the world much as our young children do today.[9]

After attendance, we would form a circle and greet the day with a morning verse:

> The sun, with loving light,
> Brings brightness to my day.
> The soul, with spirit power,
> Gives strength unto my limbs.
> In sunlight shining clear
> I reverence, O God,
> The strength of humankind
> Which thou so graciously
> Hast planted in my soul,
> That I may love to work
> And learn with all my might.
> From Thee come strength and light:
> To Thee rise love and thanks.[10]

This verse helped us begin each morning for four consecutive years. The words grew on us as time passed. The children first experienced the lines as pictures, only gradually awakening to the deeper meaning in them, as it unfolded in the context of the curriculum and their own personal development.

We then launched into a series of opening exercises intended to engage the whole child, especially the will. This meant that we learned by moving and experiencing before we conceptualized. We did circle songs: "The Farmer in the Dell," "Oats, Peas, Beans, and Barley Grow," and others. We did rhythmic clapping that involved partners left and right, we took a visit to "the curly house of snail" as we contracted and expanded the circle, and we did concentration exercises. Much of the movement work also prepared the way for arithmetic, since the rhythmic counting was easily transformed into multiplication tables: 1 **2** 3 **4** 5 **6** 7 **8**. Using full gestures and moving gradually toward the center from the periphery of the circle and then back out again, we often spoke the poem "The Key of the Kingdom":

> This is the Key of the Kingdom:
> In that Kingdom is a city;
> In that city is a town;
> In that town there is a street;
> In that street there winds a lane;
> In that lane there is a yard;
> In that yard there is a house;
> In that house there waits a room;
> In that room an empty bed;
> And on that bed a basket—
> A Basket of Sweet Flowers;
>   Of Flowers, of Flowers;
>   A Basket of Sweet Flowers.
>
> Flowers in a basket
> Basket on the bed;

Bed in the chamber;
Chamber in the house;
House in the weedy yard;
Yard in the winding lane;
Lane in the broad street;
Street in the high town;
Town in the city;
City in the Kingdom—
This is the Key of the Kingdom.
  Of the Kingdom this is the Key.[11]

The forward and backward progression in this poem (beginning and ending at the same place), and other poems such as "This is the House that Jack Built," had a healing effect on the children. I found it gave them a sense of security, a feeling of belonging, and a sense that everything has its rightful place in this world, our kingdom. After moving in and out with these and other activities, the children usually had ruddy cheeks and sparkling eyes. Their capacities were stirred and awakened, and we were now ready for the further work of the main lesson.

In first grade, the academic tasks of writing, reading, and arithmetic were embedded in the rich world of fairy tales. Since children of this age still live very much in a form of "picture consciousness," they learn best when rich, imaginative stories help lead the way toward academic learning.[12] Thus our first-grade letters were born out of stories: S came from "The Six Swans," F from "The Fisherman and His Wife," and G from "The Golden Goose." I chose my stories not only for their potential to give birth to a letter but also because of the intrinsic message or flavor of the tale. I tried to sense which stories my group needed to hear and to bring diversity in terms of content, culture, and style.

For example, although there are many stories about kings, any of which could have helped us learn the letter K, I chose the Grimm's tale "The Water of Life" because of the relational aspects of the three brothers and the quest for higher knowledge and renewal.[13]

In brief, "The Water of Life" portrays a king who is ill and cannot be healed, despite the attempts of all his doctors. The king hears of a substance called "the water of life." It alone can heal, but it is hard to find. His three sons volunteer to seek this source of renewal. The first two set off in succession. Both are unkind to a dwarf and are consequently trapped in a ravine, an image for the cycle of cruelty and unkindness that abounds today. The youngest son sets out shortly thereafter. Unlike his two brothers before him, he speaks kindly to the dwarf and consequently receives good advice, which leads to the palace in a far-off land where the water of life springs from a special fountain. Along the way, he has to use an iron wand to open the doors of the castle, feed two loaves to the hungry lions, and fetch the water of life before the clock strikes twelve. The youngest son succeeds and meets a beautiful princess, who waits for his return in a year's time.

But on the journey home to his father, he takes pity on his older brothers and has them freed, only to suffer their treachery when they secretly exchange his water of life for sea water. The old king becomes even more ill from the sea water, and the two older brothers present him with their flask, which promptly heals him. The youngest son is banished. After the year has passed, the princess has a bright, golden road made to the gate of her palace, instructing her servants to deny entrance to anyone who does not ride up the center of the road. The eldest son, eager to cash in on the situation, sets out early, but when he reaches the golden road, he turns away to ride up beside it because he does not wish to break or damage the gold. He is denied entrance. The same thing happens with the second son. But the youngest one is so preoccupied with his love for the princess (a representative of the higher self) that he rides right up the center of the road without noticing anything else. The old king is invited to the wedding, and everyone lives happily ever after.

This story was told on a Monday, after which we drew pictures of the old king in his castle. The next day, in our circle time, we thought of words that started with a *K* sound. Back at their desks, the children drew another picture, this time of the king after he had drunk the water of life and become whole again. He stood upright and looked much like a *K*. On Wednesday, we practiced writing *K*'s and hunted for more words that started with *K*. We also learned letter verses composed for *V* and *K*:[14]

> This verse is about a valley
> With a view of velvet vapors
> Where vain and vengeful brothers
> Vanished in a rocky vault.
>
> The kind old king
> With his key and his ring
> Kindled love in his kinsmen
> And kept wisdom in his kingdom.

We took this story one step further. Because of the quest nature of the story, I found a special wooden vessel and filled it with water. I then constructed an imaginative obstacle course: a few chairs became a mountain range, a plank became a narrow ravine, a few desks helped us make a tunnel. Then the children were invited, one by one, over several days, to take that journey with the water of life held carefully in their hands. I made sure to pour in slightly less water for some; others needed the challenge of a full cup. I wish my readers could have seen the expressions on their faces as they took that journey. It was with the utmost reverence and care that they traveled over mountain and dale, always holding the cup carefully in their hands. What joy when the journey was completed! They never tired of seeing their classmates strive for and finally reach the goal, bearing the water that represented purification through life-learning.

Pedagogically, this exercise served as a metaphor for the journey they were embarking on, which would take us eight years to complete. There would be challenges and obstacles along the way, but the common effort and good will of each individual would carry his or her striving forward. Done as an early morning exercise, this journey with the water of life helped center the children and prepare them to focus on their lessons. Watching each one carefully hold the water, I often had the feeling that at the same time they were holding something in their hearts that was most precious, most pure, to them. It seems that we each, in our own way, need to carry the water of life.

During the winter months of first grade we worked on a play based on "Snow White and the Seven Dwarfs." We gradually built it up out of the original story, first through the children retelling the story, then by writing key sentences in their main-lesson books, and by reciting (in groups) the rhyming verses. For many weeks, neighboring classes could hear us stamping around the room, as we became dwarfs with heavy sacks upon our backs:

> Little dwarfs so short and strong
> Heavy-footed march along;
> Every head is straight and proud,
> Every step is firm and loud.
>
> Pick and hammer each must hold
> Deep in earth to mine the gold;
> Ready over each one's back
> Hangs a little empty sack.
>
> When their hard day's work is done
> Home again they march as one.
> Full sacks make a heavy load
> As they tramp along the road.[15]

From the group recitation and marching, I gradually drew out a few individuals to play the parts of Queen, Peddler Woman, Prince, Huntsman, and Snow White. Many had the chance to plead with the huntsman:

> I am still a child,
> And long on earth I would have whiled;
> O huntsman, pray, hear what I say,
> Let me fly far, far away,
> And never homeward will I turn,
> My fate the queen will never learn.[16]

Once again, these lines really spoke to the children at their particular stage of development. The youngsters were experiencing what it means to set forth from home and journey on the earth with new friends. They loved playing the dwarfs who befriended Snow White, as well as the wicked queen in her many disguises. I will always remember my two first-graders Maria and Mary trying to outdo one another in stamping and anger as the evil queen, while the mirror continually spoke of Snow White as the fairest of them all. Abbie and Anthony enjoyed using beguiling, sweet words as the peddler woman, and seven children, costumed in burlap capes and little pointed red hats, marched in unison as our seven dwarfs: Zachary, Marc, Joseph, Jonathan, Stephen, Jules, and Eben. Because the seven were of varying heights, they were neatly arranged from the tallest to the smallest! Lucy was simply beautiful as Snow White. In the performance for the parents, we began and ended the play with singing.

In the early grades, a birthday was a special occasion. In addition to a special snack that the child's parents brought in, each birthday child received a crown and royal cape to wear for the day, and a special verse to learn and live with for the new year. The lines were chosen with care, using images that represented

qualities inherent in the birthday-child's being, while also suggesting possibilities for future growth. In the few samples
below, the reader is encouraged to imagine the children who
received these poems and who are mentioned again in later
chapters. For example, a student's role in a play in later years
may make more sense when seen in the context of these early
verses:

DOUG:

Courage to do what is right,
Courage to speak what is true,
With this as my goal I can do no wrong
For my heart will always be strong.

MARC:

Once I saw a tall, tall tree,
A mightier tree I never did see.
The roots held firmly the ground below
While the branches to the heavens
        did grow.

With my feet firmly rooted below me
And my trunk as straight as can be
Wisdom of the stars will my heart soon know
And like the oak, will ever grow.

MICHAEL:

Swirling and twirling and dancing with mirth
Little snowflakes fall gently to earth.
This way did I come on the day of my birth.
And if I listen, oh so well,
I might just hear the snowdrop bell.

LUCY:

In heaven shines a golden star,
An angel led me from afar
From heaven high unto the earth
And brought me to my house of birth.

Welcome, welcome lovely day
With sunshine bright and flowers gay,
With painted birds that sing their song
And, me, kind and good and strong.

At the end of first grade, each child received a handwritten copy of his or her birthday verse with illustrations shaded in color. Some of the children later told me that these illustrated versions had remained on their bedroom walls for years.

Despite my frustrations at never having enough time to do all that I planned, and despite my constant feeling that I needed more expertise as a poet, illustrator, storyteller, and dramatist, I was continually rewarded by a group of children who seemed to soak up everything I could give. Much of what we did together in first grade seemed to sink into deep pools of potential understanding, which was reflected in comments and observations in later years. The children seemed to be able to round out the imperfections of what I brought as they listened. The images became whole and true for them, thanks to their wonderful senses of imagination. Thus, even when I knew for sure that some element of my main lesson was not as it should be, I had at least tried to give them living material that could be taken up by their imaginative capacities.[17]

This work also nourished *me*. I found myself learning wonderful stories, playing new tunes on my recorder, expanding my repertoire of poems, and finding new ways to teach math through the use of jewels, nuts, and pebbles. My imagination was constantly being stretched; I felt active and alive, and that energy translated into a high level of student involvement.

I was not permitted to rest on past accomplishments nor grow stale by doing the same grade over and over again. After just nine brief months, we were ready to move on to second grade together.

2. The High Road and the Low Road

*O*ne of the greatest misconceptions I have ever entertained was that after the first grade I could simply "move to second grade" by teaching the next lesson the following September. Of course I knew there would be a new curriculum, but now I had an entire year of experience behind me and would be teaching the same group of children. I thought I would be teaching the same group of children. Wrong!

The names were the same, but practically everything else was not. After the first day of second grade I found myself scratching my head and asking: Where are the real Doug, Marc, Kirsten, Michael, Eben, Susan, Jacob? Did they forget to show up? After the second day my inner questioning was more intense: what had happened to the open-hearted, naive, reverent, respectful children I had enjoyed last year? Was this some kind of cruel joke? After the third day, my only feeling was: Help! Fortunately for me, the first week of school only lasted three days.

Over the weekend I slowly processed the experience. The children had changed, and my acceptance of that was necessary. How had they changed? They were more lively, that was certain. They were in movement—constantly. Also, they seemed to live in extremes. One moment they were joyfully engaged in an activity, and the next some social disruption would turn everything upside down. Most frustrating, the cause of this major event in the classroom would prove, after I had sorted the debris, to be an outrageously small infraction, such as a "borrowed" crayon. Worst of all, each child seemed to have opinions about everything. If they could at least have developed one "class opinion," I naively thought, then life would be simpler. I could deal with "their" opinion. But no, there were twenty-three separate opinions on everything! Never in my wildest dreams had I ever stopped to consider that there could be so much feeling and such diversity of opinion about whether the drinking mugs, neatly lined up on the shelf, should have their handles facing in or out! Finally, my shy, reverent first-graders seemed to have been transformed over the summer into jaded students, who actually looked down on the mere first-graders next door. My first week of teaching second grade convinced me of one thing: the status quo of the first week was not acceptable. Either the class would have to change—or I would. In the end, it seemed that my chances of success would be greater if it were I. Could I become a new teacher?

I began by intensifying my work with the morning circle. If they want to move, we'll move! We stamped and clapped our numbers, we marched around the room as gnomes and goblins, we galloped as horses, we wove in and out as we sang "Round and Round the Village" and other country tunes. Basic skills such as spelling, reading, and arithmetic were practiced with rhythmic clapping and movement during the circle, continuing and intensifying our work from first grade. With each child wearing a letter, we called for new and exciting words that would magically appear as the appropriate children skipped forward. We continued our first-grade work of walking in the circle while emphasizing different number patterns: 1 2 3 4 5 6 7 8 was a lame old woman who could only hobble along; 1 2 3 4 5 6 7 8 9 was a lad, light and gay, who jumped on every third number, thus helping us learn the three table in multiplication.[1]

These activities engaged the wills of the children, who worked with all their youthful energy, putting themselves into the movements with their limbs and all their senses. In this way each child's whole organism was stimulated, rather than the brain alone, and in the process, a deeper connection with the study material was fostered, along with a long-term memory.[2]

Rather than "force-feeding" the children with short-term memory work, I found that the time devoted to our circle actually enabled us to learn in a far more economical way than if we had skipped it: circle time made us more efficient. The children retained more because they were active in the learning process. They remembered their numbers because the tables had now become part of their whole being.[3]

The morning activities also gave me an ideal opportunity to practice child observation. In second grade I was particularly interested in seeing how each child walked. Michael would trip lightly around the circle, hardly seeming to put his feet down on the earth. When not lost in thought, Mary walked with a spring in her step, while Maria and Jacob walked in a determined, heels-down-first manner. Kirsten and Marc walked with a shuffling gait as if their feet were too big, dragging them along as though moving them were an inconvenience. For all his athletic abilities on the playground, Doug walked as if he were asleep, bumping into people and things and expressing absolute astonishment when he was rudely awakened by these encounters. Lucy, Abbie, Margaret, Anthony, and others walked with wonderful grace and harmony.

Observing how a child walks can help the teacher sense how the child is relating to the earth. Indeed, one task of education is to help children find their proper relationship to the world. We are working to enable the child's individuality, or ego, to gradually take hold of the physical organism and come into a balanced relationship with the earth, with the force of gravity.[4] A child who trips along, not connecting very much with the ground beneath his feet, may—and the word "may" is important because these are only indications—may have difficulty taking hold of other tasks as well. In fact, all through the grades Michael struggled with writing and spelling, among other things, and every task demanded extra effort from him. My job was to motivate him, awaken his interest in things, and give him examples to copy. Those who walked with their heels first in a definite way seemed to be strongly present in their physical bodies, and my goal was to draw forth the treasures that these children had brought with them. I made an extra effort to get them to share their insights with the class. Kirsten and Marc, whose feet seemed to be especially heavy, needed to bring more consciousness and awareness into their extremities—they needed to practice "knowing where their feet were." So we did exercises such as jumping and stepping over rods on the floor as we spoke the rhyme "Jack be nimble, Jack be quick, Jack jump over the candlestick." I tried never to isolate a child in such an exercise. In fact, we all did "Jack be Nimble," but I made certain that some children did it more often, and that I was particularly attentive to their efforts.[5]

In morning circle, we worked on things that went beyond traditional classroom "learning" yet in many ways seemed more important in the big picture. For how a child finds a connection to the earth is related to his or her finding a connection to the physical body and to the "self" who inhabits it and who is transforming that particular body to suit its own needs. In the early grades when the children were living so strongly in their life forces,[6] I knew I had a real chance to help them work at balancing and harmonizing themselves in preparation for their lives on the earth.[7]

One further aspect of child observation is worth mentioning at this point, before moving on to the second-grade curriculum: a tooth inventory. Several times in the early grades I took stock of how many teeth each child had lost, bearing in mind that tooth loss was yet another sign of the coming-to-earth, or incarnation, process and particularly of readiness for learning. Upon entering the classroom in the morning, each child would individually greet me with a handshake. We would exchange a few words, and these precious moments became a regular one-on-one "safe" time when personal items could be shared. In first and second grades, the big news first thing in the morning was often a wiggly or lost tooth. Without sitting them all down as a group to take my "inventory," I was able to do the survey informally over several days. (Similarly, I found that some of the most significant things that happened in my classroom often occurred in a seemingly informal setting. An outside observer might have thought, "Oh, what a friendly exchange." But the teacher has a responsibility beyond "being friendly" to pursue an active study of the children and to try and meet each moment of the day in full consciousness.)

So, the Tooth Inventory, February 1983, indicated the following tooth loss in my class: Susan (4), Liza (6), Mary (6), Kirsten (8), Joseph (3), Jonathan (2), Zachary (9), Samuel (7), Jacob (5), Marc (9), Lucy (2), Maria (8), Anthony (0), Jules (0), Ned (1), Edward (4), Michael (4), Doug (3 wigglies), Annabelle (4), Margaret (2), Abbie (6), Olivia (3 wigglies), Eben (1 wiggly). I then compared these figures with other information at my disposal and found that the extent of tooth loss did not always correspond to birthdates. That is, the youngest children did not always have the fewest teeth missing (Mary, Abbie), but the oldest often did have the most missing (Kirsten, Maria, Zachary). Among the youngest, tooth loss proved to be a more helpful indicator of learning maturity over the years than anything else I could find. Anthony, Eben, Doug, Lucy, and Margaret held on to what I call their "picture consciousness" longer than the others. Because they were enrolled in a Waldorf school, they were allowed to do this without being labeled as inferior. In fact, in light of some of their achievements in the upper grades and thereafter, I am very glad that they were allowed to grow at their own pace.

Rather than penalize a slow learner, I tried to find the pictures and images that would build confidence in the potential of slow growth. Lucy's second-grade birthday story is an example of this and also nicely illustrates the kind of nature stories that would be sought for in a Waldorf second grade:

THE BLOSSOMS OF THE HEATHER

When the earth was still very young, the trees and plants came to live on it. They were happy and contented. The lily was glad because her flowers were white, the rose was glad because her flowers were red. The violet was happy because, however shyly she might hide herself away, someone would come to look for her and praise her fragrance. The daisy was happiest of all because every child in the world loved her.

The trees and plants chose homes for themselves. The oak said, "I shall live in the broad fields and by the roads, and travelers may sit in my shadow." "I shall be glad to live on the waters of the pond," said the lily. "And I shall be happy in the sunny fields," said the daisy. "My fragrance will rise from beside some mossy stone," said the violet. Each plant chose its home.

There was one little plant, however, that did not have the sweet fragrance of the violet, and the children did not love her as they did the daisy. No blossoms had been given to her, and she was too shy to ask for any. "I wish there were someone who would be glad to see me," she said.

One day, she heard the mountain say, "Dear plants, will you not come to my rocks and cover them with your brightness and beauty? In the winter they are cold, in the summer they are scorched by the sunshine. Will you not come and cover them?"

"I cannot leave the pond," cried the water lily.

"I cannot leave the moss," said the violet.

"I cannot leave the green fields," said the daisy.

The little heather was trembling with eagerness. "If the great, beautiful mountain would only let me come," she thought, and at last she whispered very softly and shyly, "Dear mountain, will you let me come? I have not any blossoms like the others, but I will try to keep the wind and sun away from you."

"Let you?!" cried the mountain. "I shall be very happy if you will only come."

The heather soon covered the rocky mountainside with her bright green, and the mountain called proudly to the other plants, "See how beautiful my little heather is." The others replied, "Yes, she is bright and green, but she has no blossoms."

But the very next day, the little heather was bright with many blossoms, and blossoms she has had from that day to this.[8]

In attempting to let the pictorial elements in the story speak for themselves, I did not use any words of introduction or conclusion. The class knew it was Lucy's birthday when I quietly lit the birthday candle and placed it on her desk before the story. Although everyone could benefit from the environmental and social meaning of the story, I tried to hold a particularly strong inner picture of the birthday girl as I told it. Beset by parental concerns over whether she would ever learn to read, lacking in confidence about her own abilities, Lucy could have this moment just for herself.

In addition to continued work with basic skills in reading, writing, and arithmetic, the second-grade Waldorf curriculum emphasizes fables and legends.[9] Because children at this age can so easily live in extremes, the fables and legends connect the child's feeling and experience to two different aspects of human nature: the fables expose, and even accentuate, our human foibles, while the legends speak to the striving human being of individuals and saints who have accomplished extraordinary physical and spiritual tasks. The images are rich, and the juxtaposition of the humorous, mischievous animal exploits and the supra-human achievements described in the legends engages the feelings of those listening and participating.

In second grade, participation meant more than listening. The day after the fable or legend was presented, I led the class in recalling the story by asking simple questions designed to elicit responses from the children. After the story had thus been retold, we often entered into a discussion about the crafty fox, the yapping lapdog, or the angry father of the blind Odelia. The children had many thoughts and feelings to share, and I often felt that the real artistry in teaching was in the way one worked with these student contributions. Sometimes the recalling session needed prodding; at other times many children were simply bursting to tell the story in their own words. In any case, it was then only a small additional step for me to write some of their sentences on the blackboard and introduce elementary composition writing. The children enjoyed writing sentences on their own paper, drawing illustrations with beeswax crayons, and then adding the new page to their growing main-lesson books, which served as a record of what we were learning in second grade.

I selected particular fables and legends according to my personal connection to the content, to what I felt the class needed, and to the particular issues faced by individual children. The latter were also addressed through continued use of the "birthday story." Let me give two examples.

Maria was an active, confident, and talented second-grader. Despite the passage of several years, I can still see her vividly in my mind's eye with her dark, sparkling eyes, black hair, ruddy complexion, supple movements, and her attentiveness and eagerness to learn. She experienced each lesson deeply and shared her impressions in colorful, bold crayon drawings. She worked and played hard all day and enjoyed ten to twelve hours of sleep each night. Maria could sing, play her recorder, and do all our rhythmic activities—and she enjoyed every minute. On the playground at recess, she often challenged others in foot races; this was her favorite sport. She would race Doug, then Jacob, then Zachary; even older children would be drawn into the fun. Her favorite refrain was, "Someday, I will even beat Mr. Finser!" Even when I successfully withstood yet another challenge, Maria was always a good sport. Her flushed face would show only momentary disappointment, and then with a smile and a flash she would be off to another activity.

Because of the special intimacy made possible in a group that stays together over so many years, the children understood Maria and really enjoyed her birthday story as much as she did:

> A hare was continually poking fun at a tortoise because of the slowness of his pace. The tortoise tried not to be annoyed by the jeers of the hare, but one day in the presence of the other animals he was goaded into challenging the hare to a footrace.
>
> "Why, this is a joke," said the hare. "You know that I can run circles around you."
>
> "Enough of your boasting," said the tortoise. "Let's get on with the race."
>
> So the course was set by the animals, and the fox was chosen as judge. He gave a sharp bark and the race was on. Almost before you could say "scat," the hare was out of sight. The tortoise plodded along at his usual unhurried pace.
>
> After a time the hare stopped to wait for the tortoise to come along. He waited for a long, long time until he began to get sleepy. "I'll just take a quick nap here in this soft grass, and then in the cool of the day I'll finish the race." So he lay down and closed his eyes.
>
> Meanwhile, the tortoise plodded on. He passed the sleeping hare and was approaching the finish line when the hare awoke with a start. It was too late to save the race. Much ashamed, he crept away while all the animals at the finish line acclaimed the winner.[10]

In many ways, Maria was an exceptionally balanced child and in fact possessed qualities of both hare and tortoise. Her written work was always "slow and steady wins the race." But the story reminded her that she needed to appreciate all the qualities in herself and others, and that foot races were fun but not "everything." I tried to minimize competition in the class, and this fable helped in that direction. It was wonderful to see Maria's classmates jokingly challenge her in the subsequent weeks: "Hey, Tortoise, want a race?" With never-ending spunk, she would give a big smile, indicating that she understood our new class vocabulary, and then wholeheartedly comply.

Margaret was a slight, slender redhead. She had been born five weeks early and flown by helicopter to another hospital for care. She had learned to walk late, at twenty months; until then she had raced around on her knees. When she was upright, she stood on her ankle bones. She had struggled with myopia from her earliest years, yet her glasses did not dim the bright, sparkling eyes that looked out on the world. In second grade she appeared physically frail; her energy was quickly expended. Yet her spirit remained strong.[11] She had a passionate sense for social justice, yet could be overlooked in her large extended family and in a class of twenty-three children. Like Maria, Margaret was talented in drawing with crayons. She could draw for hours on end and produced pictures that were populated with many cheerful people and lots of flowers. To use a phrase from the French resistance fighter Jacques Lusseyran, when Margaret colored her pictures she was "holding light in her hands."[12]

As I prepared for sleep each night, I often spent some time thinking about the children in my class. When focusing on Margaret in second grade, I wondered, "How can I help her find the strength she will need for life?" My image of Margaret was often that of a bright star, sparkling with radiance, only recently descended to the earth.[13] In asking the question "Who is this child?" I was filled with reverence. With a slight body and a great spirit, she must have accomplished much on her star journey before entering my classroom. A legend was needed for

Margaret's June birthday; I told the tale of Queen Sunniva, who was as "slender as a young birch tree, as lovely as the green hills of Ireland," and who had beautiful, rust-colored hair. Forced to flee her native land, Sunniva led her people by boat to the northern islands of Scandinavia. Without weapons, without even oars or sails, Sunniva traveled with complete faith in God. Even when the Vikings threatened to attack her eventual home on Selje Island, Sunniva's prayers brought protection for her people (though in a most unusual and dramatic way!). Her complete trust in God inspired confidence and brought comfort to all around her.[14] Margaret listened to this story with rapt attention. Meeting her after her high school graduation and learning of her role as news anchor on a local station, I realized she had indeed become a leader! (Maria has become an incredible artist, and Lucy graduated high school with high honors in science, art, English, and Spanish.)

To help my lively second-graders settle in and focus on their tasks, I turned not only to the imaginative pictures contained in fables and legends but also to arithmetic—lots and lots of it. On many a morning we would first practice math through movement in our circle; then the children would return to their desks and take out the acorns they kept for number journeys. Instead of asking the children to add $5 + 8 + 3 + 2 + 4$, I would begin with the whole pile in front of me and build up the sequence with a narrative. First I would say, "Let's make sure we each have all our acorns. How many do you have, Eben?" (He almost always had the right number, whereas others often found that some of their acorns had slipped out of the little sacks my wife and I had made for each child.) "Twenty-four? Great! Is everyone ready for Squirrel Nutkin?" When the expectant faces confirmed that all the children were indeed ready, the number journey would begin, and the children, working individually at their desks, would put aside the required number of acorns as we went along.

On a bright fall day, Squirrel Nutkin was frolicking along, hoping to find lots of nuts for his winter hoard. As he hopped along the old stone wall, he discovered five acorns tucked between the rocks. Then he had a mischievous idea: "Perhaps my brother Flick has found some nuts today." And in a moment, Squirrel Nutkin scampered up his brother's tree to the hollow place where the nuts were kept. Squirrel Nutkin found eight round, fresh acorns, which he rushed over to his own house under the fallen maple. On his last trip back to the maple, he found three more nuts under some dried leaves. Not content with all this wealth, he hopped down to the old rusty hay baler, where he found two nuts under the left tire. Squirrel Nutkin took the long way home, and managed to find four more among the roots of an old oak tree. How many nuts did he have altogether?

On other days, nuts were stolen or lost (subtraction), shared with friends in need (division), increased when Brother Wind blew through the branches of the oak trees (multiplication). I tried to show, with the help of Squirrel Nutkin, that the processes were related—for instance, that multiplication is a fast way to add and that numbers are needed for everyday life. Only after thorough practice would we put the more abstract numerical representation of a sequence on the board, or do practice problems in our arithmetic main-lesson books.

Having had the good fortune to teach the upper grades before taking this class, I tried to do my second-grade number work with an eye to algebra. Rather than "solving for the unknown," however, we would sometimes take number journeys that involved a "missing" quantity. Also, by stressing the opposite processes (how division can undo multiplication, for instance), I tried to lay a foundation for the resolution of simple equations in seventh grade. I found once again that having the same group for several consecutive years of main-lesson work allowed for "economical" teaching.[15]

The marvelous thing about working with Squirrel Nutkin was that the exercise appealed to all the children, but in different ways. There were those who needed to focus on counting, and there was time in the story for them to carefully count out their acorns. Other children (the sanguine ones) did the numerical work quickly but enjoyed listening to the ever-changing adventures of Squirrel Nutkin. Some really got involved in the accumulation of the hoard of nuts when we worked with addition (the phlegmatics), others loved the drama of it all (the cholerics), and still others (the melancholics) lived into what I call the "character development," namely the trials and tribulations of loss, separation, and subtraction. Rudolf Steiner encouraged teachers to draw upon a variety of learning styles and temperaments so that the lesson not only engaged all the children but could also become more than the subject taught and might thus foster human development.[16] It was therefore of greatest importance to me, whether I was teaching arithmetic, fables, legends, composition, or reading, to try to give the children a content of some kind that could live on—images and experiences that would have meaning beyond the specific lesson on any given day.

Abstract ideas and concepts are quickly rendered irrelevant from the perspective of the soul, but imaginative pictures have a wonderful way of growing over time.[17] I cannot blame the "so what?" attitude of children in conventional settings who are asked to fill out countless workbooks with answers to such dull, colorless instructions as, "Please state the sum of $5 + 8 + 3 + 2 + 4$." Look at their faces, read their gestures! If given nothing but dry abstractions, they will be saying "So what?" with justification. What lives in children's souls is far greater than anything I have ever seen in a published workbook, yet so many educators try to squeeze this immense life of soul into dull, dry lessons, created by adults who have lost the glowing life of childhood.

In order to become a new teacher in the second grade, I had to become a second-grader again. I painted the same pictures with watercolors, I took part as the wolf or lamb in our second-grade class play, I enjoyed the same songs. And living with the images of the saints and legends gave me something to strive for—again and again I found that it was only *after* telling the story that I began to comprehend the meaning of the words I had spoken. The artistic practice of teaching was demanding—exhausting—yet renewing, all at the same time. After a really good main lesson, I always noticed a change in my breathing: it was somehow deeper, more health-giving.

Learning to teach all over again had one major disadvantage. It was not until the end of the second-grade year that I felt I knew how to teach second grade. I remember so clearly the feeling in early June: Now I really know what second-graders need; now I am conscious of what I have been developing all year.[18]

3. Toward Community

$\mathcal{T}$he first two chapters might easily convey the impression that I was the only one who taught my group of children. Yet this was certainly not the case. In many ways I could not have begun to do the work I did as a class teacher if my efforts had not been supplemented by a community of subject teachers who taught my group every day after the main lesson was over. Therefore, before going on to an account of the third grade, I would like to indicate the breadth of the special subjects taught in a fully developed Waldorf school and mention the foreign-language curriculum in particular.

I would also like to emphasize the community aspect and experience of working together with a group of colleagues. One might describe a community as an on-going creative event where people work together in celebration of a common vision, where the talents and achievements of each individual are honored, where diversity is not divisive, where process is valued, where "the whole" becomes greater than the sum of its parts, and where the "work" remains unfinished. Our close-knit group of teachers worked together out of such a picture, and we knew that our efforts to build a working community were not lost upon the children—our efforts formed part of their educational experience.

My class was exceedingly fortunate in having a talented group of subject teachers who taught them two or three times per week in lessons that lasted forty-five to fifty minutes each. I tried to be in the room to introduce my colleagues and would occasionally stay on to visit their classes, but otherwise I used these times to meet with parents or other teachers, or do administrative work for the school. Because this book is a narrative of my personal journey as a *class teacher*, I can only indicate the subjects taught, knowing that in many ways each one could become the subject of a full volume. These subjects included eurythmy, music, physical education, handwork, woodworking, and foreign languages.

EURYTHMY: This form of movement was developed under Rudolf Steiner's guidance and can be described as "speech and music made visible."[1] Every sound—whether mechanical, musical, or human—also creates a spatial form that, although not immediately visible, can be recognized (see Chapter Six, the Chladni plate experiment). The eurythmist recreates and experiences the variety of movement forms that are connected with the sounds of speech and music. The children worked with a specially trained eurythmist who guided them in age-appropriate experiences of these movements. Much of the main-lesson curriculum was transformed in a dynamic way into meaningful movements and simple dramatizations as the children learned to find themselves in space (see Chapter 4 and our dramatic rendition of "Iduna and the Golden Apples").

MUSIC: In addition to singing and playing the recorder, which I incorporated into the main-lesson period, the children worked with a musician once a week to further develop their repertoires, practice the recorder, and, in the fourth and fifth grades, learn notation and basic music theory. In the middle school they participated in an orchestra, which in itself developed their community-building skills, though their teachers did not draw attention to this aspect of their music or lead it into any conceptual form: the teamwork was simply an experience for them, as was the similar discipline of the school chorus, reserved for seventh- and eighth-grade students, all of whom participated.

PHYSICAL EDUCATION: The children always welcomed a chance to go out onto the large outdoor field behind the school and learn new games. The circle and tag games mentioned in

Chapter One were gradually replaced by more demanding games; later the children learned to work as teams in a variety of outdoor settings. In winter, they ice skated and skied. Occasionally we were fortunate enough to have Jaimen McMillan as a visiting instructor who did some Bothmer gymnastics with the children: these age-specific gymnastic exercises were developed at the first Waldorf school in Stuttgart, Germany, by Count Fritz von Bothmer, out of pedagogical indications given by Rudolf Steiner. I always found it helpful to observe my class when they were doing sports and eurythmy, since their movements revealed so much; I could thus enhance my understanding of the individual children in my care.

HANDWORK : Beginning in first grade the class had handwork twice a week. This subject fosters "an all-around understanding of life" by building an awareness of how things are made.[2] My class had the same wonderful teacher for the whole eight years: they knitted scarves and hats in first grade, crocheted pot holders and mats in second, did various sewing and knitting projects in third, made cushions and pillows with cross-stitching in fourth, knitted socks and mittens in fifth (I joined in during that year), created stuffed animals in sixth, and undertook various sewing projects in seventh. Their handwork culminated in the use of the sewing machine in eighth grade. Thanks to the rigor and consistency of this work, many children were able to make their own clothes and even sew costumes for our eighth-grade Shakespearean performance of "Twelfth Night."

WOODWORKING : Beginning in fourth grade, my class learned to work with rasp and chisel, sandpaper, and other woodworking tools. Over the years I was treated to hand-carved forks and spoons, boats, candle holders, and picture frames. Many a struggling speller was able to work through his or her frustrations with the rasp and chisel, building confidence and an object of beauty at the same time.

FOREIGN LANGUAGES : A fully developed Waldorf school offers two foreign languages from first through eighth grade, and through twelfth grade if there is a high school. My class enjoyed both Spanish and German, taught twice a week in the younger grades and three times per week in the middle-school years.

In *A Modern Art of Education*, Rudolf Steiner speaks about languages and speech and describes how the "mother-tongue" is deeply rooted in the whole constitution of the child, especially in the breathing and circulatory system, and how "different languages in the world permeate man and bring the human element to expression in quite different ways."[3] If we attend to the difference in our inner experiences of the words *arbre, Baum,* and *tree,* we see how very different aspects of a single object are expressed in different languages—in this case French, German, and English. When I say "arbre" I feel the flowing up and out of the tree's branches, as in a willow. When I say "Baum," I inwardly experience the trunk, and more of an enclosing, inward gesture, whereas "tree" draws me up into far-reaching height. Thus, in a sense, any one language is an incomplete picture of the world; only by experiencing many languages can we begin to see the many different aspects of our inner, soul experiences and, thus, of the contributions offered by different cultures. It is as if each of the blind men who perceived the famous elephant spoke a different language.

It was my good fortune to teach German for six years at the Great Barrington Rudolf Steiner School. My last two years of language teaching occurred while my class was in first and second grades, the period described in the first two chapters of this book. During these years the child is still "pre-eminently an imitative being."[4] I wanted to give my students an immersion experience in the language—i.e., with no English translation. But how could I engineer this, since they spoke English with me all morning in main-lesson period? What could I do?

At the last minute, just before my first German session with the first grade, I had an inspiration: I told the class that my twin brother would be visiting them. He looked just like me, and acted just like me—but he spoke only German. At first they didn't fully believe this, but as the German classes went by, and Herr Finser obviously understood no English when addressed in class, the children gradually learned to use gestures, pictures, and halting German to express their thoughts. We created a German environment, using German poems, songs, and circle games. We learned to count and identify simple objects in the room. Thanks to the children's capacity to imitate, my job was easy: all I had to do was bring in a basket of fruit and say the name of each one in German, and by the second or third round they were all vigorously at it. Many of the poems and songs were accompanied by gestures, which helped immensely. The class gradually came to accept my "twin brother," as vividly demonstrated one day toward the end of first grade: Eben had brought in a German book which he proudly presented to Herr Finser. With a gesture he indicated that he wanted it read to the group at the end of class. Unfortunately, Herr Finser got so involved in his lesson that day that he forgot to read Eben's book. When the bell rang, Eben was furious. He demanded (in English) that it be read, even though class was over. Herr Finser refused and, worst of all, seemed not to understand. Eben pushed his desk over and started to throw his chair around. Ultimately, Herr Finser was forced to take Eben out into the hallway as a safety precaution. My colleague, the eurythmy teacher, inherited the situation. At lunchtime, when Mr. Finser returned, Eben ran up to me and said, "Mr. Finser, you wouldn't believe what your horrible brother did today...," "and he proceeded to tell me the whole story of what had happened in German class. At that moment I realized that I had really succeeded in becoming two persons—something that many schools implicitly expect of their teachers.

Another reason for highlighting the special subjects at this juncture relates to the observation that children in third grade long to participate in a wide variety of activities, which are represented by the full circle of colleagues. The child at the age of eight or nine wants to see the connections between things in the world, is interested in how people work, and wants to participate in the processes of building, baking, and farming. The third-grader turns to the outer world in a more conscious way while simultaneously feeling more separated from it. The children at this age seemed more individualized, yet they were keenly interested in everything around them. They were more observant than ever before, even critical at times.[5] Instead of a morning exclamation of, "Oh, Mr. Finser, what a beautiful blackboard drawing!" (which had always made my day in the earlier grades), a child would now comment, "Nice picture, but you left the gearshift off the tractor!"

Third-graders are also capable of lots of energetic work. Fortunately for me, the third-grade Waldorf curriculum met the children with activities and content that addressed the above-mentioned needs and characteristics. The main-lesson blocks for third grade included Bible stories, arithmetic (especially measurement), housing (especially Native American), grammar, form drawing, more Bible stories, farming, a class play, many field trips, and a building project.

We also did a lot of skill-building. With the desks pushed aside for morning circle, I often took our long jump rope and, with a helper at the other end, began to practice our multiplication tables. I built up the sequence gradually. First the children would just run through as the class counted, "Two, four, six, eight..." Then one child would jump an entire table while we all counted, "Three, six, nine, twelve..." Gradually, children volunteered to jump and recite the table simultaneously, then two jumped at the same time. Our tables went up to twelve times twelve. Later on, a child would enter and begin jumping while I would call, "Ten times eight is..." and the child could practice multiplication facts out of sequence. (Toward the end of fourth grade we even managed "double Dutch"—two ropes at the same time!)

While giving a class report at a faculty meeting that year, instead of calling the children by name, I described the way each one jumped rope during multiplication practice. In most cases, my colleagues were able to identify the children correctly: the short nervous hops, the heavy thumps, the sky-high jumps that were arhythmical, and the even, graceful jumps were all symptoms of other classroom behaviors that were familiar to everyone who taught them.

Third grade was also the time for a stronger emphasis on reading. The children had been learning to read since first grade, of course, but I felt no compulsion to push them. (In fact, I had warned the parents during my pre-first-grade home visits that we would allow time for a slow maturation of reading skills so as not to endanger the health-giving, imaginative picture consciousness described in the last chapter.) The first book that the children read in first grade was "The Seven Ravens," an adaptation of the Grimm's story.[6] Each beautiful, oversized volume had been handmade by a school faculty member. The teachers had gathered in a workshop some years earlier and, with a common text, had each lettered and illustrated a copy of the story. Thus as the first-graders' read their first book, they simultaneously experienced it as a gift from the teachers. (This experience also helped stimulate the care and maintenance of library books later on.) We had a similar treat in second grade with "The Fox and the Crane."[7] In addition, the children read their own main-lesson books and thus avoided depersonalized, black-and-white print for as long as possible. By third grade, however, they were ready for more conventional texts: we especially enjoyed the Laura Ingalls Wilder series, as well as stories about American Indians.

We read aloud in both large and small groups, and twice a week we divided up according to reading ability. Library visits were introduced, and silent reading was encouraged. Thanks to a third-grade parent, we even established a class library in our own room of books that individual children had especially enjoyed reading. The class took up the library project with characteristic zeal, and by the end of the year most of the class was reading at or above grade level.

Over the years I was able to make the following observation: Most of the children who had started the eight-year cycle with me, and were allowed to awaken to reading in a gradual way over three years, actually became high-achievers in the upper grades, whereas those who entered along the way from a more conventional reading background plateaued early and seemed less motivated in later years. The analogy I thought of at the time was one from botany: one can force a plant and produce blossom and fruit early, but this is at the expense of long-term health and vitality. My responsibility was primarily to the human beings in my care, *not* to yearly Iowa tests and scores. As their literature teacher in the upper grades, for example, it was satisfying to explore classics such as *A Tale of Two Cities*, while we were studying the French Revolution. Such juxtapositions engaged the students' interest so that they read for deeper meanings and identified with the characters in their development; in other words, they were not tested for what I call "short-answer comprehension," which only touches the surface of things. Thus, our class discussions were exciting and stimulating. I was also very grateful to our parents for taking time over the years to talk with their children about their reading.

The third-grade year began with the story of the Creation, as told in the Old Testament. Taking one day at a time, we tried to experience the creative process through watercolor painting. On the page opposite each stage, we wrote simple sentences, some of which I include here:[8]

In the beginning God created the heaven and the earth. And the earth was without form and void; and darkness was upon the face of the deep.

(*The blues flowed across the painting opposite the text, with just a hint of the darker depth below.*)

And God said, "Let there be light": and there was light.

(Yellow began shining forth from the midst of the blue.)

And God said, "Let the waters under the heaven be gathered together unto one place, and let the dry land appear." And the earth brought forth grass, herb, and tree.

(In the meeting of yellow and blue near the bottom of the page, green grass and trees appeared.)

And God made two great lights, the greater light to rule the day and the lesser light to rule the night; he made the stars also.

(With a darker yellow, the stars, sun, and moon appeared on the wet page, with the surrounding blue firmament helping to make them all the brighter.)

And God created great whales and living creatures in the waters, fowl to fly through the air, and animals to live upon the earth.

(Some red and purple was brought in here, and new oranges and yellows to help paint the creatures of the land and sea. The children especially enjoyed this stage.)

And God created Man in his own image.

(Finally, the human being, surrounded by plants and animals was painted.)

The mood in the room during these painting sessions was often one of concentration and reverence—not enforced or required but arising out of the beauty of the watercolors and the content with which the children were working.

Although we were able to do only the days of creation in painting, the children carried some of the movement and fullness into the crayon drawings they did for other third-grade lessons. Painting continued once a week right through the grades, often picking up a theme from the current main-lesson subject.

My class was eager to discuss the story of Adam and Eve, as well as of Cain and Abel. At this age, the children seemed to want to explore such questions as, What does it mean to have knowledge of good and evil? Where does evil come from? I especially remember the long discussion on sibling rivalry that we had after the Cain and Abel story. Parents were surprised to hear that their children had been so philosophical and objective about such a vexing family reality.

In three separate blocks during our third-grade year, we covered most of the Old Testament, including Noah (the class wrote compositions about the ark and made wonderful illustrations), the Tower of Babel, Abraham and Isaac, Rebekah, Esau and Jacob, Joseph, Moses through Joshua, Samson, David and Goliath, and Solomon.

The images contained in these stories are vivid, the action dramatic, and the tone often authoritative. God creates, gives commandments, and punishes those who disobey. The individuals mentioned above are strong, decisive leaders of their people. It can be hard for some adults living in our modern times to find a relationship to the authority principle so strongly present in the Old Testament, yet the third-graders seemed to find security and guidance in these stories. Let me say more about this.

Rudolf Steiner described how the principle of imitation, which is prevalent in the first two grades (and is demonstrated by the ease with which the children learned language in the Herr Finser story), gives way to a new element that becomes necessary for eight- and nine-year-olds. This new element is the need for authority.[9] No longer at one with the environment, the third-grader now experiences the world "outside" as being separate from the Self. The child at this age wants to make decisions but is only gradually developing the inner resources to do so. The natural authority figures of mother and father are often questioned at this age. Children in the middle grades need to experience wisdom that is connected with authority, which comes through the story content of the main lessons. One might call this a need for guidance through recognizing the voice of authority—guidance that develops the children's own growing ability to discern truth from untruth. Encountering the guiding authority that permeates the Old Testament can ignite the *inner process* of finding the *inner voice* of authority, which can become the ultimate authority for life. In this way, the experience of outer authority during one epoch of childhood can create the possibility for real freedom later on, a freedom that comes from inner strength, from the resources of the individual soul.[10]

The nine-year change represents one of many instances when parents and teachers need to "let go." The old patterns of interaction with the child may no longer suffice; a new way of resolving issues needs to be developed. For me, the story of Abraham and Isaac illustrates the peculiar dynamic of child rearing and letting go, often before one might feel ready. Just as Isaac was spared in the end, so our children can also come back to us if we let go a bit in their ninth year.

The October of our third-grade year was a main-lesson block in measurement. I struggled with the preparation. Instead of bringing out a few graphs and abstract tables, was there a way I could introduce measurement in an imaginative yet realistic way? The children seemed to enjoy solving riddles at this time, and in addition to introducing measurement I also wanted to appeal to their different temperaments. Exposure to another culture would also be a good thing to include. The reader can well imagine the impossibility of finding just the right story, given this set of requirements. So, as frequently happened in the midst of class teaching, when I couldn't find the story I needed, I wrote one myself. It was not as polished as I might have wished, yet my own creations seemed to sink in deeper and affect the children more strongly than stories I found in books, perhaps because of the effort invoked in writing a story with a very specific purpose. Despite its imperfections, here is "The Miller's Riddle." The different temperaments that are addressed while telling the story are indicated in brackets:

In a country called Holland far across the great Atlantic Ocean, there once lived a boy named Hans. When he was nine years old, his father and mother died quite suddenly, leaving Hans all alone in the world [melancholics].

The farm where he had lived all his life now seemed dreary, and Hans was ever so lonely. He went to the barn, harnessed his faithful horse to a bright red wagon, and set out for the fields. He was a hard worker. Within a matter of days, Hans had harvested the wheat, and it was piled quite high in the red cart. He then set out, horse, cart, and all, to seek his fortune.

Hans drove for miles, over fields and meadows, down country lanes, and through villages. At noon, he led the horse to the side of the road and rested a while. Just as he was about to resume his journey, he spied something bright and shining in the middle of the lane. What could it be? [sanguines]. As Hans bounded up, he thought, "Oh, if only it were a sparkling piece of gold!" But when he picked it up, it was not money. It was small and round, with a long thin part, too. A key! A shining golden key. "I wonder," thought Hans, "what this little key can open?" He tucked it deep inside his pocket and resumed his journey.

As the day advanced, Hans began to feel hungry [nine-year-olds can have quite an appetite]—he had not eaten since breakfast. As he rounded a bend in the road, he spied a great windmill in the distance. "Ah, perhaps the miller will give me a meal, and grind my wheat as well," said Hans as he hurried along.

The windmill was standing still. "No doubt the miller is at lunch," thought Hans, and he hurried around the back to the adjoining house [phlegmatics]. As he passed an open window, he saw the miller and his wife at the table, and what a meal they were having! The smell of roast meat wafted toward Hans—mashed potatoes, piping hot rolls, pies, and other delicious things that Hans longed to eat.

As you can well imagine, Hans lost no time in knocking smartly on the front door. He had scarcely ceased knocking when the door opened, and he was invited inside. The friendly, easy-going miller immediately asked Hans to pull up a chair and join them. Hans did not need a second invitation!

When the meal was over, Hans told the miller about his red cart full of wheat. They went out together, climbed the steps to the deck, and were about to enter the great mill when the miller turned, slapped his thigh, and declared, "The wind is from the north today—I can feel it for sure." And with a long pole he adjusted the direction of the wings. Then, without another word, he turned to enter the door. But it was shut—and locked. Oh, what anger ensued [cholerics]. "My apprentice always does this to me! Every time we make a trip to town, he insists on locking this door before we leave, but who is going to steal a windmill?" The miller stamped his feet, clenched his fists, and was about to break down the door, when Hans happened to slip his hand into his pocket and found what was deep inside. The miller was just raising a sledgehammer for the first stroke when Hans brought forth the key from his pocket. "My key! You have found my key!" said the miller. And with a smile that appeared as fast as his anger had disappeared, the miller took the key, which opened the door like an old friend recognizing a comrade from years past.

The miller released the brake on the "wings" of the windmill as he entered, and Hans could see the huge oak cogwheels, one leading to another, and a strong axle beginning to turn. All had been quiet a minute ago, but now Hans heard a slow swishing sound as the wings began to turn, then a creaking and grinding as the oak wheels rotated. The miller jumped about, adjusting one thing here, another thing there. The wheels turned faster, the wings swished louder, and then came a great rattling and grating as the big stones below began to turn.

The miller poured Hans's wheat into the chute, and the dust began to rise. Now the whole mill was shaking and rattling as Hans watched in awe. Slowly, a thin stream of flour poured out of a funnel into a large sack that was attached to it. When all was done, the miller lifted the sack and, holding it in one hand, balanced it against another sack that was standing in the corner. Holding one sack in each hand he lifted them with a grunt and a groan, testing to see if Hans's sack was as heavy as the other. The sweat was pouring from the miller's brow by the time he had finished weighing Hans's sacks: all told, there were ten!

Hans was so excited by what he had seen that he asked the miller forthwith, "May I become your apprentice?" The miller considered for a while (no doubt remembering the golden key Hans had found) and then said, "I will let you work for me. One condition however, shall be set before you. Help me solve a riddle, which if solved will make our work here easier. You have three days to accomplish it."

This was the riddle that the miller gave to Hans—one that you, third grade, will help to solve:

"My arms grow tired of lifting and weighing thousands and thousands of sacks of flour. My back is no longer so strong. Find a way to help with this work, a way that is good and is fair. Some farmers complain that their sacks are too full, and others say I'm cheating by not filling them enough. How can I prove that they are wrong and I am right? How can I rest my weary arms from my work? Solve this riddle, and you shall be like a son to me."

The class spent some time working at this. They found a long board. With a fulcrum, they tried balancing the sacks of flour. Some used a rope hanging from a hook in the ceiling to construct a simple balance. Others hung ropes from a tree branch outside. Ned brought in an old-fashioned grocery-store scale, which we used with counterweights: I remember even having some children become human scales, weighing various things with blindfolds. I wanted them to have an *experience* of measurement, which, in its archetypal sense, has to do with comparison and with an inner assessment and weighing. Achieving a sense of balance—through the use of scales—is also a natural introduction to the algebra that we would be learning in seventh grade. In short, we performed lots of experimentation before arriving at the conventional units of measurement: ounces, pounds, pecks, bushels. The class also enjoyed working out simple conversions with the help of pencil and paper, such as changing twenty quarts to five gallons, and using the four processes (addition, subtraction, multiplication, and division) with units of measurement.

Our housing block came in November, just as the weather began to change and the "nesting" instinct set in. The block began with a project that at first seemed like an extended recess: I asked the class to build a shelter in the woods behind the school, a shelter that could keep out the worst of the winter weather that would soon arrive. They were encouraged to work in small groups, and the only materials that could be used were things readily available in the woods—no living thing could be harmed or disturbed. I was not really concerned about the latter because a recent incident around the discovery of an orchid in the forest had demonstrated to me how sensitive most of them were concerning nature (they built a small moss garden around the orchid, with a ring of stones for protection). The children greeted the shelter project with great enthusiasm and scampered away to begin.

I tried to stay on the periphery so as not to influence the group process or the final results. It was soon apparent that they would construct a small village of fort-like structures. It was wonderful to watch them heave giant logs, hoist dead branches, and experiment in various ways as they went along. My group had a fluid leadership structure throughout the grades, and this was evident in the shelter project. Boys and girls interacted easily, each working from acknowledged strengths. Occasionally I was asked to arbitrate over a disputed forked limb or a territorial infringement. Within a morning, they had succeeded in constructing several imaginative, if not quite waterproof, shelters.

In the three weeks that followed, we took up a study of housing, which focused on the environmental basis of various types of shelters, with special emphasis on those of Native American cultures. Thus the class explored the wickiups of the Woodland Indians, the teepees of the Plains Indians, and the alcoves of the Cliff Dwellers. We also looked at adobe houses from the southwest and igloos from the far north. We used beeswax to model and assemble miniature villages of each type, complete with people at work, and animals native to that geographic region. Unfortunately, the warm sun of an Indian summer day was the downfall of a beautiful set of wickiups on our window display shelf, just before a parent evening. Nevertheless, many colorful drawings and my memory of the children's work live on. Looking over their main-lesson books, which several of my former students loaned me for this project, I am reminded of the Navajo poem that we recited in our third-grade housing block:

Beauty goes before me,
Beauty goes beside me,
Beauty follows me.
Mountains sing with me,
Bluebirds sing with me,
Tall pines talk with me.
I see the smoke coming from my hogan.
My heart is good,
My spirit is good,
All is beauty.[11]

My third-graders seemed to deeply appreciate the Native American sense for beauty and goodness, two essential themes in Waldorf education. Through the study of housing, the children also had yet another chance to explore the idea of community, since the housing arrangements of most cultures also express how they wish to live together.

The housing block resumed in the spring, and the class studied carpentry, which afforded us an excellent opportunity to apply the lessons learned in linear measurement. As a special project, the group built a bell tower on the playground, which also helped cover up an unsightly well. We built a trapdoor in the floor so as to maintain access to the well. Several strong posts supported an old-fashioned bell, which we hung at the top of the tower beneath the roof. It became a favorite task to ring the bell before and after classes. Even the youngest children could pull the long bell rope.

Our practical work was not restricted to special projects such as the bell tower, however. Right through the grades the children had daily chores, such as sweeping, vacuuming, erasing the blackboard, watering the plants, and emptying the compost bucket (an assorted collection of apple cores, banana peels, and such things that went out to the compost pile, which the third grade traditionally tended at our school). The tasks rotated weekly, and some new ones were added along the way, such as recycling. In addition to helping keep our learning space clean and beautiful, these tasks were planned to foster a relationship to the environment. I felt the children needed help—in an age of central vacuuming systems and disposable everything—in making a conscious reconnection to the essential ingredients of life. Distinguishing between recyclable paper and compostable material was accepted practice in Waldorf classrooms long before it became fashionable in the larger community. These daily chores built a foundation for future main-lesson blocks such as the unit on papermaking in fifth grade and the farming block at the end of third grade. When we planted our third-grade garden in the spring, we used *our own* compost!

During the month of December, the class did many form drawings and also began working with grammar. Grammar was introduced gently, with the help of *doing* words (verbs) and *naming* words (nouns). Just as Adam (in our Old Testament block) had named—with words—all natural things after they were created, we now looked at the activity of naming with words: the verbs helped us experience the active, creative side of life while the nouns expressed objects at rest. We used our red pencils to write verbs and our blue pencils for nouns. Soon adjectives and adverbs came along to help modify our doing and naming words. Thanks to a skit written by a colleague at the school, we had a chance to act out our work with words:[12]

The royal family sat at the front of the room, each wearing a crown. Queen Noun had a blue crown, King Verb a red one; Princess Adjective had a green crown, and Prince Adverb an orange one. The action went like this:

CLASS: Tell us *who* or *what*?
QUEEN: Horse! [The queen gives a different noun each
    time which keeps the game lively and fun.]
CLASS: *What kind* of horse?

PRINCESS: A black-and-white-speckled horse.

CLASS: What does the black-and-white-speckled horse *do*?

KING: Gallops!

CLASS: *How* does the black-and-white-speckled horse gallop?

PRINCE: Swiftly!

CLASS: The black-and-white-speckled horse gallops swiftly.

The children took turns wearing the crowns and giving key words. The rest of the class remained engaged by asking the questions and forming the simple sentences. The repetition allowed a moment of breathing space for the "royal" child to think of an answer. We never knew just what sort of sentence would emerge, so there was always a skit quality to this exercise—spontaneity was encouraged. It helped the class learn about sentence structure, expanded their vocabulary, and gave them opportunities for humorous social interactions—again, active practice in community-building skills.

In the winter and spring months of third grade we revisited many subjects that had been introduced in the fall: Bible stories, arithmetic, English, housing, and farming. A major event was the production of the third of our class plays, "Joseph and His Brethren."[13]

This particular story was chosen at the last moment, as I wanted to see which Old Testament tale sparked the most interest. After telling the story of Joseph and how he was sold into captivity by his brothers, interpreted the Pharaoh's dreams, and tested his brethren when they came seeking grain, the children had many questions and observations.

Their conversations spilled into recess and lunchtime, with much debate about loyalty, slavery, favoritism, and family. I introduced the play as a reading text to further test the waters, and they responded by eagerly asking to perform it.

We had a fluid cast to begin with, as each child wanted to try many parts. Eventually we settled on Margaret and Lee sharing the role of Joseph, Susan and Lucy sharing Pharaoh, Samuel and Mary as Judah, and Joseph, Michael, Zachary, Ned, Doug, Anthony, Maria, Jacob, and Kirsten as brethren. Everyone else participated in the chorus and was available for substitution. In all our plays, right through to Shakespeare in the eighth grade, the children did not seem to mind trying a variety of parts, regardless of the gender called for.

I was glad to see how strongly they took the parts in this particular play in third grade. The content of the Joseph story helped them maintain a lively connection to soul/spiritual realities in a year of many practical activities. Through Joseph they came in contact with questions of individual destiny, never overtly discussed in class yet experienced by all who had "walked in his shoes." Youngest of all the brothers, the father's favorite, blessed by childhood dreams, Joseph stands in contrast to the conniving, plotting group of older siblings. What was his calling? Why the captivity and long service to the Pharaoh? It was an event of his destiny, which resulted in the long years of servitude for his people and was only resolved much later with Moses.[14] The prominence of dreams in Joseph's story served as a reminder to the third-graders that even in a world of house-building, farming, and measurement there is another world—with riddles to ponder.

This deeper aspect of life was further enhanced when Francis Edmunds, founder of Emerson College in England and teacher of teachers, visited my main lesson at the end of third grade. In his eighties at the time, he filled the children with awe and veneration for his bearing and manner as he stood before them in the room. His sparkling eyes saw everything, and the children seemed to be gathered up into his protective gesture. In an overly cynical age, we need people, and lesson content, that inspire veneration.[15] At the end of his visit, I asked Mr. Edmunds if he had a poem or verse to give the class as a reminder of his visit. I thought he would agree to send us one after his return to England, but instead he gave us a simple one that he shared right then and there:

> The sun makes life to grow
> And my heart also.

We all carried these words into our third-grade summer.

4. Trials by Fire

$\mathcal{M}$ ost teachers struggle to find the right balance between personal and professional needs, between family and work.[1] This issue was a natural part of my daily juggling as a Waldorf teacher, as there was never enough time to do everything that was needed. Somehow life seemed to chug along merrily—until a crisis prompted serious self-examination and reappraisal. My year as a fourth-grade teacher was so influenced by events outside the classroom that this narrative would be seriously lacking if the following story were not told.

Two years before I decided to take a new class—in fact, just a month after my wedding—my wife, June, and I opened our home to a handicapped teenage boy, who, for the purposes of this story, will be referred to as "Max." In addition to suffering from Williams Syndrome and congenital heart disease (which meant that he could die at any moment), Max had been neglected as a child. One account related that he had been left in his crib until the age of six and had never been able to make any attempts at walking—let alone at speaking or socializing.[2] His three older sisters had been abused by their father before he left, and Max had witnessed the murder of his mother at the hands of her boyfriend. He was placed in a series of institutions, which further contributed to his unusual habits and behaviors. Before he came to us at the age of sixteen, he had been diagnosed as having the social skills of a six- to seven-year-old and the mental capacities of a two- to three-year-old.

Max had a warm heart and could often play the role of "gentleman," extending his hand in greeting with a big smile and using his few favorite phrases to best advantage. Yet on a daily basis, he displayed strong antisocial tendencies: wolfing down his food, evading responsibility for things he had done, muttering obscenities to his clenched fist, and, at times, beating his head against the wall.

My wife and I entered into the task of caring for Max with high ideals. We really believed that we could help him change. The innovative program under which he came to us was excellent. It was felt that a family setting would be exactly the right thing for such a "moderately" handicapped individual. My wife had worked with autistic children in Montreal and had a Camphill training,[3] and I had hopes of using some of my Waldorf inspirations at home. We managed to involve him in baking, gardening, and seasonal festivals. We taught him to brush his teeth and dress himself with only moderate supervision. Even so, he sometimes came down in the morning with his undershirt over his sweater. Life with Max was a constant struggle, and we had very little respite. He had to be included in most of the social functions we attended, along with his flatulence, grabbing of food, and inappropriate advances toward other people.

Our son, Thomas, was born on December 17, 1982. My first-graders had their wonderful handwork teacher for main lesson that day and heard the news just before departing for the Christmas vacation. It was a joyous holiday season.

Max stayed with us after Thomas's birth. I felt a moral responsibility not to return him to the institution from which he had come. My wife, however, felt that our family should now come first and that we had done all that was possible for Max. With hindsight, I believe she was right. Yet he remained with us for three long years more, during which time I also took on additional responsibilities at school.

Waldorf schools are faculty-directed, which means that those most connected to the classroom—the teachers—set and carry out the pedagogical policy. This meant that in Thursday afternoon meetings, and often on Tuesdays as well, we would hear class reports, discuss children, take part in a study to deepen our understanding of Anthroposophy, or plan the details of running a school, including such things as schedules, dismissals, and supervision. This system, wherein policies and decisions are based on classroom needs, not on community or school-board politics, gives teachers a strong feeling of ownership in the school. We had a board of trustees composed of elected community members, but their domain was mainly the legal and financial affairs of the school.

The faculty could not do everything while working as one large group, so committees were formed with specific mandates. These groups prepared assemblies, festivals, and parent-teacher evenings. Rather than appoint a principal from the board, as is done in most schools, the faculty selected a teacher to serve as chairperson each year.[4] I was asked to take on this role when my class was in third grade. The charge was not to end until five years later, when my class had finished the seventh grade. My responsibilities included chairing Thursday meetings, setting the agenda, communicating with parents on behalf of the school, attending the board of trustees meetings once a month, and handling much of the correspondence involved in hiring teachers.

Through careful planning, I managed to keep a daily and weekly rhythm that allowed for both teaching and administrative work. For instance, I kept the first part of the day for my teaching and, if possible, only entered the faculty-chair office *after* I had given my best to the children. What put me over the edge at times were the crises that a school seems to experience every so often: a budget shortfall, a failure in communication with parents, an emergency involving the physical plant. One year, all the pipes froze during Christmas vacation due to a furnace failure. There were days when family mealtimes were continually interrupted by phone calls, and the family began to feel the effects of my over-involvement.

The two strands of extra responsibility—our care of Max and my school administration—created the conditions that were ripe for a "wake-up call." I was not fully aware of how broadly I had stretched my consciousness until April 1985. The events of that month prompted the most serious revaluation I have ever had to make, both personally and professionally.

It was a bright, sunny day during the spring vacation. Thomas and I were out turning under sod for our garden. However, the expression "turning around in the sod" would be a more accurate description of what he was doing at age two-and-a-half. Max and June were doing a spring-cleaning project—cleaning out the garage. About midmorning, when Thomas had accumulated enough sod for the day, I took him to the garage and exchanged him for Max. June and I had agreed that each boy needed one-on-one adult supervision. However, the exchange of boys this morning had not been planned. It was a sign of our stretched consciousness that we did so without stopping to take a mid-morning break at that point. Instead, we blindly resumed our respective tasks. A sharp cry from the garage a half-hour later first alerted me, followed by the image of June running toward me with Thomas over her shoulder.

She had been stacking old lumber, mostly molding strips, on a pile in a corner while Thomas played contentedly on the *opposite* side of the garage. She had turned her back for what seemed like only a second to retrieve some more pieces and had then tossed them toward the pile across the garage. It was only when a particularly sharp one was already airborne that she simultaneously saw Thomas running toward her, arms outstretched. The end went straight into his right eye.

Need I describe the pain and agony we all endured in the hours, not to mention the days and weeks, that followed? The rescue squad could not be reached, so I called for a police escort as I piled everyone into the car and drove at breakneck speed for the hospital. In the lobby of the emergency room, while I was trying to give the necessary vital statistics, Max kept asking if it was lunchtime yet, and June collapsed. Meanwhile, my little boy clung to my shoulder with blood streaming down his face and his eye in shreds. Thomas did not let go of my shoulder for the entire ambulance ride to another, bigger hospital in Albany. I experienced the full depth of fatherhood. During those hours in the hospital I realized that something in my life had to change.

All the doctors present wanted to remove the remains of my son's eye, put in a glass eye, and hope that the uninjured one would not react and cause total blindness. They spoke of the risk of infection no matter what happened, and of the potential damage to the brain and future learning. One doctor alone, a man who is through and through a humanist, spoke of something called *hope*. He said that if there were even the slightest hope of saving the eye, we should try. Only his gentle expression of hope stood against the opinions of all the other surgeons and the weight of the medical establishment. We decided to put our trust in hope and in this most remarkable individual.

The operation lasted many hours, the eye was sealed for three months, and June slept beside Thomas every night during his two-week stay in the hospital. My class of children was without me for three weeks but fortunately had the kind guidance of an intern from the Waldorf Program at Antioch New England, who had been working with me in the classroom for the past ten weeks. When I returned to school, the children, who so vividly remembered Thomas's birth and had enjoyed his presence on many of our field trips, asked for daily bulletins on his eye. For three months there was not much to tell. What would we find when the eye was reopened and the bandages permanently removed?

The extended family gathered in the waiting room to await the news. My parents, who had jumped in to help soon after the accident, were there and every bit as anxious. When our doctor of hope entered the room, I knew from the smile on his face that the news was good. He expressed himself cautiously. The physical basis for sight had been restored through the operation. The question that remained was whether the eye could be brought back to *function* again. We rejoiced nevertheless.

In the months that followed (and indeed even prior to the good news), we used a series of homeopathic remedies prepared by the Weleda Pharmacy, which are used in anthroposophical medicine. These remedies were mainly in the form of drops administered directly to the eye, but some were taken internally. The substances used were taken from natural sources and then potentized so that their activity could help restore the injured eye.[5]

My mother is a curative eurythmist and had specialized in color therapy for vision impairments.[6] Her grandson now needed all her expertise, and it was given with an abundance of love over the months to come. Seeing his "Oma" was always a joyful occasion, now even more so because he could visit her studio and look at all the beautiful colors. June also did watercolor painting with him, and we patched his uninjured eye for several hours each day to stimulate the functioning of the damaged one.

After each visit that Thomas made to the opthalmologist, and each new fitting for a lens, which had been lost in the accident, my class asked for the latest news. They made things for Thomas, visited and played with him, and in fact adopted him in every sense of the word. It was their victory when, at the end of fourth grade, we received the results of Thomas's latest eye test: his vision in the injured eye was back to 90/20, and the good eye had remained 100% perfect throughout the ordeal!

The accident left him with a scar across his iris. He could never be a fighter pilot, but almost any other tasks in life would be his for the choosing. The combination of hope, skillful surgery, color therapy, and lots of love had accomplished more than we had dared expect.

From this experience of Thomas's eye accident, I woke up to new realities in life. Rather than stuffing, cramming, and overachieving on all fronts in a way that can only result in imbalance, I began to look for simpler ways to work and live. Conversations that had been "useful business transactions" were replaced by more time to simply share human concerns. I started spending more time with my family, and I looked for ways to help colleagues when they were experiencing stress. Outwardly, my school responsibilities and teaching assignments did not change much, but I began to feel a subtle difference in the quality of my time at home and work. I began the slow but steady upward climb along the path of renewal.

Thanks to the nature of the Waldorf curriculum, I was also given many opportunities to renew my joy in teaching by plunging into subjects I had never taught before. In fourth grade alone, I had a chance to teach Norse mythology, fractions, local geography, grammar, zoology, form drawing, painting, and speech. It was wonderful to embrace new subjects out of the perspective and reorientation that had been gained from the personal trials at home. Teaching always has been, and I hope will always remain, an intensely human endeavor. We become what we teach and teach what we are.[7]

The opening-day assembly each year offered an opportunity for each teacher to give an overview of the coming school year from a personal, human point of view. I often chose some object or theme that I had experienced in a personal way and used it to characterize and describe some of the subjects we would be meeting. On opening day in our fourth-grade year, I brought in a shell found on the beach during our family vacation on Cape Cod and said something like this:

> As I was walking along the beach yesterday morning, I found this shell. [I held it up.] At first it seemed quite ordinary. One can find them all over Cape Cod—but then I saw something remarkable. One after another the subjects ahead of us in fourth grade began to unfold, just like the rings on the outside of this shell.
>
> First of all, I observed the rounded exterior and remembered the story of Ymir, the frost giant, and how his rounded skull was placed so as to form the sky above. Then

I saw the beautiful patterns on the outside of the shell and imagined some of the new form drawings we shall do.

Then I counted the spirals and rays, and found sixteen. One whole shell with sixteen parts, each being one sixteenth of the whole. Yes: the shell spoke of fractions, too!

Then I remembered the sea creature who must have lived in this shell when it was still in the great ocean, and I thought of the other creatures we will discover in our zoology block.

Just as I was about to walk away, I saw the mark on the sand that the shell had made, a sort of "earth-writing" to mark the spot where it had landed. That mark in the sand reminded me of our study of "earth-writing," the writing God used to create rivers and mountains; the writing human beings use to divide towns and states. We shall learn all about this in geography.

Finally, I saw a tiny grain of sand in one corner of the shell, and realized how *little* we have learned thus far and how *much* is still ahead of us.

In the classroom, we continued the tradition of starting each main lesson with the morning verse described in the first-grade chapter—"The sun, with loving light..." (the new version would begin next year in fifth grade). Two lines in particular seemed to sum up the dominant quality of my fourth-graders:

> The soul, with spirit power,
> Gives strength unto my limbs.[8]

They entered the room with greater certainty and confidence, assured of a place in the world. Inner and outer realities were now clearly defined, and they enjoyed the challenge of complex forms that involved intricate weaving patterns, many from traditional Celtic designs. They were able to practice a kind of inner distancing as they asserted their individual needs and wants.

This showed itself in vocal assertions of opinion, the keen observation of everything around them, arguments, and at times, critical thoughts about people close to them. They enjoyed exploring the *differences* among people, such as, "My mother does such and such when I.... What does your mother do?"

At times, it seemed to me that fourth-graders were discovering themselves through their likes and dislikes, or through the alternation between sympathy and antipathy.

In the second lecture of his pedagogical course *Study of Man*, Rudolf Steiner states, "We create the seed of our soul life as a rhythm of sympathy and antipathy."[9] Antipathy, through the boundaries and distance it creates between observer and observed, helps us to make mental pictures and concepts, transforming the past into conceptual knowledge, whereas sympathy, with its merging of boundaries between observer and observed, leads us into activity and helps us to change our soul life into the will for action, which works toward the future.

Most conventional classroom situations work extensively (and almost exclusively) with what I would call the forces of antipathy, such as memorization and testing through short-answer, factual responses using paper and pencil. I felt that my role as a Waldorf teacher was to bring as much balance as possible into the equalizing of sympathy and antipathy. Yes, we did do ever more demanding academic work, but our morning-circle activities and recitation helped to engage the rhythmic/circulatory system of each fourth-grader in vigorous activity, flowing between and helping to integrate the two polar spheres of sympathy and antipathy, which are physiologically connected with the brain and nervous system on the one hand and the organs of metabolism on the other. Not only are perception and memory enhanced through such activity but also the possibility for deeper understanding, or comprehension.[10]

Inspired by the ancient Norse myths of the *Poetic Edda*, the children began each morning with choral recitation, speech, and drama. Using verse peppered with mighty alliterations, they stamped, clapped, and spoke with Norse vigor. Stamping on every accent and crossing arms every other time, we fashioned the famous hammer for the Norse god Thor. When I mentioned that the old Norse warriors would march into battle shouting such alliterative lines, and striking their shields on the accents, my class responded with, "Let's do it!"

THE FORGING OF THOR'S HAMMER

Blow, bellows, blow,
Set the sparks aglow!
For Sindri of Swartheim,
The shaper of swords,
Is molding and making
Gifts for the Gods.

Blow, bellows, blow,
Set the sparks aglow!
A ring of red gold
For the master of men;
A boar with bright bristles
For Frey and his friends,
But Thunderer Thor
Needs weapons of war!

Blow, bellows, blow,
Set the sparks aglow!
Fierce and fiery
Flames and furnace,
Molten metals gleam like gold;
Clash and clang of hefty hammers
In the hands of sweltering smiths.
Hard and heavy, strong as steel,
Mighty Mjolnir's forged and fashioned.
Blow, bellows, blow,
Set the sparks aglow. [11]

The alliteration—even without the benefit of shields (to spare our neighbors)—promoted deep breathing, strong circulation, and increased mental alertness. The children's ruddy cheeks and lively expressions demonstrated the inner involvement and heightened sensory awareness they had gained from doing such a recitation.

We covered a wide variety of poems and verses, of which the above is but one example. Occasionally, as we walked and stamped around the room in recitation, I mentioned as an aside that lines in a verse have "feet," and that poets alternate long and short feet for different effects. I reminded the children of the many iambic poems we had learned in the early grades and of the dactylic forms we had learned this year. In such ways I began to lay a foundation for the formal study of poetry that we would be doing in seventh grade.

The above-cited poem contains a healthy dose of repetition, which builds inner confidence. We often returned to the same activity many days in a row, and my experience was that the repetition of "old" material often brought clarification to the "new." [12] Children learn not only from single experiences but also in the flow that moves from day to day, bringing about the juxtaposition of old and new material. As a class teacher, I had many opportunities to experiment with these patterns.

Our morning recitation also included more and more tongue twisters as we moved to the higher grade levels. Our familiar "Peter Piper" was replaced by many new exercises that emphasized consonants and clarity and dexterity in speech:[13]

Round the rough and rugged rocks the ragged rascal ran.

A cup of coffee in a copper coffee pot.

Spitting and spewing,
Splitting and splattering,
Spilling and spoiling,
Spellbound: the sprite.

Red leather, yellow leather.
A lump of red leather, a red leather lump.

Thrice times three
Twice times two.

These two were especially good for my fourth-graders:

Whether the weather be cold,
Or whether the weather be hot,
We'll weather the weather
Whatever the weather
Whether we like it or not.

Never noisy,
Only nimble!
No! No! Do not nettle
Your neighbor!

We would say them in unison, once for clarity, then several times in succession for the challenge of it, and then ask for individuals who were ready to try saying one on their own. My method of teaching tongue twisters was playful: on the spur of the moment I would invent a new way of reciting them, perhaps alternating lines between children, or having one child say the whole thing, except for a chorus at one point. After a vigorous fifteen minutes of recitation and speech work, the class was much readier to begin our main lesson and help build a recollection of what we had done in main lesson the day before. This rosy freshness energized their schoolwork for the rest of the day. I, too, felt refreshed.

In keeping with the characteristics of fourth-graders described earlier, we began the school year with our study of Norse mythology, plunging into the strong alliterations of its verses. The children were surprised to hear an entirely different Creation story from the one in Genesis: this time the world was created out of "burning ice, biting flame." Where the frozen rime of Niflheim in the north was met by the warm breath of air from Muspell in the south, the ice melted and formed drops, which quickened into life and became the giant Ymir.[14] The class delighted in the strong images. The first man and woman grew out of the ooze under Ymir's left armpit. Odin, the one-eyed leader of the gods, displayed some all-too-human shortcomings. Loki, the trickster, was always getting himself and others into trouble. Freyja, mistress of the disguise, had a falcon skin that allowed her spirit to enter the underworld and come back with the gift of prophecy and the knowledge of destinies. The children wept when they heard the story of "Balder the Beautiful," who could only be slain by a shaft made from the mistletoe. Loki managed to contrive a contest and put into the hands of Hodur the blind the fateful dart, which found its mark and killed Balder. As a representative of purity and innocence, Balder stood for the spirit of childhood as the children in my class had known it thus far. His death marks a turning point in pictorial form. Loki, our cunning intellect, allows for a mighty separation, a kind of descent into physicality, which—ultimately—leads to the Twilight of the Gods. After the last battle (Ragnarok) was fought, my students did not want to speak for quite some time.

The Norse myths provided a marvelous opportunity for writing compositions and for making bold, colorful crayon illustrations. The class was really ready at this stage to take on longer assignments and even to do some independent work at home.[15] In fact, much of our mythology and, later, our history blocks were also English workshops. The children continually worked with spelling, grammar, and expression in writing as they processed the images of the presentations.

Our fourth-grade class play dramatized one of the Norse stories. We chose "Iduna and the Golden Apples." Briefly, the myth describes magical apples that renew the gods and prevent them from aging. Only Iduna had the power and capacity to pick these apples. Through a mishap with the giant Thiassi (disguised as an eagle), Loki is forced to promise that he will assist in the abduction of Iduna and her apples. With characteristic cunning, Loki succeeds in luring Iduna out of the garden, whereupon Thiassi swoops down and carries her off to his stone castle in the north. Instantly, the gods begin to age. Their skin wrinkles and sags; they walk with stiff, limping legs, and their vision and hearing grow dim. Odin, also affected by this frightening phenomenon, calls the gods together and discovers that Iduna and Loki are the only ones missing. They know immediately who must be behind this disaster! After an intensive search, Loki is found and compelled to rescue Iduna. With the help of Freyja's magical falcon skin, he makes amends by flying off to Thiassi's castle. Because the giant is out at the time, Loki manages to find Iduna, change her into a nut, and begin the homeward journey. However, Thiassi returns in time to see them depart, and a great race ensues. Will Loki make it back to Asgard in time? Odin, from his high seat, Hlidskjalf, can see everything, and when he spies Loki pursued by Thiassi in eagle form, Odin summons the gods, worn out as they are, to help build large piles of plane shavings around the walls of Asgard. The gods can see the falcon with the eagle close behind. From the heights, the falcon swoops down into Asgard, still holding the nut between its claws. "Light the shavings!" cries Odin. The flames leap up just as the eagle comes through, too late to stop. Thiassi plunges to the ground, and Loki speaks the magic runes that change the nut back into Iduna. Her golden apples soon restore the gods to their previous good health.[16]

When we performed this myth as our play, we opened and closed by singing a round featuring Iduna picking her apples. Joseph and Abbie shared the part of Loki, and Marc and Jacob were superb as Odin. Lucy was a natural, graceful Iduna, and Mary and Eben flew across the stage as Thiassi. The final scene was done with half the class as a speech chorus and the other half doing eurythmy. The audience experienced the following fire scene through flowing veils and dramatic movement:

Fire! Fire!
Leaping and soaring,
Flaming and flashing,
Shine afar.

Guide our falcons
Through the darkness,
Waken courage,
Make swift their flight.
Fire! Fire!
Leaping and soaring,
Flaming and flashing,
Shine afar.

Swifter, swifter,
Swoops the eagle.
Now their strength
Begins to fail.
Can they reach
The fiery beacon?
Can they gain
Valhalla's height?
Bliss, bliss,
They gain the beacon
Now they rise
Above the fire.

Swoop to safety
Through the smoke cloud,
Gain their ground
Among the gods.

Fire! Fire!
Burn more brightly,
Flash more fiercely,

> Seize Thiassi,
> Clutch him closely.
> Flames enfold him,
> Fierce and full.
>
> Lo! They seize him,
> Leaping, flashing,
> Burning, blazing,
> Fast enfolding,
> Fiercely holding.
>
> How he falleth,
> Swiftly sweeping,
> Down he crashes,
> Dark and dead.[17]

Because of the movement and color, and the alliteration with its repeated consonants and crescendo and decrescendo, the experience seemed to touch the children in the very depths of their feeling. They were inwardly and outwardly engaged, and the forces of sympathy toward Iduna and antipathy toward Thiassi were quickened. They loved the action and drama of this myth, the image of the mighty gods growing so ridiculously infirm, and the magical quality of Iduna's apples.

Just as in the earlier grades, I did not "explain" the myth to them, but rather let the images ripen within each individual, knowing that each child would extract meaning from them as needed. This is the marvelous quality of living pictures. The alliteration and images from mythology brought their own kind of "wakefulness," which I respected and therefore left the children to experience in time. An explanation would have weakened the power of the images to work on as an enlivening undercurrent toward future understanding. As an adult I, too, explored, questioned, and examined the myth as we rehearsed. I wanted the challenge of searching for meaning myself, and felt that my inner activity would also enliven our class work. So I pondered the role of Iduna as goddess of fertility, youth, and death. I asked myself, Why apples? Is there a connection between the apples that brought knowledge of good and evil to Adam and Eve and the apples that brought eternal youth to the Norse gods? The nut in the story of Iduna also intrigued me. I was fascinated to read that in Scandinavian folklore, the nut ensures life after death, and that in Irish sagas nuts are symbols of eternal youth.[18]

The vivid pictures of mythology do not grow stale. As a teacher I never tired of living anew the images and events so fully portrayed. It was always hard for me to move on to the next subject.

When the autumn leaves were turning brilliant reds and golden yellows, and the frost lay white on the grass in the early mornings, we turned our attention to arithmetic. I always favored October for math. It seemed that the children and I could think more clearly during the sparkling days of autumn. The waning outer luxuriance and growth of nature seemed to promote the opposite process in the soul life of the children: their powers of concentration and inner activity seemed to increase.[19] For me, math in October always worked.

I began fourth-grade math by reviewing everything we had done to date. Having had the same children for the past three years, and a minimum amount of change in the enrollment each year, I was able to zero in on individual as well as group review. We went back over number placement, the four processes, measurement, Roman numerals, the special role of zero in multiplication, prime numbers, and mental arithmetic. When I felt the group was ready, we launched into the world of fractions.

Because of the nine/ten-year change referred to earlier, fractions are an ideal subject in that they directly mirror the *separation of the world as a whole into the world in its parts*. We started with a large, red apple, which I ceremoniously cut in half and then quarters. I spent some time that first day building the essential concept behind fractions, namely that they are parts of the whole and that one can go from the whole into parts and back again. In the days that followed, we all made large pizza pies out of heavy construction paper, each time discovering different fractions: quarters, fifths, eighths, and tenths. After coloring them in, the children had a chance to cut out the pieces and begin "trading." They could have gone on for hours: "I need some eighths. Does anyone have two to trade for my quarter?"—and so on. Because we had constructed our pies to have the same radius, and equivalent slices were the same size, the children could actually experience that two eighths were needed for one quarter. Because of the wide assortment of colors, not to mention the prestige of having "Abbie's fifth," the children were eager and active in their trading. Only after a firm grounding in the tactile experience did we progress to paper and pencil, as we learned to add and subtract fractions, find the lowest common denominator, reduce, and work with mixed numbers. We did not take up the multiplication and division of fractions until the second main-lesson block in math, later that year.

In that later block we also tackled long division. Few subjects seem to promote more tears of frustration, and more notes from perplexed parents assisting with homework than long division. Considering the infrequent use of long division in everyday living, I was at a loss to understand what all the hoopla was about and tried to make it less of a "big deal." Yet the myth that long division was "so hard" filtered down into my group even before I had begun. Thanks to a little ditty composed by my godmother (and long-time Waldorf teacher), Dorothy Harrer, I was able to help bring a rhythmic, musical quality to the four stages of long division: "Divide, multiply, subtract, bring down."[20] We did problems on the blackboard, worked in pairs, and even sent some problems home.

In the end, most of the children mastered long division. The real achievement was not in the computation skill itself but rather in the development of a capacity to work a problem through in stages and in sequence according to instructions. Many schools stress skill-building above everything else. I do not share this belief: the skills needed for life change. I felt that my real goal as a Waldorf teacher was not only to drill the children in specific skills but to help them *develop capacities*, capacities that were transferable to a multitude of life situations and needs. These included not only learning to follow instructions and sequences but also developing flexible thinking and imagination, learning to solve problems, and gaining experience in group work—all things that we pursued during those eight years together.

Teachers can grow quite egotistical about their successes when they pour information into their students and then test to see how much of what *they have taught* is reflected back by the students. Because of the control mechanisms and the strong role of the person dispensing the information, the process of education can easily be subverted. Teachers need to guard against egotism.[21] The more I taught in a Waldorf setting, the less confidence I had in standardized tests, educational "norms," or the conventional picture of the teacher as dispenser of information. Rather, I felt that my role was to work—as *artistically* as possible—in a way that would help the children gradually awaken to their inherent capacities and to the world around them. I tried to draw forth rather than pour in. [Isn't this what education is all about?]

The children's awakening to the world around them in fourth grade was encouraged by an introduction to geography. The initial presentation described the course of a stream as it started from the melting snow high in the mountains trickling over rocks in high passes, then gathering sister streams along its way through mountain meadows, flowing past villages, down slopes, into the valley, and eventually, into the sea. With the help of a large blackboard drawing, I spoke about the "earth writing" [*geo-graphia*] that resulted from the flow of the river: natural boundaries were carved out over time by the flow of the water. We went down to look at the stream behind our school at recess and found that its course had, in fact, changed slightly since last spring—it had left its traces in the earth.

I also introduced the children to the four points of the compass. Outside, with arms outstretched, we became human compasses, turning north, then east, south, and west. We spoke of the four directions in terms of the path of the sun and of familiar landmarks around the school.

Back in the classroom in the days that followed, we did a floor plan of our classroom, a "bird's-eye view" of desks, chairs, and plants as seen from above. The children insisted on labeling each person's desk and including even the smallest details in the room, such as the exact location of the pencil sharpener. Then we did a drawing of the school, which proved more difficult. I asked the class to do a rough sketch from memory first, which they thought would be no problem at all. Yet when we all went through the building afterwards, we discovered many corners, and even entire offices, that had been overlooked. As a result of this exercise the children became much more observant of their surroundings, and the final drawings were done with great care.

Continuing the process of moving from the center outward, I then asked each child to make a floor plan of his or her room at home, and then a simple map of the road from home to school. Some were so used to chatting up a storm each morning in their carpools that they really could not remember which route they took. In one such instance, a child across the room pitched in with explicit instructions, and the frustrated mapmaker exclaimed, "But you have only been to my house once!" Everyone stopped work to take note of the dialogue. Here was one example of the many instances where students taught each other better than anything I could have said. The capacity of *attentiveness* was given a mighty boost that day!

As a final project, we made a map of our county with the school at its center. The four directions were incorporated, and everyone's house was clearly indicated.

In the spring geography block we studied the history of the Housatonic Valley and of Berkshire County, Massachusetts, in the early days. A highlight was a canoe trip down the Housatonic River. We ended with a study of the state of Massachusetts.

In teaching geography I tried to begin with familiar surroundings and gradually awaken the children to a new sense of space and a new relationship to the physical world. Moving from the center out was a natural progression that built confidence and kept things anchored in reality.

Before Christmas vacation, we returned to grammar, expanding our third-grade work on the parts of speech, and now taking up punctuation as well. Of course, we had always used punctuation in our compositions, but now the class seemed ready to consider it much more consciously.

I tried to introduce this grammar segment with characterizations that personified the quality and style of each form of punctuation:[22]

> I am the period.
> I like to sit quietly.
> I bring each sentence to a close.
>
> Oh, I am lusty,
> Lively, and brave,
> A nimble, jolly fellow.
> In most sentences
> I am well known,
> For Comma is my name.
> Sometimes I become so excited,
> That I talk on, and on, and on . . . .
>
> Oh Ho! Hurrah!
> I'm here! I'm here!
> All move aside!
> For the exclamation point!
> Make room! Make room!
> The exclamation point is making a sentence!

The period sits down
And closes the sentence,
Unless a comma comes rushing along
When they are together,
The period and the comma;
You know them well;
They become the semicolon.

The period says:
"I like to sit quietly."
So two of them say:
"Listen to us:
We make up a colon."

I am a dash—as dashes go—
Though some call me—they call me—
Those who remember—they call me
Call me—me—the hyphen: -[23]

I'd like to know,
What is your name?
Where do you live?
What do you know?
What are you doing?
Say, do you know me?
The question mark?

If anyone speaks some "important words,"
We lead them on.
No spoken words are ever lost,
Because we hold them on both ends,
and carry them forth.

The apostrophe
Shortens a word.
The last sound
may be wiped quite clean.

Making illustrations and examples in color, the children soon felt at home with their punctuation friends. The class especially enjoyed correcting "mistakes" in my sentences on the blackboard by calling out what the correct punctuation should be. All this work also helped us practice forming sentences and strengthened our composition skills.

Many of the spring main-lesson blocks have already been alluded to, but before closing this fourth-grade chapter, I want to describe my favorite block of the year—zoology, otherwise known in Waldorf circles as "Man and Animal."

In the second grade, fables helped us understand certain qualities of the human soul that are represented in our images of particular kinds of animals. Thus we use phrases like "sly as a fox," "brave as a lion," and "timid as a mouse."[24] Now, in our fourth-grade study of animals, we moved from image to form. We tried to examine the form of each animal, in every respect, in relation to the human form. As with geography, fractions, punctuation, and all the fourth-grade subjects, the emphasis was on *our relationship* to things—now, to the animals.

Rudolf Steiner indicated that each animal reflects some portion of the human being, but in an extreme form. In one case the legs predominate, in another the neck, or the sense of smell or of sight—whereas in the human being, the various attributes are balanced and blended.[25] I did not present this as a theory, however. I simply described and characterized each animal and allowed time for discussion in relation to the human being.

To give a framework in which to consider specific animals, I began by calling the children's attention to the threefold nature of the human body. The *head* is carried like a king on a chariot, sitting quietly on the shoulders yet always keeping its goal in view. It needs to rest quietly on high so as to allow for reflection and undisturbed thinking. The head is the home of the senses: sight, hearing, balance, smell, and taste.[26] Through the senses, the head can awaken to the surrounding world. The *limbs* are our strong workers, helping us to move and act. Our legs and arms are our trusty servants, serving our every command. Because we stand upright, we are able to enjoy the free use of our hands for purposeful activity. The head is hard on the outside so as to protect the softness within, while the limbs are the opposite: soft on the outside and bone-hard inside. The *trunk* of the human being gives a home to the rhythmically working heart and lungs. In our breathing and heartbeat, we find nourishment in rhythm and time, which weave between our heads and our limbs, helping the process of integration referred to earlier.[27]

The animal world helped us study examples of the above. The octopus, with its glaring eyes and coiling tentacles, appears as all head and limbs. The children enjoyed hearing how the tentacles have suckers that help the octopus crawl along the ocean floor. We learned about lions and their African habitat. The lion, with its mighty roar and full mane, proclaims the strength of the chest and trunk. The mouse, with its nervous energy, speaks to us of the head-oriented sense world. We all practiced being mice one day. Such chaos! The children captured the quick, frightened, nervous energy of the mouse as they darted on all fours around the room. We also took up a study of the eagle, the penguin, the beaver, and the musk-ox (rather than the cow, which is traditionally done in Waldorf fourth grades). The latter got us into a comparative study of teeth. We then discussed rodents, carnivores, and ungulates as groups, with special emphasis on incisors (rodents), canines (carnivores), and molars (ungulates).

My background reading for this block was unusually extensive and included a study of the anthroposophical insights into the human being in relation to the animals.[28] I reread Chapter Ten of Rudolf Steiner's *Study of Man*, which speaks of our threefoldness, and also another marvelous lecture series by Steiner called *Man as Symphony of the Creative Word*. In the latter I found much food for thought. Steiner asks us to observe the nature of the lion, for example, immersing ourselves in it, to feel the joy, the inner satisfaction, that the lion experiences through living in its surroundings. We must live into the lion's own processes of breathing and circulation to gain a sense for this feeling of satisfaction: between its blood beating upwards, and its breath pulsing downwards, the lion lives in a perpetual, dynamic state of balancing, in which it joyfully masters opposing forces. A few pages later Rudolf Steiner describes how the cow—in the very position of its body, the expression of its eyes, and every movement of its body—expresses *digestion*. The cow lifts its head upon hearing a sound and asks: "Why am I lifting my head now? I am not grazing. . . ." For the cow, there is no point in any exertion unless it is to graze.[29]

The children entered into the qualitative aspects of animals and wrote many compositions incorporating their own experiences. Here is Maria's contribution on the mouse:

> The timid mouse has many enemies: the fox, the badger, the snake, the owl, and the cat. They all love to catch the poor mouse for supper.
>
> The paths of the house mouse are in cellars, in walls, and in the attic. He makes tunnels in the insulation of the house.
>
> If you watch a mouse you can see him shake because he is a frightened animal. At the smallest sound he will run away.
>
> He can be a pest when he gets into food. He also runs up and down the walls at night and wakes you up. He can keep you from sleeping. It happened to me and I was very tired the next morning.

My only frustration with the four-week block was that it went by so quickly—next time I would choose to do two three-week segments instead.

I would like to conclude this chapter as it began, on a personal note. Toward the end of my fourth-grade year, I participated in an international Waldorf teachers' conference in

Dornach, Switzerland. Knowing what I had been through during the past twelve months, one of my colleagues drew me aside
and asked, "Wouldn't you like to take an extra week and have
some time to yourself after the conference?" The conference
itself was scheduled during spring vacation, but any extra time
off would mean missing a week of school. At first I responded
with the attitude, "That's impossible!" Yet she stubbornly persisted, "But would you like to?" When I finally acknowledged
that I would enjoy some time to write, hike in the Alps, and
reflect, she insisted on pursuing her initiative. Before I knew it,
my substitutions, schedule, and finances had all been arranged.
Her deed did as much for my personal renewal at that point as
the actual week of vacation in Europe.

I had a glorious time. My room in Arlesheim overlooked the
valley and the mountains beyond. Just a short way up the road
were the ruins of a castle that had figured in the Parsifal legend,
and beyond that the trail climbed up into the mountains. I read,
wrote, hiked, and sat in outdoor cafes. I practiced my German,
met people, and walked through downtown Basel. But most of
all, I found myself again.

We teachers spend a lot of time involved in the act of giving.
I would not want to change that aspect of teaching. It can also be
re-creative and renewing. I found in Switzerland, however, that
time away from one's responsibilities and the possibility of
uninterrupted *solitude* restores inner balance. I will also never
forget the kind intervention of my colleague.

5. In Balance

*A*t the end of every school year I wrote lengthy narrative reports on each child. These reports helped me characterize my students at each stage of child development, formulate an overview of the curriculum, and maintain a dialogue with the parents.

Before beginning a sequential review of the fifth-grade year, I would like to share my introduction to the reports I wrote at the end of that year and develop the theme of parent/teacher cooperation in a Waldorf school:

On the first of May, 1987, an event that my fifth-graders had anticipated for five years finally occurred: Skipping in and out, expanding and contracting, the children danced together to weave the colorful braid of the maypole at the annual May Day festival. Smiling faces and joyous glances bespoke their feelings on this special occasion, as they moved together, in harmony with each other.

Graceful movement and balance characterize the fifth-grader. The step is still light, the joy still natural. New capacities of thought are awakening, yet the children are still immersed in an intrinsic sense of beauty and order. The fifth-grader wants to succeed, to achieve, but is able to temper his or her individuality to the pulse of the group. Music and poetry speak to the nobility that lives in eleven-year-olds, while the great battles of Marathon and Thermopylae awaken their sense for adventure and their love of action. The student readily identifies with Jason's quest for the

Golden Fleece, the struggles of Heracles, and the exploits of Perseus. Working with students of the fifth grade, one is presented with a glimpse of the true spirit of ancient Greece.

In addition to the maypole dances that the children performed, the May Day festival also included Morris and garland dancers costumed with bright ribbons and bells. They danced to lively accordion music, surrounded by a wide circle of spectators. Jack-in-the-Green often appeared mysteriously from out of the woods, with a newborn lamb tucked under his arm. The dances were followed by a picnic lunch, with children, parents, and teachers sitting together out on the grass. In the afternoon there were games, including a tug-of-war between winter (the adults) and summer (the children). In the end, summer always seemed to win.[1]

Parents and teachers also participated in a variety of festivals during the course of the school year, each marked by a special assembly at which the children shared their accomplishments. Michaelmas was celebrated at the end of September, Halloween at the end of October,[2] Thanksgiving at the end of November, Advent in early December with the Advent spiral, and Christmas at the final assembly before Christmas vacation. These festivals linked us with the passing of the seasons and brought us together as a community. By celebrating these rites of passage together, I found that the bond between parent and teacher grew stronger.[3]

Two or three times each year I also met with the parents of my students at class evenings. We explored aspects of the curriculum together, often engaging in some of the activities that the children had experienced during the day. We performed morning exercises, painted, drew, recited verses, and played the recorder. Parents always seemed to have more appreciation for the Waldorf method of instruction after having actually participated in these activities themselves. At these evenings we also discussed the social and developmental changes that were taking place in the children, along with the field trips, class plays, and special events that called for everyone's participation. I was exceedingly fortunate to have a high level of parent support. Class nights were well attended. We had high group expectations. If a parent missed an evening, I would call the next day to schedule a "make-up" session. Parents also came twice a year for individual parent-teacher conferences. These conversations were essential for my work insofar as we developed a common picture of the child in question. I kept notes on these conferences, which helped me write the year-end reports and follow up on any issues raised by parents.

Rudolf Steiner placed a high priority on parent-teacher interaction.[4] He felt that it was really a two-way street: while teachers need to enlist parental support for their educational objectives, the parents also need to express their hopes and aspirations for their children. A continuous human contact between parent and teacher represents the single greatest security for an independent school. If the government, with all its state mandates and legal/political directives, finally gets out of the business of education, the vacuum will need to be filled by mutual trust and a harmony of feeling between parents and teachers.

In the course of working with my circle of parents over the eight years that I was their children's teacher, I discovered what wonderful human beings they were, with rich life stories and varied interests and talents. These were often put to use in our classroom in the form of guest presentations. With only the conventional one year to work with a particular group of parents, the tendency of a mainstream teacher might be to view them only as "so and so's mother and father." But over the years, they became vital figures in my life. They knew me well—perhaps too well—and were often ready with a kind word or helpful hand when I most needed it. Yes, there were frustrating, even annoying, moments too. One or another parent could become narrow-minded about an issue or event and not let go, even after many conferences and/or phone calls. There were times when I was actually ready to throw in the towel. However, time often served as the best helper. I would begin to see an overactive parent in a different light, for instance. In time we would find a new basis on which to work together. The commitment of eight consecutive years required that we not walk away from difficult situations and that our images of one another remain flexible enough to grow and change.

In a series of lectures that has been printed under the title *Awakening to Community*, Rudolf Steiner speaks of a process that he called the "recasting of judgment."[5] This involves a soul process in which one resists the temptation to form final, fixed conclusions, but rather tries to keep inwardly open and mobile, deepening and transforming one's opinions. Even if the content of the judgment remains the same after a recasting, the nuance changes, due to the warmth one has brought to it through inner effort. One gains a new perspective through each recasting, the personal element is somewhat withdrawn from the judgment, and one can begin to form a new faculty of perception. The exercise of recasting takes time and a lot of patience, but it can act as a social leaven, enhancing relationships between human beings who are striving toward a new social consciousness.

If I were to take another class, I would redouble my efforts to work with my parents on all fronts, not just for the sake of the children, but for the health of society as a whole.

My fifth-graders were able to observe how things change over time, without hindrance from the modern "mind-set" and attitudes that often cloud an understanding of history. And so we launched into an extensive study of ancient times, with emphasis on ancient India, Persia, Babylon, Egypt, Crete, and Greece.

As I prepared for this study, I tried—rather than collecting a host of facts and events to lay out in chronological order—to find symptomatic examples that reflected major changes in human consciousness.[6] In a sense, I considered the outer events of history to be the expression of an inner, more hidden process. My fifth-graders were deeply touched by this study because, in their own development, they were recapitulating the stages of consciousness through which humanity had passed historically. They experienced the mood and forms of ancient cultures in a very intimate and personal way; I often felt that they were *participating* in the stories as they were told. As they followed the "dynamic process of humanity through many different evolutionary phases,"[7] the children saw themselves as the heirs of a growth process that continues through history and still needs to be carried forward in our own time. Learning history was therefore a learning about ourselves.

The following paragraphs attempt to capture the essence of some of the historical symptoms and changes of consciousness that we covered in fifth grade:

INDIA: The class listened to yet another Creation story, this time from an entirely different point of view. Brahma created the waters, and breathed warmth into them. He placed his seed in the waters, which became a golden egg more glorious than the sun. In that egg, he, Brahma, was born.[8] After this tale, of which the foregoing is but a fragment, the children heard about "Manu and the Fish" and recognized shades of Noah and the Ark.

They listened to the teachings of great sages and learned about the caste system. Our discussions were extensive at this point. "How could people be divided into groups like that? It's not fair!" I told them about the Brahmans (priests), Kshatriya (warriors and protectors), Vaisya (merchants and farmers), and Sudra (servants). The students really wanted to examine this more deeply. We even considered the question, "Which caste do you think you might have belonged to?" Bold remarks were made about one another. Everyone agreed that Anthony would certainly have been a Brahman. When reviewing the story of Rama and Sita, I expected that the Indian notion of reincarnation would also be a "hot" topic. Yet the children surprised me again; their response was, "Of course—reincarnation makes sense."

The story of Gautama Buddha figured prominently in this block. The class heard how his birth had been foretold, how the Wise One had warned his mother and father that if their son should ever witness poverty, illness, old age, or death, he would leave them. The royal family went to great lengths to protect the prince, surrounding him with a pleasure palace and luxuries of every description. All those who were ill, poor, or old were removed from his environment. He was not allowed to witness death in any form. This effort failed, however. One day, during a chariot ride, the prince encountered an old beggar, then a sick person, and later, a funeral procession. His soul was so agitated by the sight, and he was so shaken by the existence of such suffering in the world, that he left his palace, gave away his possessions, renounced the throne, and set off on foot to seek wisdom. After many trials, the story continues, he settled under the Bodhi tree, determined not to move until enlightenment found him. It was there that he became the Buddha and that Truth was revealed to him. In his visions he saw that suffering exists wherever there is life on earth but that it can be resolved through successive earth incarnations, until the soul reaches Nirvana where it is freed from the great wheel of repeated lives.[9]

The image of Buddha under that tree, at one with the world, is really a symptom of Indian consciousness. The ancient Indians felt that the supersensible world was the true home of humankind and that the sensory world was unreality, or Maya.[10] They had a great longing to reunite with that supersensible world, to be at one with it. The eight-fold path of self-development was a means to this spiritual union.[11] When we had finished the story of Buddha, and our time in India, a deep peace settled over the children; they had entered into the mood of "wholeness," and it resonated within them.

We moved from the experience of unity in India to that of duality in PERSIA:

Ahura Mazdao was the creator of the world of light. Ahriman, the second-born, loved darkness. He created the daevas to help him oppose the light. So the battle between good and evil began in the beginning of time.

Ahura Mazdao created perfect lands, but to them Ahriman brought ice and snow, storms and floods. Ahura Mazdao's best weapon against Ahriman was human beings who could think good thoughts, speak good words, and do good deeds.

Ahura Mazdao told Djemjid to build a great shelter with high walls and to take into it all kinds of plants, animals, and human beings. When Ahriman created the evil winter and the flood that followed it, only those inside the shelter were saved.[12]

Into this picture of duality steps the figure of Zarathustra (or Zoroaster), a key figure in understanding ancient Persian culture. We spent several days on the life and teachings of Zarathustra, of which only a few glimpses can be shared below:

When Zarathustra reached the threshold between childhood and adolescence, a noteworthy change occurred in him. His otherwise cheerful glance became downcast. He would now wander for days at a time, alone, through forests and pastures. Finally, he fell ill and lay listlessly on his cot.

The Daevas celebrated and conspired to send poison in the guise of medicine. One day a doctor appeared and promised to cure the sick youth. He went to the sickbed and handed the invalid a cup filled with deadly poison. Zarathustra took the cup. Yet as he held it, his hand shook so badly that he could not drink from it. Quickly, the false doctor stepped forward to assist him by holding the cup to his lips. But then Zarathustra raised himself. He had now seen through the evil intent. He took the cup in both hands, poured the contents on the ground, and cried aloud: "For naught has the devil conspired. The Daevas shall lose all their strength through my victory."[13]

As I told this episode, I was mindful of the preadolescent fifth-graders in front of me and of the many temptations they would face in the years to come. Inwardly dedicating my words, I continued with the narrative:

The Turanians were accomplished warriors, far better armed than Zarathustra's people. These enemies' spears had stone heads, and their daggers were sharp. They hid behind hills and in treacherous moors, then came out in wild swarms, outnumbering the bewildered farmers.

Zarathustra deliberated: should he train his neighbors to be equally good in combat, or should he honor the ancient tradition of his people and keep the golden dagger as a peaceful plow? Was not service to the land a service to God, to Ahura Mazdao?

The harvest was once again in. The nights were clear and cool. The mountains beckoned from afar.

In a state of inner turmoil, Zarathustra took his bow and arrows and went up into the mountains. Perhaps there, alone, he could find an answer to the riddle of his people's fate....

Carefully following the stream, Zarathustra eventually arrived at a clear mountain lake, surrounded by steep cliffs. Not far away, a maiden clad in white appeared at a watering hole. Her black hair was held by a golden band, framing a noble face. She raised her water jug to her shoulder, turned, and noticed the strange youth.

The amazing sight of her had left Zarathustra speechless. Finally, he broke the silence to ask, "Who are you, and to whom does this valley belong?"

"You have now entered the valley of our sun-priest, Vahumano."

As Zarathustra approached, she continued: "And my name you wish to know—I am called Arduisur, after this lake."

"Arduisur," repeated Zarathustra in a halting tone (for he was now realizing the importance of this meeting). "Arduisur means 'source of light' in my tongue. My name is Zarathustra. Please let me drink from your jug. I have traveled far."

Arduisur remained motionless and fully upright as they gazed upon one another. Finally she raised the jug and, with a mixture of love and pain on her face, handed it to him.

Zarathustra placed the jug to his lips and drank, and it was as if he were drinking the fulfillment of his life in that water.

"You have had enough," said Arduisur. But as he drank further, she warned him, "He who drinks this water shall develop a burning thirst, which only a god will be able to quench."

Zarathustra returned the empty jug to her.[14]

As I paused in the telling of the story, I contemplated the central dilemma raised early in the above passage: For the sake of victory, even of simple preservation, is it acceptable to sacrifice one's spiritual ideals and become like the enemy? Inwardly, I also compared the archetypal meeting of Zarathustra and Arduisur in the pure mountain air with the crude images of male/female relations portrayed on many television shows. Would any of the wonder and innocence of this meeting work creatively at some later time in my students' lives? Would they then recognize the inevitable "burning thirst" and the wish to drink too deeply? For now a truly oppressive scene unfolds as Zarathustra, with his followers, decides to enter the Turanian camp and look the enemy in the eye. The story continued:

On great stone pillars rested the king's seat. Intertwining snakes formed the backrest. As darkness fell, the Turanians began a powerful, insistent beat by clapping their hands. Some used bones as drumsticks. The sound rose and fell—hour after hour came the same rhythmic beat. Midnight arrived. Suddenly the drumming stopped. An eerie silence preceded a new, more intense beat. At the highest possible crescendo, Argaspa appeared under the arch, red in the light reflected from the nearby flames.

The drumming continued madly as Argaspa ascended the steps to his throne. His bald head glistened. The shadows flickered.

Accompanied by high, shrill tones from hollow wooden instruments, a black figure appeared, holding a staff in one hand and a whip in the other. This was the high priest of the black magicians. Two enormous snakes were brought forth. At a signal from the black priest, the snakes were set down around a large vessel filled with blood.

A cry, not loud but nevertheless heart-rending, broke through the devilish chanting. A woman, half-naked, with her hands bound behind her back, was led by two Turanian servants to the central fire. A great pain coursed through Zarathustra: he recognized the stranger from the mountain lake—Arduisur.

"We shall feed this woman to the snakes," called out King Argaspa, "unless someone offers his blood instead and places his head beneath my foot for as long as I command."

A shudder passed through Arduisur. Zarathustra stood motionless. His glance had met hers.

Then a bull-necked Turanian stepped forward. He took a dagger, pierced his arm, and let his blood flow into the vessel. Then, holding his wound, he climbed the steps to the high throne and placed his head under the king's foot. "We will not witness the sport of the snakes' feast tonight," said Argaspa. "You shall have her. She is yours. Lead her away."

Triumphantly, the Turanian sprang up and approached Arduisur. A cry came from her throat. Then Zarathustra, with drawn dagger, fell upon the Turanian. Chaos ensued. Yet before the army of Turanians could interfere, Argaspa had separated the two and stood before Zarathustra. "You may have her: will you give the blood sacrifice and swear to obey me thereafter?"

Zarathustra lost his senses. He could have strangled the Turanians with his bare hands. His knees shook. Then his followers rushed forward and swiftly carried him away into the dark night.[15]

Some may feel that the above scene is too strong for fifth-graders. Certainly, if it were not followed by the final episode, it would be. Yet because the experience of polarity was so strong in ancient Persia, I felt that the final scene, in which Zarathustra is initiated by the sun god, Ahura Mazdao, would speak more powerfully if the Turanian scene were not omitted. (It also illustrates the fact that a strong light casts a strong shadow.) And, although I discouraged television viewing by my students, I knew that those who were watching Indiana Jones and the like were being exposed to every bit as much and more—but without the balance of positive scenes, and with little opportunity to discuss and process their experiences as we did in the days after hearing the Zarathustra story. I also felt that the imagery and compelling hand-clapped beat of the Turanian scene was a true expression of what I would call the "subhuman," as it is experienced at times in history. I found a disturbing similarity in the Nazi propaganda rallies of the 1930s.[16] The use of an unrelenting, rhythmical beat can awaken base instincts and submerge human consciousness in a way that can place people firmly under the foot of a dictator. We referred back to this scene in the eighth grade when we studied Nazi Germany. By building up a series of experiences, such as this one from the Persian period of history, I felt that the students would have an opportunity, by eighth grade, to begin to *understand*, and not simply "know."

In a sense, balance becomes possible not by eliminating polar experiences and achieving a kind of gray neutrality, but rather by entering into polar opposites in a strong but age-appropriate way so that the individual can wrestle with and find an inner equilibrium, a personal relationship to the dynamics at work in a given situation. The final scenes from the Zarathustra story, when placed before the children shortly after the Turanian scene, gave us just such an opportunity to explore the opposite pole:

Seeking out a hermit, Zarathustra opened his heart, shared the anguish of the Turanian experience, and asked how justice could be achieved. The Wise One answered that the Turanians could not be conquered by weapons of war.

"And it is really not the Turanians that we are fighting. The real enemy is their god, the evil spirit Angra Mainyu [Ahriman]. The Turanians serve him. They sacrifice to him. He is a god of error and lies, yet the Turanians cannot see their error because the god of darkness has clouded their vision, closed their ears.

"The true strength in the battle against the dark forces is Ahura Mazdao, the great sun spirit. All living things are nourished by Him: grasses, flowers, sheep and horses—he lives as spirit in all human beings. Man's life on earth is transitory. Yet in his immortal soul, the human being is open to the sun spirit—everyone wears this garment of light. The physical eyes, however, see only the body that perishes.

"Climb the Albordsch mountain. There, where the eagles rest on the boundary between heaven and earth, there you shall live and pray to Him. Beware, however, for Angra Mainyu will move in the depths and try to block your way.

Prepare your soul by day through prayer; by night open your soul to the great, far-reaching, resounding tone of the cosmos. In time, He will speak and you shall hear."[17]

Zarathustra took this advice, climbed to a high mountain cave, and began his vigil. During the day he suffered from hunger and cold; at night he was tormented by terrible dreams. Weeks and months went by. His prayers remained constant. His only companions were the eagles that circled in the air outside his high cave. Snow and winter froze his limbs. In his misery, and after particularly hellish nightmares, the image of a child often appeared to him. Who could this child be? Gradually he learned to overcome his fears; he spoke his prayers with greater warmth and intensity. The child appeared again, yet this time there was a change:

> The following night the figure was of shimmering white, and its size was larger than the child's. The eyes sparkled, and their glance sought for Zarathustra, touching him gently between the eyes and the forehead. A stream of warmth coursed through his body. The figure rose up and moved away. He gazed—as it vanished into the light.
>
> When Zarathustra awoke, the sun was high in the sky. His whole being felt warmed through as the dream came back to him in memory. Light filled his soul; that which had filled him so with warmth could only have been Arduisur. Where was she, who as light-filled being had vanished into the ether?
>
> Zarathustra stood erect in his cave and gazed out over the mountaintops, over the earth as far as his eyes could see. The earth clouded before his eyes and the mountaintops swayed as a stream of tears poured forth from the lonely one. He would never again see Arduisur on this earth, never again. This certainty now arose as he contemplated the dream experience. He swayed, the precipice looming

before him; he groped along the wall of his cave, and fell to the ground. All bodily and spiritual resistance was broken. He lay there unconscious

Held in space and time, his soul expanded like a ringing tone, and his spirit rose upward toward God. A fireball filled the heavens, and out of it an image appeared. Like thunder echoing through the world, the words resounded: "I will speak! Hear my voice, Zarathustra, thou who art the highest of human beings. I am Ahura Mazdao, the Creator, the one who has chosen you. My voice will henceforth speak to you and impart to you my living words."[18]

Thus at his lowest moment, when all outer and inner supports had been removed from his life, Zarathustra began to hear the voice of Ahura Mazdao. I feel that this scene contains archetypal images and messages—for teachers, parents, and fifth-graders. The experience of the abyss, the loss of all support, is a twentieth-century experience. Many people often feel that they stand alone, without the old community structures, the extended family, and the simple rhythms of life that were present even fifty years ago. Yet through the experience of the abyss, one can cross the threshold and gain new consciousness.

A last note on Zarathustra: When he asked Ahura Mazdao what in all the world is best, second best, and third best, the reply was: "The best are good thoughts, the second best good words, and the third best good deeds."[19] I found this sequence intriguing, since Western culture often seems to place deeds first, undervalues the spoken word, and gives very little consideration to the power of thoughts.

When I reviewed Ahura Mazdao's answer with the fifth-graders, however, their attitude was, "Yes, one has to have good thoughts first, in order to speak good words and do good deeds. You have to think something before you can do it." Again I was astounded by their matter-of-fact acceptance of a great spiritual truth.[20]

It was hard to tear myself away from the mighty experiences of ancient civilizations, but October had arrived and it was time to allow the "potion of oblivion" to take effect in regard to history.[21] Part of the wisdom behind the block system of teaching involves a "letting go" of the material so that it can ripen quietly over time. Many teachers concentrate exclusively on remembering; my aim was often to promote healthy forgetting. When this happened, as in the case of dropping history until November, I found that the children came back to the subject with new perceptions of the old material. Just as a field left fallow over a season can garner new strength for growth, so the fifth-graders seemed eager and ready for a resumption of history after a healthy interval.

In the meantime, we visited Decimal Island. As an introduction to this new unit in arithmetic, I described a logging operation in the north country (thanks to my wife, who was raised in Newfoundland), where loggers used a river for transporting their timber. After the lifestyle and customs of the loggers had been described in suitable detail, I created a picture on the blackboard of a fictitious island in the midst of the river:

> Standing at the tip was one logger who had a long pole. As the logs floated by, he sent whole trunks down the left side of the island toward the lumber mill, and parts of logs down the right side toward the paper mill. At night he returned to his hut on the island. Because of his keen memory, he was able to make notations in his "log" book, giving the daily totals. He wrote the number of whole logs on the left and the number of log parts on the right. In between, he represented the island with a dot (.). Today, we call the Decimal Island dot a "decimal point."

In the weeks that followed, we found many uses for decimals. We solved word problems with money and learned to keep the decimal point aligned when adding and subtracting, but to move it for multiplication and division. Each time we took up a new aspect of arithmetic—such as the decimal unit in fifth grade—I found that all our basic skills could be reviewed without the children realizing it. Rather than simply practicing the same things over and over again each year (which would have grown stale rather quickly), by introducing a new theme each time, we brought freshness and vitality to our work. Having known so many adults who had dreaded math throughout elementary school, I was grateful for the opportunity to "disguise" our practice—but practice was definitely needed for those students who "forgot" their arithmetic.

In November, when the trees were bare and exposed, we returned to our study of ancient cultures, this time focusing on EGYPT and the mythology of Isis and Osiris.[22] If Persia had presented an experience of dualism or polarity, Egypt stood for the trinity: this was seen in the surfaces of the great pyramids and also in the dynamic of Isis, Osiris, and Set (or Typhon). As retold by Lucy in her main-lesson book, this is their story:

> Osiris was once a king in Egypt. He was strong and good; his people loved him. His wife's name was Isis. She was beautiful and wise. She guarded Osiris from his evil brother Set.
>
> Set was jealous. He made winds rush across the desert; he hated to see growth and happy people.
>
> One day, Osiris was standing alone when Set came up from behind and measured his shadow before sneaking away.
>
> A few days later, Set had a big party and everybody came, including Osiris. Isis was not able to attend.
>
> At the party a chest was placed in the middle of the room. It was very pretty, with lots of precious stones embedded in it. Everyone admired it. Then Set stood up and said, "Whoever can fit into that chest can have it." So

everybody tried, but no one could fit inside. Osiris tried and he fit perfectly. Seventy-two men rushed up and slammed down the lid and threw the chest into the Nile.

When Isis heard about this, she cut off a lock of her hair, put on mourning clothes, and went out to find the chest. She followed the Nile for a long time. One day she heard that a big chest had come to shore and a tree had grown up around it. The king of this land had then used the tree to hold up the ceiling of his throne room.

Isis did not know what the king would do if he knew who she was, so she said she was a nurse and took care of the queen's baby.

One night, the queen went by the baby's room and saw that the baby was in the fire. She rushed up and pulled her baby out of the flames, but Isis looked sad and said, "If you had let me keep the baby in the fire for just one more night, he would have gained immortality." Then she told the king and queen who she really was, and they gave her the tree that had her husband in it. She opened it and found both the chest and Osiris.

On her homeward journey, she stopped to see her son, Horus, whom she had not seen for a long time. While she was visiting with him, Set came and pulled Osiris into fourteen pieces and scattered them throughout Egypt. But Isis did not give up. So she went all over and buried all fourteen parts, and at each spot where Osiris rested, a temple of learning was later founded.

This story indicates—in picture form—yet another change in human consciousness. Whereas Zarathustra had climbed to the pinnacle of the mountaintop to come as close to the heavens as possible, Osiris was enclosed in a chest, later in a tree, and was finally buried in the earth. Whereas in the contest between the evil Turanian god Angra Mainyu (Ahriman) and Ahura Mazdao (god of light), Zarathustra was still able to achieve direct communion with the supersensible world, the Egyptians could find the spiritual worlds only through the portal of death.[23] The complex process of mummification and the elabo rate burial rites in the pyramids indicate this focus on death and on the preparation for life after death.

A subtle indication of this change in consciousness can be found in a detail of the Isis story. Her journey to find Osiris takes her to the palace of a king and queen in Phoenicia. Without the insights made possible through Anthroposophy, this small detail might remain insignificant. Egyptian culture at the time used hieroglyphs, or picture-script, while the Phoenicians were already using a letter-script. The old mysteries of Egypt had pre served the ancient, spiritual Imaginations in picture images, whereas the Phoenicians had already entered a more abstract, modern consciousness that enabled them to write with letters.[24] In order to reassemble the life-giving being of Osiris, Isis brought a new consciousness of symbol and letter back to Egypt. A direct experience of reality was replaced by "putting the pieces together," with the help of the human intellect.[25]

We did not discuss these aspects in class, but we did do a lot of writing and drawing in our main-lesson books that reflected these changes in consciousness. The class enjoyed practicing the picture-writing of the Egyptians, and those who had felt some what overwhelmed by the complexity of English grammar and spelling felt especially comfortable with the hieroglyphs. "Why can't we always write like this?" was the repeated question. The children were confirmed in their love for Egyptian writing when they heard that the scribe had been held in particularly high esteem by the ancient Egyptians.

In addition to exploring the pyramids and their construction, we spent considerable time describing the preparation and edu cation of the pharaoh. I felt it was important to fully describe the outer splendor of Egypt: the processions, in which the pharaoh was carried on his great shield, followed by the royal household, temple initiates, pontiffs, dignitaries, and guild members, each with their special emblem and their banners flying in the breeze. And at night members of the royal orchestra, their costumes flashing, would play sweet music beside an artificial lake that sparkled with lights. I also described the inner preparation required for rulership, beginning with the applicant's knock on the outer gate of the temple:

> With majestic countenance, the hierophant (teacher) approached the new arrival. His dark, impenetrable eyes gazed piercingly at the would-be student. It was impossible to hide anything. Questions were asked about the student's background and family. If he was considered unworthy, a simple gesture indicated the path homeward. But if the hierophant found in the aspirant the sincere desire for truth, he was allowed to enter the temple.
>
> Once inside, they passed a disguised, life-sized statue of Isis. Seated in an attitude of meditation and contemplation, the goddess held a closed book on her lap. Her face was veiled, and beneath the statue one could read the inscription, "No mortal has lifted my veil." The student was then warned that acquiring higher knowledge required crossing an abyss. He was asked to work for a time in absolute silence while performing menial tasks in the outer courtyard.[26]

At this point, as we reviewed the lesson the next day, the class discussed what it would be like to observe a vow of silence. Some thought it would be challenging, but Lee, one of my most energetic and talkative boys, exclaimed, "Oh, that would be easy. Just don't talk! No problem." As so often happened in my classroom, in part because of the social insights made possible by having been together for several years, Lee's classmates took him up on his boast. "Oh yes? Why don't you try it!" The next morning Lee arrived with a roll of masking tape and asked me to seal his mouth. He took his seat that day with an air of satisfaction and managed to spend the entire day without even attempting to say one single word. Afterwards I asked him to share his experiences. He gave us a most remark able account. He had heard things he would never have thought possible; he had learned more in that one day's classes than in many previous weeks. He now appreciated some of his classmates whom he had scarcely noticed before. Ancient Egypt really came through for me that day.

But to continue the story:

Only after fulfilling this vow of silence did the student gain admittance to the next trial. He was given a small, lighted lamp and told to enter a dark opening in the wall. The door of the sanctuary closed behind him with a loud bang. There was no turning back.

The next stage is beautifully recounted by Edouard Schuré:

The novice could no longer hesitate; he had to enter the corridor. Hardly had he eased through by crawling on his knees when he heard a voice at the end of the tunnel saying, "Fools who covet knowledge and power perish here!" Because of a strange acoustical phenomenon, this sentence was repeated seven times by echoes at various points. Nevertheless, he had to move forward; the corridor became wider, but inclined downward more sharply. At last the daring traveler found himself before a shaft which led into a hole. An iron ladder disappeared into the latter; the novice took a chance. As he hung upon the lowest rung of the ladder, his frightened gaze looked downward into a terrifying abyss. His poor naphtha lamp, which he gripped convulsively in his trembling hand, cast its dim light into endless darkness. What should he do? Above him, impossible return; below, a drop into the blackness of awful night. In his distress he noticed a crevice on his right.

Stretching forward with one hand on the ladder, and his lamp held out with the other, he saw steps. A staircase! Safety! He climbed upward, escaping the abyss. . . . Finally the aspirant found himself in front of a bronze grating leading into a great hall. . . . On the wall could be seen two rows of symbolic frescoes. . . . A guardian of the sacred symbols opened the grating for the novice and welcomed him with a kind smile. He was congratulated upon having successfully passed the first test.[27]

The trials continued. They included experiences of the four elements—of earth, air, fire, and water. Each of the purification experiences had a strong ritual character, for the student was expected to undergo a moral training that would cleanse the soul in preparation for higher knowledge.[28] For those who successfully passed the tests, the "veil" of Isis could be lifted, and initiation wisdom could be shared. My fifth-graders were astounded to hear that the process of initiation-education in ancient Egypt could take as long as twenty-one years.

To supplement the narrative content of this main-lesson block, we made clay models of pyramids and created a desert cluster of Egyptian monuments on our window shelf. This time our display did not melt in the sun. We even took a trip to the Metropolitan Museum of Art in New York to visit the Egyptian exhibit.

December brought an English block, this time with a focus on writing. Using the Greek myth "Jason and the Golden Fleece," every child created a personal text by writing intensively during the main lesson and continuing each evening at home with parental guidance. I fashioned daily lessons on spelling and grammar around the needs and weaknesses I found in the students' work. At a class night early in the fall, the parents and I had discussed the coming block, arranged a common standard of expectations, and coordinated personal schedules to allow for this coaching each evening. The children took a great leap forward in their writing through this intensive experience

After another block of arithmetic in January, we returned to ancient history, this time to GREECE. As we had seen, the Egyptians followed the sacred path in an inward direction, expressed in the pyramids and in the initiation process. The Greeks, however, turned outward, as seen in the Parthenon and in other temples. The Egyptian felt held and supported by the forces of the earth and the inevitability of death, while the Greek exalted in human freedom and in the joy of living. The figures in Egyptian paintings are seen only in profile. This rigid orientation is locked into a single direction of space and is bound to forces operating outside the body. The Greeks portrayed the human body as at rest within itself, rounded, relaxed, and full of vitality.[29] To convey these qualities, I began our Greek block with a sampling of myths, continued with a characterization of the Athenians and the Spartans, went on to the Persian and the Peloponnesian Wars (spiced with tales from the battles of Marathon and Thermopylae), and concluded with the Greek Olympics. It was an invigorating month!

In keeping with the theme of evolving consciousness, illustrated through the foregoing descriptions of India, Persia, and Egypt, I would like to focus on one particular aspect of the Greeks, namely, the new-found ability to *conceive*, or to conceptualize.

This quality is best conveyed through the story of Perseus, which I reviewed for parents in the school newsletter with the help of excerpts from the children's compositions:

> The evil king Acrisius sent his fair daughter Danae and her little son, Perseus, away to sea in a trunk. After many days, they were rescued by a kind fisherman.
> *—from Ian's composition*

The Greek heroes represent the decline of the old, bloodline culture and the dawn of individuality. The heroes stand as personalities opposed to the old traditions, as is dramatically represented in the banishment of Perseus when he was still an infant. He has to pass over the stormy seas, the realm of Poseidon, ruler of the depths (and of the temperamental storms of human passions). The tiny casket containing Perseus and his mother is rocked on the seas of life before a safe haven is found.

> Many years went by, and Perseus grew to be a very strong lad. Polydectis, the king of that new land, fell in love with Danae, but she would not marry him.
> One day, Perseus went sailing. When he came to an island he sat down to rest under a tree. In a half-dream, Pallas Athene came to him. She showed him a monster with snakes for hair and parched lips with venom dripping from them. She asked him if he was willing to kill this monster. Perseus said he would be. Pallas Athene told him to go back home and wait till the time was right.
>
> *—from Jonathan's composition*

The last sentence contains a strong message for any preteen! As a son of Zeus, Perseus possesses creative sun forces—but he must also prepare himself adequately. His god-given gifts are not enough: he must make an effort to develop what he has—another strong message for the gifted child. For he will fight against the horrid Gorgon, who has been left behind in the development of humankind and has become the personification of evil. I have found that evil often appears in mythology as something misplaced in time—a mode or ability that was once appropriate but has been superseded.

> "Athene," Perseus asked, "is it time to slay Medusa?"
> "Yes, it is, but first you must find the three Grey Sisters and they will tell you where to locate Atlas. Only he can

direct you to Medusa. Yet you must remember not to look at the Gorgon's eyes, for if you do, she will turn you to stone."

—from Donna's composition

The hero must pass many trials and persevere over a long period of time. Even then, knowledge is needed. Thus Perseus is instructed to gaze only at the reflection of Medusa in his shield when striking the fatal blow. Learning for the child in the early grades is perceptual, direct, and intimate. The young child lives at one with the world. The fifth-grader now begins to step back from the immediacy of experience and starts to develop conceptual skills. Just as Medusa's image is reflected in the shining shield of Perseus, so the knowledge of an older child utilizes the *concept*—knowledge that is a *reflection* of the world. This process, and the transition from one mode of learning to the other, is recognized and vividly demonstrated in the Waldorf curriculum. To continue the story:

Perseus traveled south until he came to a great mountain where he found the nymphs. They gave him the hat of darkness and directions to the Gorgons.

It was about midday when Perseus reached the Gorgons. They were sleeping on the beach. Medusa sat between her two sisters.

Perseus slowly descended, and then chopped off Medusa's head. Then he popped the head into a bag, sprang up, and fled. The other two Gorgons chased Perseus for the rest of the day.

—from a group effort: Joseph, Marc, Samuel

A great longing filled the Greek soul, a longing for what is truly human. Greece felt that its own soul had been born through the deeds of Perseus. The ancient, nocturnal, dreamlike consciousness as represented by Medusa is finally overthrown.

The paralyzing fear of the primal, dark forces of the past is overcome.

The human being has been given a powerful new weapon in his battle against evil: the ability to conceive, to think. Can he use it rightly?

In conquering Medusa, Perseus frees the winged horse, Pegasus. The emerging fifth-grader can catch the reflection and hold it fast. Pegasus, winged phantasy and creative genius, is the liberation of thinking that goes beyond intellectual, conceptual knowledge—it bestows the feeling of joy and wonder that can infuse a fifth-grader's learning.[30]

Each year I gave a presentation to the faculty on the curriculum and on the students with whom I was working. In fifth grade, I chose the theme of ancient civilizations and described the children in relation to each epoch. There were those who seemed most at home in the Indian epoch: these children felt a great sense of unity with the world, were receptive, open, and full of empathy. Marc, Ian, and Doug were described in connection with ancient India. Other fifth-graders seemed to experience the duality of life very strongly: my Persians were Mary, Margaret, Samuel, Zachary, and Eben. I placed Anthony in the context of the Babylonians and their celestial consciousness. We had several Egyptians, but for the purposes of the faculty report, I described Tara, Steffen, and Jonathan as Egyptian scholars. Even though in a sense the whole class was Greek throughout their fifth-grade year, I spoke of several children as most clearly embodying the balance, harmony, spirited imaginative life, and budding conceptualization abilities of the Greeks. These were Lucy, Abbie, Susan, Donna, Lee, Kirsten, Joseph, and Maria.

We ended our spring history block with a Greek Olympiad. I will never forget that glorious day in May. We were invited to the Hawthorne Valley School just over the mountain in New York State—they, too, had been practicing for this special event. Now, clad in white, and with Marc and others holding the brightly flaming torch aloft, fifty fifth-graders streamed across the field to open these Olympic games. There were contests in running, jumping, javelin and discus throwing, and Greek wrestling. Each contest was judged not on speed and strength alone but also on grace, skill, and sportsmanship. The final awards were true to the Greek tradition: many received olive wreaths (woven of willow branches since no olive trees were growing at Hawthorne Valley), which were ceremoniously placed on the victors' heads. Everyone returned home that night healthy, happy, and sunburned.

Fifth-grade geography consisted of two North American main-lesson blocks wherein various regions of our continent were studied as we continued the outward expansion begun in fourth grade. I cannot possibly relate the full extent of our explorations, but I will mention two highlights. Our Spanish teacher joined me in teaching the main lesson for an entire week while we covered Mexico and Latin America. She brought songs, poems, and personal experiences of the lands and people. Because the class had been studying languages for several years, their ears were awake to different sounds, and they could appreciate the subtle differences in expressions and customs in the various countries. I found this instance of team teaching to be personally rewarding: I learned along with the class. We ended the week with a piñata and a Mexican feast.

A second highlight involved a book that we used in conjunction with the geography of the Northwest. In *Naya Nuki—Girl Who Ran*, by Kenneth Thomasma, we met the spirited story of a Shoshone Indian girl who was captured in 1801 by a rival Indian tribe. She and her best friend, Sacajawea, were forced to march from their native region in western Montana to an unfamiliar part of North Dakota. Naya Nuki managed to escape and traveled alone for over a thousand miles as she retraced her steps homeward. The remarkable aspect of this story, from the point of view of teaching geography, was that she had practiced such

keen observation of her natural surroundings when she was captured that she was able to retrace her way, following the landmarks of streams, fields, and animal life. The story is also one of
survival and initiative—it is a gripping account of human
achievement.[31]

In fifth grade we also studied botany. We did it in two stages,
first when the leaves began to fall and nature to withdraw for
the winter, and again in the spring when new growth returned.
Whereas our work with animals in second and fourth grades
had helped us understand human soul qualities, the realm of
plants now extended our gaze to include the realm of the forces
streaming between heaven and earth, the cosmic-earthly forces
that are at work in nature. We looked at the big picture of the
interdependence of soil, sun, air, and water, and the types of
vegetation found in different parts of the world. We followed
the path of the sun at the equator and at the poles. We looked at
tundra, lichens, mosses, ferns, and trees. We did a lot of drawing
to capture the gesture of each type of tree, learning to recognize
the difference between the willow and the spruce by the gesture
of its branches. I remember one morning during the daily
review when I gave the class an impromptu quiz in which I used
my arms to indicate one or another tree. The children sang out
the name. As in all things in Waldorf education, the subject studied is related to the human being, with the hope that this inter-
connectedness will instill in the children an appreciation of our
vital role in preserving the environment.

We also looked at what Goethe called the "archetypal plant,"
examining the relationship of root to stem, stem to leaf, and leaf
to blossom.[32] We learned to identify the sepals, corolla, pistil,
stigma, style, ovary, stamens, and anthers. Reproduction was
treated in the context of renewal, and specific plants were looked
at for their medicinal value. For instance, a parent came in one
day to talk to the class about ginger root. She brought specimens
from which we made ginger water for upset stomachs, not to

mention car sickness. We touched on the theme of natural versus synthetic substances, a theme taken further in seventh grade, when we studied cotton.[33]

We ended our school year with a myth—"Demeter and Persephone"— that seemed to tie many of our fifth-grade themes together. Persephone is enjoying the bounty of nature one day when she is captured by Pluto and taken to the underworld. Demeter, her mother, is so distraught that she holds back all growth upon the earth; plants wither and die. In the end, the gods intervene, but only after Persephone has already eaten one pomegranate seed in the underworld. As a consequence, she is forced to alternate between the world of mortals for six months of the year, and the underworld of the dead for six months. Through this alternation, the yearly seasons of growth and death are created.

This myth has continued to intrigue me since I first taught it in fifth grade. The children experienced it as a story that captured the theme of the year: they discovered *balance* in the world of nature between growth and decay, in relationships between mythological figures, and in the whole versus the parts (decimals), although again I did not expound on the fact that we had learned about balance but simply let the images and experiences bear their own weight. As an adult, however, I wanted more. I needed to take the story of Persephone further. I am still not finished with this quest for meaning, but I have found two other seekers along the way:

Robert Bly, in his *Iron John*:

We could say that the Greek goddess Demeter owns the surface of the earth, the wheat fields, barley fields, olive groves, vegetable plots, pastures. We remember that her daughter, Persephone, is playing one day on one of these flowery fields when Pluto, or Hades, takes her downward and inward. She goes to live with Pluto, whose name means "wealth," and so all of us go, when we go into the walled garden, to encounter the wealth of the psyche, which is especially rich in grief.

For men an unnamed god of duty holds down the surface of the earth; and all stock markets, all football fields, all corporation parking lots, all suburban tracts, all offices, all firing ranges, belong to him. There a man makes a stand, makes a farm, makes an impression, makes an empire, but sooner or later, if he is lucky, the time comes to go inward, and live in "the garden." The Wild Man here is like Persephone. It is in the garden that a man finds the wealth of the psyche.[34]

A few pages later is a statement that is ever so applicable to the life of the modern teacher: "Making a garden, and living in it, means paying attention to boundaries, and sometimes we need the boundaries to prevent caretaking from coming in and occupying all our time."[35]

In the middle of Plato's *Meno*, I discovered yet another seeker in the voice of Socrates. After suddenly quoting a verse about Persephone, Socrates says:

As the soul is immortal, has been born often, and has seen all things here and in the underworld, there is nothing which it has not learned; so it is in no way surprising that it can recollect the things it knew before, both about virtue and about other things. As the whole of nature is akin, and the soul has learned everything, nothing prevents a man, after recalling one thing only—a process men call learning—from discovering everything else for himself, if he is brave and does not tire of the search, for searching and learning are, as a whole, recollection.[36]

So the Greek philosopher Socrates takes us back to the start of fifth grade, and the ancient Indian awareness of the soul's continual rebirth and immortality. So—recollecting or recalling is more than the daily, weekly, or yearly review: it involves a calling up and comparing of distant experiences. So—this whole thing we call education is much more than at first meets the eye.

No wonder I finished the year feeling inspired, puzzled, and overwhelmed.

6. With Both Feet Firmly Planted on the Ground

*M*ost people refer to the growth of children as "growing up." A common refrain from aunts and uncles, hated by most children, is the famous "My, how you have grown!" This implies that since the altitude is increasing, the direction is from below upward. But in my experience, children do not grow up, they grow down.

Sixth-graders present a striking example of this downward momentum. A student at this age stands resolutely, with both feet firmly planted on the ground. He or she is physically more solid than before—muscles and bones are now bound together in a way that leads to new strength.[1] The earth is his or her domain. Twelve-year-olds think in practical terms. Cause and effect becomes an increasingly important factor in their understanding of human motivation, history, and science. Concepts such as justice and loyalty can be fiercely debated but must in the end pass the acid test of life experience. For indeed, sixth-graders want to *experience* the world and, if possible, make it their own.

The Waldorf curriculum at this stage of child development allows for learning through the practical, physical applications of the material being studied. Arithmetic becomes useful for everyday life when the mechanics of compounding interest to make money are explored. Although the student still finds delight in beautiful things—for example, in the coloring of geometric designs—now, as the light of conceptual thinking dawns, it is the tools of a trade that hold a special fascination.[2] As an eager geologist, a twelve-year-old literally touches and holds the physical earth while discovering the secrets of its minerals. The phenomena of acoustics, heat, magnetism, and optics are explored through concrete application and experimentation. The culture of ancient Rome is studied, with its emphasis on the material and practical. Such is the world of the Waldorf school sixth-grader.

When my students returned in the fall to begin their sixth-grade year, I found them to be more aware of clothes, food, money, and social issues. They could be bubbly, eager, and pleasant one moment—and then in an instant become sulky, restless, and even resentful.[3] Most of them showed interest and readiness to take on more responsibility for independent work, and they could move mountains when a subject or task interested them.[4] Periods of intense physical activity would alternate with intervals of lethargy and sloppy postures at their desks.

After a few days of school, Maria made the comment that "Mr. Finser has changed so much." I was glad to hear this, because in fact *they* had changed so much that a new teaching style was called for. They wanted and needed someone who was matter-of-fact, clear, and above all, fair. Concepts and ideas were now realities, and they could argue like lawyers. They did not want any obvious references to spirituality and felt most comfortable in cause-and-effect relationships. Above all, in the name of being "just like everybody else," they rejected anything "Waldorfized." The class was ready for a new kind of teaching and for new subjects.

We began the year with geometry. Our preparation for it had already begun in the early grades with extensive form drawings. In the first two grades we made freehand drawings that emphasized repetitive patterns; in third grade we did a lot of symmetry (mirror-image) exercises. In fourth grade we drew braided forms and Celtic designs, and in fifth grade we made circle designs that prepared the way for geometry. Now, in sixth grade, the students were presented with new tools: the compass, protractor, triangle, and straightedge. They had used rulers since the third-grade measurement block. As an introduction to the compass, I gave them an outdoor problem-solving assignment in which they had to find as many ways as possible to inscribe a circle in the sand. They experimented by forming a circle with the class, by using a rope, and by attaching the rope to a pivot point at the center and drawing a circle with the rope taut. When we came inside, we further experimented by attaching string to our pencils and drawing circles on paper. All these activities built a healthy anticipation for the presentation of their compasses. When they finally had these sparkling tools in their hands, they were able to experience a deep appreciation for them because of all the experimentation they had done beforehand. This appreciation grew as they discovered more and more things that the compass could do. The tools were respected and better cared for as a result of this preparation. It always shocked me to see a teacher pass up an educational opportunity of this magnitude by simply taking the supplies out of a box and saying, "Here are your compasses." I found that preparing the class for a new subject actually saved time in the long run because *the students formed their own relationship to the subject or the materials* and were far more responsive and quick to cover ground than they would have been otherwise—another example of economy in teaching.

We began our sixth-grade study by making circle designs that were partly an artistic exercise (we used colored pencils to shade them) and partly simple practice in using the compasses. We drew concentric circles, expanding each one from a common point, and made many, many drawings of circles divided into six parts—opportunities to discover that the radius of any given circle fits exactly six times around the circumference of the same circle.[5] By drawing full circles at each of six points around the circumference, the class created a variety of flower forms that could be carefully shaded in a whole palette of colors. We then went on to drawing families of triangles—of acute, obtuse, right, and corresponding angles—and of squares, parallelograms, and much more. The emphasis in this first block was on the beauty and clarity of geometry, and on conventional concepts and theorems, which were arrived at through discovery and drawing.

Because the students were so engaged in their own hard work during the geometry block, I was able to practice child observation and adjust my teaching according to what I observed in them. Geometry emphasized *their* activity, whereas history and other subjects mostly emphasized mine. I feel that the block schedule should alternate between these two emphases in order to achieve a balance. One might also see this as an alternation between contraction and expansion: the students pull into themselves when doing geometric drawings, and their consciousness expands out beyond themselves when they are living into history.[6] In any case, the group was sorry to leave plane geometry after only three weeks, so we continued making geometric drawings in our extra main-lesson periods later in the day, and in the spring months made geometric string designs with small nails hammered onto large wooden boards.[7]

In the final days of September, we plunged into Roman history. In the pages that follow, I have attempted to do three things: tell the *story* of the Romans that we heard in class, share my thoughts and insights, and by way of endnotes indicate some of the anthroposophical perspectives on Roman history, especially regarding the essential nature of the human being.

After the fall of Troy, Aeneas journeyed far in search of a new home. He and his company first sailed to Macedonia, then to Sicily, and finally to the territory of Laurentum, or present-day Italy. In the course of their wanderings, they lost all their possessions.

Once on shore, they began to search for food and, while doing so, came across a force of armed natives led by King Latinus. He inquired why Aeneas and his men had come to Laurentum. The king was deeply moved by their tale of

Troy and their search for a place to build a new city. Latinus gave Aeneas his royal pledge of friendship. A treaty was made, and the Trojans built a settlement that they named Lavinium.

After many years had passed and many kings had ruled the town, it happened that one ruler, by the name of Proca, fathered two sons named Numitor and Amulius. The father left the kingdom to Numitor, the eldest son. But Amulius had no respect for his father's will: he drove his brother out and seized the throne. One act of violence led to another. Amulius even murdered his brother's male children so that there would be no heir to the throne. Amulius also forbade his niece, Rhea Silvia, to have any children. Yet despite the royal edict, Rhea Silvia gave birth to twin boys, Romulus and Remus, and declared that their father was none other than the god Mars himself.[8]

Thus Mars, the mythological god of war, enters the stream of Roman history through the birth of Romulus and Remus. Mars represents that which leads the human being down to the earth, into hard, physical form.[9] The iron we find in the earth (and in human blood) can be experienced as physical manifestations of the influence of Mars. The Romans later proved to be Mars people in every respect. Their warlike ways, their emphasis on physical accomplishment, and the strong personalities of their leaders brought the influence of Mars to the European continent. My students, with their new hardening muscles and intellects, were ready to meet the fierce realities of the Romans.

The shadow of Mars fell heavily on the two boys, Romulus and Remus. The cruel king, Amulius, bound their mother and flung her into a cold prison cell. The boys were condemned to death by drowning. Yet because the Tiber had recently flooded, it was impossible to get to the actual river channel. Thus, the king's servants set the twins afloat at the edge of the floodwater. Eventually, the basket was left high and dry as the water receded. A she-wolf, coming down from the hills to quench her thirst, heard the infants crying and went to investigate. She found the boys and, according to the legend, took them back to her cave and nursed them. Later on, a shepherd found the twins playing in the cave and adopted them.

My sixth-graders interrupted me at this point to mention the similarities to the stories of Moses in third grade and the Fenris wolf in fourth grade. I acknowledged this observation and remarked that people of different cultures seem to have similar pictures and stories (in adult terms, archetypes) that actually unite people of different nations. I also used this opportunity (the closest I ever came to an outright "plug" for Waldorf education) to say how glad I was that they had worked together as one class for so many years and could make these comparisons in history and mythology. Our hope as Waldorf teachers was that through subtle guidance the older students would see the big picture, the relationships between subjects and cultures, which would not be possible in the same way if each course were taught by a different instructor.

But to continue the story of Rome:

As young men, the brothers were seized by a desire to found a city at the spot where they had been left to drown as infants. (In the meantime they had revenged themselves on the wicked Amulius.) A dispute arose as to which twin should be king of their new city, so the brothers decided to ask the gods for guidance. As the story goes, Romulus took the Palatine hill and Remus the Aventine as their respective stations from which to look for an omen. Remus was the first to receive a sign: six vultures flying overhead. Yet soon thereafter, twelve vultures appeared over the head of Romulus. The followers of each promptly saluted their master as king, one side basing its claim upon priority, the other upon number. Angry words ensued, followed by blows. In the course of the battle, Remus was slain by his brother. Thus the city was named Rome, and Romulus became the first king.

(Other stories relate that Remus was killed after mockingly jumping over the partially built walls of his brother's new settlement. In a fit of rage, Romulus is said to have slain his brother with the words, "So perish whoever else shall overleap my battlements.")[10]

The class had already encountered fratricide in the third-grade story of Cain and Abel, yet in this sixth-grade version the two characters are less clearly differentiated. Nevertheless, one can note the fact that it is the more headstrong Romulus who wins—and community and cooperation thus lose: twelve vultures overcome six. *Quantity, might, conquest,* and *expansion* stand as the four pillars of the foundation of what was to become the Roman Empire. For my sixth-graders, who frequently seemed to value the same qualities (often in the vocabulary of athletics), it was important to objectify these aspects through Roman history as well as to see some of the consequences.

Strong walls do not a city make, as Romulus soon discovered. Faced with the necessity of finding a population, he opened his gates to all those who had no home—the ragtag vagabonds roaming the countryside. This unruly mob, slaves and fugitives included, became the *res publica* of Rome.

Here we come to a crucial point in the narrative. I tried to present this picture to my twelve-year-olds as vividly as possible: all the riffraff of society enter what would later become the greatest city on the continent. I then asked my class, "What kinds of problems would you foresee for the rulers of such citizens?" It took some time to build up this conversation, but in the end the class appreciated the fact that the chaotic, rowdy populace required exceptionally clear laws and a legal system, one that is still part of our lives today.[11] Likewise, the need for law and order, for consequences based upon cause and effect, represents an essential concept for the preteen, who is searching—often in an intensely personal way—for a new relationship to authority. Thus when Romulus created one hundred senators, he was building up a political structure that could temper strength with polity. These "fathers," or *patres* as they were called, were the forefathers of our U.S. Senators and Congressmen. Thus the foundation for understanding our constitutional convention was prepared not in a U.S. history block but in the origins of the Roman legal system.

After Romulus disappeared in a wild thunderstorm, the senators could not decide upon a successor. Who could best follow such a strong founder? Finally, after a year-long interregnum, they decided to approach Numa Pompilius, a man known for his justice and piety. Originally a Sabine, Numa was a learned man, versed in the laws of both man and God. Yet much to the senators' surprise, Numa Pompilius at first refused to accept the crown. Only when he was told that government can be seen as a service to God and humanity did he relent.

Rome had been founded on the principles of physical force and material possession. Now Numa set about building another foundation: a cultural life based upon the needs of the heart and soul. Religious observance and human consideration now became the guiding principles. Numa set a personal example when a breathless messenger once arrived with the news that an enemy force was approaching. Instead of immediately responding, Numa replied, "And I am sacrificing."

Numa built a temple to Janus. When the gates were open, war was at hand, but when they were closed, peace reigned. Thanks to his skillful negotiation of treaties with neighboring communities, the gates of the Janus temple were closed throughout Numa's tenure. He also encouraged farming and forbade the selling of children. Numa even left his influence on the calendar, for the year now began in January (Janus, god of peace) instead of March (Mars). Included for the first time was February (from *februa*, meaning "purification").[12]

Without much discussion, the children were able to appreciate the contrasts between the Roman kings:

In the name "Hostilius" one finds a clear indication of the nature of Rome's third king. Indeed, the reign of Tullus Hostilius was a time of war and aggressive militarism. The third king viewed the forty-three peaceful years under Numa as a reflection of abject senility and sought any and every excuse to ignite the self-interests and self-glorification of the citizens of Rome.

One incident is a picture of both the warlike nature of Hostilius and the cleverness and cunning of the Roman consciousness:

After a skirmish with the neighboring kingdom of Alba, a dispute over territory arose. Mettius, the Alban leader, proposed that the armies avoid excessive bloodshed and instead appoint three brothers from each side to resolve the issue by hand-to-hand combat. In fact, each army boasted of triplets who were the same age and equally strong. These two sets of brothers were now appointed to fight, and the victorious team would confer the disputed territory to their nation. Tullus would have preferred an all-out battle but finally, and reluctantly, agreed to this proposal

The Roman historian Livy describes the battle as follows:

> The six champions now made ready for battle. As they stepped forward into the lists between the two armies, their hearts were high.... The rival armies were still in position; danger there was none, but every man present was tense with anxiety. The stakes were high; upon the luck or valor of three men hung empire or slavery.
>
> The trumpet blared. The brothers drew their swords and, with all the pride of two embattled armies, advanced to combat. Alba's three champions were wounded; a Roman fell, then another—a cheer burst from the Alban army. One Roman survived, surrounded by his three adversaries. They were wounded, while he was unhurt. He knew he could not face them together but that he did have a chance in single combat.
>
> With this purpose in mind, he took to his heels, sure that they would be after him with such speed as their wounds allowed. After a while, the Roman looked back. His three opponents were strung out behind him. Quickly he turned and attacked the first one, who was swiftly killed. Then he performed the same feat with the second Alban, and then the third. The Roman army burst into cheers.[13]

Another time Tullus punished a traitor by tying his arms to one chariot and his legs to another. Then the populace watched as the chariots were driven in opposite directions, demonstrating the results of divided loyalty. Only once, at the end of his life, did Tullus try to consult Jupiter instead of Mars, but he used the wrong incantations and the palace was struck by lightning. Tullus perished in the flames.

Again, one might wonder whether to describe such events as the above to sixth-grade students. Certainly they are not "politically correct," but they are very much a part of Roman history. Clearly we are also still influenced by our Roman heritage, and aggressive militarism is by no means absent from our society. The crucial question for me as a teacher was: How can these images promote discussion and thereby help the students to see Roman traits as soul characteristics that can either run wild or be harnessed and serve a higher authority? What is the difference between outer and inner authority? As sixth-graders, the students were no longer always willing to accept things on my authority as their teacher, but the objective lessons of history were another matter. They could see Numa as one who had lived in harmony with nature and the divine, one who believed in the life-engendering force of a rich cultural life. My students were also able to see Tullus Hostilius for what he was yet at the same time identify with his aggressive nature because of their own early adolescent hormonal changes. Although we did not discuss their personal developmental changes at this point, I felt that they were being *indirectly* addressed long before we arrived at our physiology and health block in seventh grade. Throughout my eight years with the class, my aim was always to address the more complex issues of life on a feeling level first, and then to bring in the facts and figures. My position—contrary to that of most programs designed to deter drug use, teenage pregnancy, and AIDS—was that to reach the children, one had to begin with something other than the nuts and bolts of physical detail.

The question however remained for me: What is it that can awaken within the human being in such a way as to exercise control over the severe mood changes and the aggressive behavior that every person experiences at some time or in some way? I was delighted to find in Ancus Marcius, the fourth king of Rome, a figure who represented the ego (that principle which can assert rulership over the tumult of the human soul).[14] Ancus had some of the qualities of both Numa and Tullus, yet he was in charge of his own destiny, planned for both war and peace, built bridges across the Tiber, passed measures to deter lawlessness, and knew how to serve as an administrator—one who ministers to others. He even introduced an element of control to the battlefield by establishing specific formalities for declaring and conducting war. The twenty-four years under Ancus were a time of balance and order.

Although the Romans were practical people, they still had a healthy sense for auspicious omens, especially if they were favorable to their own interests: A wealthy man by the name of Lucius was traveling in his open carriage with his wife when an eagle dropped gently down and snatched off his cap. It rose with a great clamor of wings until, a few minutes later, it swooped down again and, as if sent by heaven, neatly put the cap back upon Lucius's head. His wife immediately saw this as a good sign and exclaimed, "Did it not declare its message by coming to your head—the highest part of you? Did it not take the crown, as it were, from a human head, only to restore it by heaven's approval, where it belongs?"[15] Lucius moved to Rome, used his wealth to get close to the king, and soon became his trusted advisor. When Ancus died, Lucius sent the king's sons out of town on a hunting expedition. He made a political speech for support in the Senate, and was easily elected king of Rome.

Even the sixth king was preceded by an omen: A little servant boy by the name of Servius Tullius was lying asleep one day when his head suddenly burst into flames. Someone was about to throw water on them when the queen stopped him because she recognized the portent. Sure enough, in a few moments the child awoke and the fire went out. The royal couple adopted Servius, and he later became king.

Perhaps the most dramatic period in the early history of Rome involves the last king, Lucius Tarquinius Superbus, just before the consulship was established. Because his rule involved so many of the classic issues of Roman history, this period seemed to offer good content for a class play. Dressed in Roman togas, and with a double cast to accommodate all my eager players, we performed the play after three weeks of intensive rehearsal. The cast of characters included:

LUCIUS TARQUINIUS SUPERBUS, *the last king of Rome*: Torrey and Kirsten
SERVIUS, *the reigning king*: Zachary
TWO SONS OF TARQUINIUS: Jonathan F. and Michael
BRUTUS, *nephew of Tarquinius*: Susan and Mary
PRIEST *of the delphic oracle*: Joseph
PONTIFEX MAXIMUS, *first initiate of the college of priests*: Jonathan B.
CENTURION: Tim
LICTOR: Anthony
SYBIL OF CUMAE: Emily
TULLIA: daughter of Servius, wife of Tarquinius, Kirsten and Torrey
SERPENT: Lucy
SENATORS: Samuel, Maria, Donna, Tara, David, Abbie, Marc, and Margaret

The play began with a speech chorus that recounted the early kings, followed by scenes in which Servius is ruthlessly deposed by Tarquinius. After the body of the old king is trampled by the horses and the chariot driven by Tullia, the chorus warns:

Beware the pride that finds a place above the clouds
Beware the sword that has too many blades.
Beware ... beware the time
When satisfaction turns to shame.
Beyond the brow of every man
Still stand the Gods who see the heart,

Who know the heart!
Tarquinius Superbus!
Your days are autumn days
That ever shorter grow
Toward wintertime.[16]

The scene with Sybil, the wise woman with her nine books, is symptomatic of the change in consciousness that was taking place during the Roman era:

SYBIL: I am a wanderer out of Cumae.
TARQUINIUS: What do you want?
SYBIL: I have come to offer you these nine books.
TARQUINIUS: Does a king of Rome need books, woman?
SYBIL: No. You would do well not to buy them.
TARQUINIUS: Buy them, you say.
SYBIL: The price is nine hundred oxen.
TARQUINIUS: Begone, woman. [He laughs.] You are mad.
SYBIL: No. You would do well not to buy them.
[She burns three of the books in the brazier.] Now there are only six left, but you may still have them for the same price.
TARQUINIUS: I will give you six hundred oxen for the six books.
SYBIL: [She burns three more of the books.]
[Enter Pontifex Maximus.]
Only these three remain. I will still give them to you for the same price.
TARQUINIUS: Who are you?
SYBIL: I am the bringer of a gift.
TARQUINIUS: You cheat me, and yet I feel compelled. A curse on you for the power which you have over me. Here is the money! [Exit Sybil.]
[Looking at the books.] Have I paid nine hundred oxen for the scribbling of a mad woman? The letters are Greek but I cannot read the words.

Roman logic dictates that six-hundred oxen should pay for six books, yet Tarquinius cannot resist the allure of the mysterious Sybil. Each time that three more books are burned, his curiosity grows. Yet in the end, Tarquinius cannot read the print: the ancient wisdom is no longer accessible, the wisdom of earlier civilizations is lost to him. Here we find the "descent" of human consciousness: the early omens (eagle and fire) have now left, and the price for achieving individual human intelligence and freedom is a closing of the books of spiritual wisdom.

The play contained many moving scenes, including one in which Lucy entered as the Serpent to haunt Tarquinius, followed by the priests entering in procession, carrying lighted candles in their hands, as an echo of the past. There was a scene at Delphi where the sons substitute their own question for that of the king about the Serpent, "Who will be king after the death of our father?" The oracle replies, "Whichever of you shall first kiss his mother." The two sons rush off, but Brutus, who has accompanied them, falls to the ground at the feet of the priests and declares, "Is not the earth the mother of us all?"

The final scene involves the uprising in the Senate when Tarquinius is deposed in favor of Roman law and the rule of two consuls who will govern for but one year at a time:

TARQUINIUS: Who is responsible for this . . . insurrection?
SENATOR 1: The Patricians of Rome depose you for the sake of justice!
TARQUINIUS: Who leads the Patricians of Rome?
SENATOR 3: The law.
TARQUINIUS: The law?
SENATOR 4: Every man is open to the powers of selfishness and ambition. Only the law stands above temptation.
SENATOR 3: We'll have no more kings!
SENATOR 1: To take the place of a king, there shall be law—impersonal, unprejudiced, equitable law.[17]

Yet the theme of laws before kings is balanced at the very end when Brutus, who now sits as consul and has passed the first law, namely that anyone conspiring to plot the return of a king shall be beheaded, is faced with his first case—his own sons. The Senate is willing to consider exile in view of "all you have done for Rome," but Brutus responds with anguish:

BRUTUS: Remember our words? Impersonal, unprejudiced, equitable law. If the law is to be just, then the eagle and the wren must be equal under it. The law must not fail its first test! Hear me! It is the will of Rome that these men, guilty by confession.... [He pauses.] Tarquinius would have given you nothing...these men, my sons...shall be publicly whipped...beheaded. Take them away.
SON 1: We are the sons of the first consul.
SON 2: You would not dare harm us!
SON 1: Father.... [They exit.]
BRUTUS: [Alone.] So this is how you reveal yourself. O, Law! You are harsher than any God. You demand more than any divinity has ever received upon an altar. What pain you cause me. Now at last I see...through my tears...through my suffering...that the law can only endure if there are people who will sacrifice of themselves out of their own free will.[18]

Mary and Susan played the part of Brutus with great feeling and pathos. Their speech and gesture really captured the inner torment of family loyalty versus impartial law. I will also never forget how well Kirsten and Torrey portrayed the proud Tarquinius, nor will I forget the marvelous group spirit of our Roman senators. As with many of the plays given by my class, I was deeply indebted to our school eurythmist, who coached the speech chorus in the art of walking for their candlelit procession, and the Serpent in making sinuous, fluid movements under her veils of green and blue. One child remarked at the end, "Lucy had no lines to speak, yet her part was one of the best in the play."

As we continued with the consular period, and later with the rule of the emperors, I found myself once again asking inner questions:

"How does the birth of the Roman legal system relate to our modern legal mentality, wherein social issues are decided not in the fellowship of the church, nor in the extended family, or even at our place of work, but more frequently in a court of law. Our critical faculties are fully awake, but where is the inner capacity that can form healthy judgments?"

"How does the Roman emphasis on laws relate to Rudolf Steiner's Threefold Social Order where he describes the sphere of rights life and the need for an independent cultural life?"[19]

"Why are so many of our public schools governed by political school boards?"

"Why is modern education so permeated by this still-prevalent Roman attitude in its concern with numbers, power, accomplishment, and preparation for business and industry rather than with cultural and spiritual endeavors?"

And finally as a Waldorf teacher, I asked myself, "How can I intensify my efforts to break through this Roman barrier in my own meditative life, in my work with colleagues, and in my involvement with cultural activities outside of school?"

As at other stages in my odyssey, I did not find easy answers, but I felt reassured in asking and living with my questions. They heightened my consciousness of the dilemmas we have inherited from Rome. Through this kind of personal research I felt that the living stream of teaching and working out of Anthroposophy was nurtured, guided, and enhanced. Each year I sensed more strongly that teaching is a practical manifestation of this inner searching.

Our next main-lesson block took us back to practical math and focused on percent and interest. We set up a class bank and learned how to compound interest. We also made our own checkbooks and enjoyed writing unlimited checks—until it came time to reconcile our monthly statements. One child asked, "What happens to checks when they are at the bank?" Instead of giving a long-winded answer, we arranged a field trip to our hometown savings institution and, thanks to a particularly friendly guide, managed to see not only the vault but also the check-processing center downstairs. The class was able to see, step by step, what happens to checks, and how savings money is recycled into mortgage loans.

In keeping with the sixth-grade qualities described at the beginning of the chapter, the English block that followed focused on business letters: contracts, letters of application, letters of understanding, thank-you letters, and so on. Besides reviewing rules of grammar, spelling, and punctuation while writing these letters, we also worked with conditional sentences. At this age the students particularly seemed to relish the many ways one might state a condition: "I will ..., if you do thus and so." Since they were employing such sentences at home and school anyway, I figured we might as well take advantage of the opportunity to develop grammar skills.

In December, when days were short and nights long, we began a preliminary study of astronomy. We spoke of the path of the sun during the seasons and of the phases of the moon. We gathered one evening for stargazing and hot chocolate. Seventh grade would bring a thorough exploration of the heavens; in sixth grade I merely wanted to prepare the way. By keeping a star journal and learning simple stellar observation skills a year ahead of time, the children would be ready for the science of astronomy in seventh grade.

After the winter holidays, we began the first of two blocks in physics. Since this subject was a favorite of mine, and of the students, I would like to describe our work in detail. The science curriculum is closely geared to the characteristic stage of child development in each grade and serves as an illustration of the new way in which children can be taught at each age.

Working with the Waldorf curriculum, the teacher tries to develop the concepts given in physics out of life itself and strives to be as inventive as possible in bringing the phenomena in question before the children.[20] In sixth grade, we covered acoustics, heat, magnetism, and optics, with the latter falling in the second block, given in the spring.

Several experienced Waldorf science teachers have suggested that acoustics be "born out of the musical," perhaps through the playing of stringed instruments and the experience of higher and lower tones.[21] With all due respect to my colleagues, I disagreed. Of course, my class had experienced music every day for six years now. As a musician, I welcomed every opportunity to fur-ther their musical appreciation. But I felt that my sixth-graders needed a new approach—they were yearning for "real science," and I felt it was time to use a phenomenological approach that challenged them in new ways. I had tried the "musical approach" with my first group of sixth-graders, and it came off as a rather ho-hum experience. This time I wanted to adopt a new style of teaching and really challenge the students in science.

So we began with the phenomena of sound. When the chil-dren walked into our classroom that first day after the Christ-mas holidays, they found a large screen shielding my desk and the front of the room. This in itself awakened their curiosity, but their questions received a "wait and see" answer. After morning exercises, in which we still did speech—now mainly working with hexameter—I passed out paper and pencils and asked the class to take five minutes to practice listening and write down all the sounds they could hear while sitting at their desks. A stu-dent commented, "Not much," but after a few moments he was writing busily. Long lists indicated that there was much more to hear than they had imagined. These included such things as doors closing, birds singing, a lawnmower, a plane overhead, and so on—things they ordinarily wouldn't have noticed at all

I then stepped behind the screen and made various sounds using coins, a glass, water, a spoon, a hammer and nails, paper, scissors, an egg carton, a plant mister, and a bean bag, and the students were asked to write down sequentially what they thought they had heard. Afterwards, we compared notes. They had identified every single object.

After experiencing the phenomenon of sound in this way, we discussed our findings. I began by asking, "How did you know what the sound was?" After the usual declarations of "Everyone knows!" or "It was easy!," they began to focus on the experience. Eventually, through discussion, we arrived at the observation that every sound reveals its source and that each object used behind the screen had made a different sound. I reminded them that the screen had prevented them from seeing anything—they had used only their ears. Then I asked them to hold their ears and block out the sound I was about to make, just as their vision had previously been blocked. When they were all tightly holding their ears, I played a high G on my recorder. They all reported hearing it very distinctly. This gave me a chance to point out that, unlike visual experiences, sound penetrates very deeply.[22] In our review the next day, someone remarked that an older sister often played loud music at home and that the penetrating sound kept him awake. This resulted in a discussion about certain kinds of music and the potential for loss of hearing at concerts where this music was played. Everyone had something to say on the subject, and at one point I steered them back to acoustics by asking, "Where is sound when we don't hear it?" This quieted them down. After the question had a chance to sink in a bit, we continued with our experiments.

We explored the phenomenon of timbre with the help of five wooden blocks, each made of a different wood: oak, walnut, cherry, birch, and pine. When we struck each one in the same way, we found that each block had a different quality of sound. Each person then tried saying the word "acoustics," and several children played an 'A' on their musical instruments. Each time, we experienced a different quality of sound and learned that this quality is called "timbre." We moved on to resonance and tuning forks. Each child struck a tuning fork and placed its base on a desk. Then we struck a tuning fork and held it parallel to another one of similar size. Finally, we struck tuning forks and dipped them in cups of water. After experiencing the phenomena, I asked them to describe their experiences. Susan wrote her observations as follows:

1. When the vibrations of a tuning fork are carried through the stem to the surface of a solid object, they force the object to vibrate and resound in the same pitch as the tuning fork. This is called *resonance*.
2. When we placed the tuning fork in the water, we observed that the vibrating end caused the water to spray out. Thus sound involves motion and vibration.
3. The vibrations of a tuning fork can set another fork of the same frequency in motion. Thus we heard a hum from the second tuning fork. One can speak of the two forks as being in sympathy with one another. Such vibrations are called "sympathetic vibrations."

In our second-day review, I touched on the larger theme of "sympathy" by asking the class how they could tell if someone was in sympathy with them or not. They offered observations such as "if they are similar to you," "if they have the same interests," and "if a friendship over time has built a common base of experience." Thus, even though we were immersed in acoustics, the subject matter gave us opportunities to continue our exploration of social and community-building issues. The above experiment also ended with a humorous twist. At the end of the block the students asked if they could do a few physics experiments at a school assembly. Tuning forks were part of the demonstration. They found a large basin and, at the appropriate time, asked for volunteers from the audience to closely observe any changes in the water. Then, with friends from the younger grades intently pressing their chins to the basin, my dear sixth-graders struck twenty-four large tuning forks and simulta-neously placed them in the water. Many younger children went home with vivid descriptions of something called physics and how it made water spray at people's faces.

Our study of acoustics also included the Chladni plate exper-iment, in which a metal plate was clamped to a desk, and table salt sprinkled on its surface. By drawing an old violin bow down the edge of the plate, a tone was created. Most exciting of all, the salt jumped around on the plate and formed intricate, regular geometric patterns. We thus discovered that sound's movement also creates forms. We then went on to the soda bot-tles the children had collected for recycling. We filled them with different amounts of water, and I gave one to each student. They were asked to arrange themselves in a line according to pitch. It was wonderful to see them sorting themselves out as they blew over the tops of their bottles. Eventually we fine-tuned the bot-tles to get a C-major scale. After some practice, we added "Mary Had a Little Lamb" to our assembly repertoire.

We ended the acoustics portion of the physics block with an examination of musical intervals and mathematics. I brought in my cello, and we fastened a long strip of paper to the finger-board, making sure it was exactly the same length as the strings. Then we folded it in half crosswise, fastened it to the finger-board with a clothespin, and played the note indicated by the fold mark. After the half, we did this with fourths, thirds, and so on. Afterwards, we charted our findings on the blackboard. When the paper was folded in half, the note played at that mark was an octave, the one-third fold resulted in a fifth, the one-fourth a fourth. I then did a quick sequence on music theory, which included sharps, flats, and major and minor modes. Through this mathematical and phenomenological approach, the children approached music from a different direction and appreciated it in an altogether new way.

Still in deep winter, with icicles hanging over our windows, we took up a study of heat. For homework the day before, I had asked the students to write two descriptive paragraphs, one on the hottest day and one on the coldest day they had ever experienced. This assignment served to "warm up" the subject, and they came to school ready for some experiments. The first one surprised them. I placed three bowls of water on a desk at the front of the room. The first was filled with hot water, the second with cold, and the third with lukewarm water. One by one each student placed his or her left hand in the cold water while the right hand was gingerly placed in the hot. Then both hands were quickly placed in the lukewarm water. They were not allowed to say anything until everyone had had a chance to try the experiment. There was universal agreement that in the lukewarm water their two hands felt quite different: the hand that had been in cold water felt hot, and the hand that had been in hot water felt cold. We had thus observed that our body reacts to heat and cold in relation to its own temperature.

Out of their recognition of the imprecise nature of the body as a thermostat, the students were ready for an objective way to measure heat. We did experiments measuring the conduction and expansion of liquids, gases, and solids when heated. The experiment that received the most enthusiastic response utilized potassium permanganate ($KMnO_4$). Here is Susan's account of it:

> We placed a beaker of water on a stand and carefully placed the potassium crystals at the bottom. We then placed a flame under the beaker. As the water heated, the crystals began to dissolve, and beautiful, thin wisps of purple began to rise up through the water. The color was incredible.

The class did not need any further persuasion that water rises when heated, and the beauty and power of the visual perception touched them so deeply that they would never forget it.

In his book on child development, John Benians mentions that the art of teaching science must always stimulate the child's observation and not merely present him or her with a book of answers. The more that each child can do individually toward finding the answers the better, and children who have been brought up in this way—so that the maximum of activity is expected from them—will not need undue time to do what is so commonly done for them in present-day textbooks.[23]

When we did experiments, I said very little beforehand but made sure that everyone was in a good position to see what happened. Here is an experiment on magnetism. We did it together:

Each child received several magnets and placed a piece of light-weight paper over them. I then sprinkled iron filings on the paper, which moved into position so that we could observe the lines corresponding to the magnetic field around each magnet (similar to what we had seen in the Chladni plate experiment). Working with large, ten-pound magnets was especially fun: we used them to demonstrate that opposite poles attract and like poles repulse, and the students actually *felt* the strength of attraction and repulsion, right into their muscles and bones. When I asked for volunteers, many hands went up. I selected two children who were having some social difficulties that year. They stood ten feet apart. I gave each one a powerful magnet. Without first introducing the concept of poles, I handed them the magnets in such a way that the opposite poles were facing each other. Then I asked them to take small steps toward one another, but not to let the magnets touch. With an attitude of "No problem, I wouldn't want to get too close anyway," they slowly walked forward. The class watched with suspense, realizing that more than a science experiment was being played out before their eyes. At a certain point the two children seemed to leap forward, and the two magnets united with a snap. The class was fascinated—everyone wanted to have a turn. I next selected a boy and girl for whom the opposite scenario was needed. I asked them to do the same as the last couple, but I switched poles so that "like poles" were facing each other. No matter how hard they tried, these two could not bring the magnets together.

In the days that followed, as we experimented further, we also discussed some of the social aspects of "attraction and repulsion" in terms of friendships and of siblings. I treated the topic gently. As with zoology, botany, and the other sciences we studied, I felt it was of great importance for the students to relate their experiences to human situations, to keep the human being "in the picture" when studying science. This theme was addressed in a more direct way in eighth grade when we looked at the advent of atomic energy with all its ramifications.

In the spring physics block we worked with optics, experimenting with primary and secondary colors, afterimages, the darkening of light, and the use of the prism. We were fortunate to have a full set of prisms so that each student had one and could first gaze through it at various objects in the room and then experiment by looking at the boundaries between dark and light shapes that had been placed on their desks. We observed that a dark surface overriding a light surface gave the red-orange-yellow end of the spectrum, and a light surface overriding a dark gave the blue-indigo-violet end. We talked about light being darkened and dark being lightened and about the seven colors of the spectrum. We then further explored the world of color through painting.

That year I continued to serve as faculty chair and as a trustee of the school. Because we did not receive any state funding, all our monies had to be raised by parents and friends of the school. We had many parents who could not afford the tuition payments, so we worked to raise money for scholarships. Each year we had an extraordinary holiday handcraft fair. Parents, teachers, and friends knitted, sewed, crafted, and constructed amazing and beautiful items that brought in the needed scholarship money. (These handcrafted items also expressed the artistic ideals that are woven into Waldorf pedagogy and so

made a statement about what the school stood for.) Nevertheless, there were years when, despite all our best efforts, the
needs of the scholarship fund outpaced our ability to raise
money. At those times we had to make painful budget cuts.

The anguish of the budget shortfall was a powerful experience for me. With hindsight I have come to realize that these
painful financial challenges were actually helpful—they made
us more conscious of what we were trying to do and of what our
priorities were. Rudolf Steiner speaks of the present time as the
age of the "consciousness soul," a time when things are
achieved only through great effort, and clarity is won through
individual striving.[24] The system of tax-supported education
that prevails in most communities can actually lessen this conscious connection between school and community because the
element of choice is often not present and active participation
not required. A Waldorf school, on the other hand, cannot exist
without the activity of its parents.

Yet I must admit that I have often looked with envy at the
Scandinavian, German, and Dutch Waldorf schools, which seem
to have the best combination: eighty percent of their budget is
covered by government funding (for essential services) and
twenty percent parental support funds for subjects not required
by the state. I feel that Waldorf schools need an active parent
body, but preferably one not always so stressed on the financial
front. The only way we might achieve the Scandinavian model
in the United States is to increase the level of understanding for
Waldorf education. Such understanding could lead to support
for choice in education and to alternative ways of funding our
schools. My hope is that more and more people on this continent
will support education, whether or not they have school-aged
children, because support for education means support for
change and growth in our society.

So, while I was spending my classroom time in sixth grade
working with physics, Roman history, and banking, my administrative time was directed toward organizing committees and

task groups, wrestling with the budget, and attending board meetings. One afternoon I came home from school to find that my five-year-old, Thomas, had hauled lots of lumber from the basement and was constructing something in the living room. After taking in the scene, and noting the effort and care with which the boards and planks were laid across the floor from chair to chair, I asked if he was building the foundation of a house. His reply showed me how far off base I really was: "Oh no, Papa—I am having a board meeting."

In addition to planning further blocks in math and English and a study of medieval history, the last months of the year also included preparation for geography and mineralogy. Before going with my family for a week of spring vacation on Cape Cod, I packed the necessary resources for a further study of rocks and minerals. I wanted to increase my knowledge of mineralogy and also find ways of awakening the students' interest through dramatic presentations and special projects.[25] Little did I know just how dramatic my preparation for mineralogy would be.

After our drive, I went to bed feeling unwell. Before long I was bent over in the bathroom, vomiting as if I had eaten the worst possible poison. This continued hour after hour, and I became so weak with pain that I didn't bother returning to the bedroom in between the bouts of retching. In the morning, the pain had become so acute that I could barely move. My wife suggested that I might have the flu (which infuriated me, but my response mechanisms were too severely curtailed to react properly to this ridiculous notion). After a phone call home to our family doctor, I asked June to drive me to the hospital. I will never forget lying in the corner of the examination room, curled up with pain the like of which I have never, ever experienced, before or since. I remember wondering, *Why me*? Too many board meetings? Once the doctor arrived, it took her only moments to make a diagnosis: kidney stones.

Thanks to pain-relief drugs, and gallons of fluids consumed in the days that followed, I was able to pass the stones without surgery. I entered the classroom a week later. In addition to the specimens of igneous and sedimentary rocks, crystals, and gems that the children found on my desk, there was a little vial with a particularly small specimen of the mineral kingdom—but one that had been earned the hard way.

With the warm months of May and June at hand, we had a marvelous time rock hounding, along the nearby riverbed and also further afield. We visited Howe Caverns in New York State, north of the Catskill Mountains, and really entered the depths of the earth, seeing spectacular stalactites and stalagmites of the most dramatic colors.

In class, we examined various minerals in depth. We focused on gold, which I found particularly rewarding: gold served as an overarching theme. We covered all the conventional aspects of the subject, such as the American gold rush, how to pan for gold, and the properties of the mineral itself. Then we looked at mining, particularly in South Africa. This study pointed to the fact that whenever and wherever the existence of gold surfaces, there is a potential for fabulous wealth, and, as a directly related phenomenon, for human exploitation. What is the real nature of gold, and what effect does it have on people? Without much prompting, the class was able to make a quick retrospect of gold as it had appeared thus far in our main lessons: Gold appeared in our first-grade fairy tales as money or wealth; we met it in ancient civilizations such as Egypt, where it was highly prized. Someone remarked that in our sixth-grade block on banking, and indeed on our visit to the bank, we had seen lots of money but no gold.

So we were able to explore the nature of gold from a scientific and historical, as well as a human, perspective. We ended our characterization of this precious metal by listing all the phrases we could think of in the English language that contained the word "gold," such as "She has a heart of gold." We found that gold is often associated with the human heart.

In my personal reflections, I pondered Rudolf Steiner's observation that gold was in ancient times a representative of

Sun-wisdom—yet today it can act as a hindrance to the development of a world economy.[26] Rather than competing national interests and a monetary system pegged to the gold standard, a world economy with fluctuating currency valuations, such as we have now, can better mirror human initiatives in business and commerce.

We capped our sixth-grade year with a bike-a-thon to begin raising money for our eighth-grade trip. The students gathered pledges from unsuspecting parents and friends. Not even I came close to anticipating just *how far* those sixth-grade Romans would bicycle! We gathered at the school one afternoon, and with my son, Thomas, on his seat behind me, we began to do laps around the rural block. Several hours later, I (no longer on my bicycle) was still there, watching, and the students were still cycling. Parents arrived to pick up their children; some students stopped from sheer exhaustion, but many continued into the evening. Much to my embarrassment, we raised over two thousand dollars that day.

What a cap to a year of Roman achievement, physics, banking, and gold. What a year! The class had done everything wholeheartedly. I was heartily glad to have been a part of it all.

7. Outer and Inner Explorations

$\mathcal{M}$y recollections of seventh grade emerge in images such as this one:

I am at sea in a small rowboat. The oars have fallen overboard. The surging, rolling waves are tossing me from side to side. The sea rises higher and higher. Storm clouds always seem to be threatening, yet the storm seldom breaks. The smell of electricity is strong in the air; I feel the atmospheric pressure. I find myself almost longing for a storm so that at least the air will clear. But the heavy clouds above and the surging sea below simply roll on. I am at the mercy of elemental forces far greater than me. It is dark outside, and I am all alone.

Such were my feelings in the early months of seventh grade. My room was the darkest one in the building. In addition, it was filled with the surging emotions of twenty-six adolescent girls and boys, who seemed to bear very little resemblance to the children I had taught over the past six years. They had made a 180° turn in attitude and bearing. They were so focused on each other that I felt almost superfluous, a "last minute addition" to the scene. The warm, morning handshakes of earlier years were replaced by, "Oh yes, good morning," as they streamed in the door toward the more important people in the room. I was, at most, an afterthought—and I didn't like it at all.

Was this how it would all end? Would I ever have a chance to come up for air? What had I done to deserve this? Hey everyone, *remember me*?

In an uncanny way, my personal life conspired, as it often seems to, to highlight the dilemma. I spent a glorious fall weekend in my backyard cutting brush, mulching, and clearing the brambles and weeds around our grape arbor. It was a splendid weekend—until I started to itch. In the days that followed, I developed the worst case of poison ivy ever. My fingers became webbed and totally incapacitated, my face soon unrecognizable. My eyes were squeezed shut. I could not eat. Needless to say, I stayed home from school for a while.

Ironically, in the midst of my enforced vacation, my family received some delightful news. After several years of waiting, our second son announced his wish to join us. I remember dancing around the kitchen with Thomas and June when the pregnancy results came in. It must have been quite a sight, blown up with poison ivy as I was.

Over supper that night, Thomas reminded us of something he had told us some weeks ago. He had been standing at his bedroom window one evening when he called out, "Mama, Papa, I see a star flashing down. Soon, we will have our baby!" He had been right, and now we could look toward next summer (1989), when Ewen Alexander would join us on July 2.

I returned to school the next week and found that some of my teaching materials had disappeared, including a valued folder with all the poems, songs, and ballads I had collected for my class over the years. I remember thinking, "Everything is changing once again in my life. I will have to learn to swim in the high seas of adolescence, adjust to new parental responsibilities, and once again change as a teacher."

Despite having a good many years of teaching behind me, I now returned to an earlier, well-tried path of inquiry and asked myself anew, "Who are these children? What can I learn about them that will help me once again become their teacher?"

I began by simply observing them. Their arms and legs were longer; they seemed to be awkward, even clumsy at times. The lightness of movement they had as fifth-graders was now replaced by stiff-jointed, irregular movements that seemed at times to defy the owner of those limbs. The girls seemed taller, more mature, and much more talkative than the boys. All seemed to avoid eye contact with adults whenever possible and preferred not to speak with teachers when surrounded by their peers. At times one sensed the profound depth of their feelings, yet the curtains were often drawn over the windows of their souls.[1]

How could I help them find a new relationship to the world and to themselves? They seemed detached from the past and from their early childhood. But they were also intensely curious. Listening to lunchtime conversations, I heard talk about the things that interested them—health and relationships, trips to exotic places around the world, and the mechanics of how things work. Their vocabularies had expanded tremendously, and they seemed to enjoy intellectual banter. I sensed a new capacity in them to form judgments about themselves and the world.[2]

Before describing how we tried to work with these seventh-grade characteristics within the Waldorf curriculum, I want to address all those parents and teachers who, like me, struggle at times to understand the children in their care. It is a remarkable thing, this exercise of observing a human being. When I devoted myself to it, and when the faculty spent time discussing and observing a class or individual children, things *seemed to change*. Only years later did I read of Heinemann's observation: "If you want to change something, observe it."[3] I feel that this is a magical effect, a spiritual reality of teaching. If observed intensely over time, our most perplexing cases, our most difficult problems, can bring unexpected, positive realizations—and the possibility for change. We have to work hard to attain any glimpse of insight, no doubt about that. But it is as if our struggles to understand the children are matched by a greater, more powerful response from the spiritual worlds. We do not travel alone on this journey.

One of the tools that I used in attempting to help my seventh-graders was an intensified use of biography: through the personal struggles and explorations of others, I tried to meet those of my seventh-graders. In her marvelous book *Practicing History*, Barbara Tuchman describes the potential of biography in a way that also speaks to the theme of soul economy, mentioned several times in earlier chapters of this narrative:

> As a prism of history, biography attracts and holds the reader's interest in the larger subject. People are interested in other people, in the fortunes of the individual.... Secondly, biography is useful because it encompasses the universal in the particular. It is a focus that allows both the writer to narrow his field to manageable dimensions and the reader to more easily comprehend the subject. Given too wide a scope, the central theme wanders, becomes diffuse, and loses shape. One does not try for the whole but for what is truthfully representative.[4]

Considering what still lay ahead of me on my way through the Waldorf curriculum, I found Tuchman's insight a great relief! If I could find representative biographies, I would have the possibility of teaching more with less. This did not by any means lessen my preparation; in fact, in order to find *representative* biographies, I had to do more.

I went through a rebellious phase. I was not interested in teaching something simply because others had, or because Rudolf Steiner had given suggestions on biographies to present in seventh grade. I wanted to choose biographies that I knew would touch my students. I wanted to meet my own friends to walk with, to teach out of my own striving to understand Waldorf education as a practical manifestation of anthroposophical insights into human nature. I knew that we would continue the broad sweep through time begun in the early grades as we followed the development of human consciousness in accordance with the yearly changes in the children. I knew that we needed to cover the Age of Exploration in history and science, the Reformation, the Renaissance, and set the stage for the colonization of America through European history and geography. The broad outlines were there, and I had no problem with that. But I wanted to find biographies generally appropriate for seventh and eighth grade that would at the same time speak to the particular children in my class.[5] In the end, the ones I selected were not so different from the ones other seventh-grade teachers were using, yet the process I went through meant that I could tell the stories from my heart because they were living in me in a way that had been enlivened and strengthened through my own feelings.

Now that we were in seventh grade and no longer so bound to sequential narrative—one that began at the beginning—I was able to begin a biography with a symptom—a characteristic scene or event that spoke to the essence of the person's life and striving. Here is an example from the life of Magellan:

> The time was a little before sunset on an evening in October 1516 (the exact date is not known). The place was a courtyard in the royal palace on the bank of the Tagus, where dom Manuel the Fortunate, King of Portugal, was enthroned in state on his dais of ebony and gold. All day a succession of supplicants had been kneeling at the King's feet, humbly begging in public those favors for which they lacked the influence to petition in private. By the time a herald was announcing the name of the last petitioner, the sun was setting and the King was tired.
>
> "Fernao de Magalhaes!"
>
> A murmur of surprise ran through the court. For Ferdinand Magellan was a person of substance, an officer (albeit a junior one) of the royal household, and certainly not the sort of man one would expect to go down on his knees in public. Heads craned forward as the short, thickset figure limped awkwardly to the dais. And dom Manuel frowned;

he had disliked Magellan when as boys they served together as pages at his aunt's Court; the years had done nothing to mellow his feelings.

In a low voice the mariner began his petition. He outlined his nine years of service in Africa, India, and Indonesia, mentioning the great battles in which he had fought and the three times he had been seriously wounded; he ended with the plea that he might be granted the extra few pence a month that would signify a rise in rank to *fidalgo da casa de El Rei*. Dom Manuel refused. Magellan had half expected this, and he stayed on his knees. He was making another petition now: that he might be given command of one of the royal caravels soon to set sail for the Moluccas, the fabulous Spice Islands of the East. Again dom Manuel refused; he had, he said curtly, no use for Magellan's services either in a caravel or anywhere else. Magellan had not expected this; his sense of justice was outraged, and his indignation was all the greater because his humiliation had taken place in open court. "Then may I be permitted," he cried, "to seek service under another lord?"

Dom Manuel rose from his throne, his commanding figure towering majestically over the insignificant Magellan. "Serve whom you will, Clubfoot," he said loudly. "It is a matter of indifference to us."

For a moment Magellan did not move. Not in his worst nightmare had he imagined anything so terrible as this. Then, automatically, he bent forward to kiss the King's hand, a ritual traditionally performed by loyal *fidalgos* at the end of their audience. But Dom Manuel put his hands behind his back.

As Magellan, humiliated once again, backed haltingly from the royal presence, his limp hampered him; he lost his balance and almost fell.

"Don't trip over your cloven hoof!" an usher shouted, and a ripple of laughter ran round the court.

Half-blind with anger and grief, Magellan stumbled from the palace.[6]

I wanted this symptomatic episode to sink in, so I stopped to allow time for the discussion of some of the issues raised by this scene. I asked what this exchange might tell about the big picture of Magellan's life, and what it must have been like to be an explorer. The above scene also gave us an opportunity to touch on such things as respect, authority, and attitudes toward disabilities. The whole tone of the exchange, and the feelings of shame, anger, and embarrassment, were "real-life" subjects for my twelve- and thirteen-year-olds. At the end of our discussion, I felt they were better prepared to absorb the rest of the narrative. Their subsequent compositions and reflections also indicated that this instance of soul economy had provided some depth of insight in a comparatively short time.

We studied other explorers, beginning with Henry the Navigator and the captains he inspired to explore the coast of Africa. The class appreciated the influence of Henry in cartography and navigation, despite the fact that he himself never left home! We also sang sea chanteys, learned about the construction of various types of vessels, and recited sea ballads with appropriate vim and vigor. We spent a session on the role of women as portrayed or not portrayed in historical texts from the Age of Exploration. I was delighted to receive a composition from Emily the next day in which she had invented a fictional explorer who successfully took over her husband's ship when he became incapacitated during a wild storm. His wife sailed the vessel to glorious achievements. Emily read it to the class, and the piece was eventually published in a children's magazine. Her twenty-five classmates got an excellent introduction to revisionist history.

In this same spirit, I decided to teach seventh-grade geography not as a separate block, as is usually done, but in conjunction with the Age of Exploration. As we covered the various expeditions around Africa, and later Asia, we looked at the physical geography of the coastlines, and at the vegetation and animal life described by the explorers. We traveled inland, following rivers toward their sources in the mountains. When we met native peoples, we tried to see them not as "those who were discovered," which is the Eurocentric view, but as distinct cultures. In this attempt we used their mythology, religious ritual, and economic life to try and understand how *they* saw the world. We took the same perspective in some of our writing assignments, such as this one:

> You have lived in the Kalahari Desert all your life. Taking into account all you have learned about your people, describe your feelings and thoughts when you first saw a company of explorers approaching your homeland.

The books of Laurens van der Post were tremendously helpful in our explorations of southern Africa.

We studied the geography of Europe, the home base of many of the explorers. Now able to research independently, the students were each assigned a specific European or African country. The Spanish and German teachers supported this effort in their language lessons by incorporating the customs, idiomatic expressions, culture, and geography of Spanish- and German-speaking countries. We even had a bake sale in which the classroom was transformed into a German cafe; pastries were served by waiters and waitresses who spoke in the appropriate language. Later, my class was treated to several weeks of Spanish dancing lessons. What began as the Age of Exploration thus became much more. I remember reading afterwards—and I must admit, with considerable satisfaction—the statement by Rudolf Steiner that in geography "the achievements of all the other lessons should meet and flow together in all sorts of ways."[7]

In mid-October, after weeks of exploring unknown lands around the world, we turned to an exploration of the unknown in mathematics. Al'jahr, or algebra, was introduced in its Arabian context, with the practical necessity of finding that which remained unknown, whether it be the weight of a bolt of cloth sold in the open marketplace, or a sum in the counting house. With the help of the large scale we had used in third grade, we looked at the need to keep it in balance by adding, subtracting, multiplying, or dividing *both* sides of the equation. The letter X came to represent the unknown as we began to solve simple equations such as: $x + 8 = 10$, or $x - 15 = 5$. I began with simple equations because they provided an opportunity for new students, and for those with less apparent ability in math, to excel. All the students moved forward rapidly, so we went on to complex equations involving many steps, and eventually to equations with two unknowns. We used commutative and associative properties, worked with higher powers, and covered positive and negative numbers. My impression was that many children could not translate math skills to real-life situations without considerable practice, so I used practical problems:

> A farmer has 465 sheep. They are divided into three flocks. The second flock has twice as many sheep as the first, and the third flock has fifteen more than three times as many as the first. How many sheep are in each flock?

The class had to learn how to set the problem up so that they could use their algebraic skills to solve it:

> Number of sheep in first flock = x
> Number of sheep in second flock = $2x$
> Number of sheep in third flock = $3x + 15$

From there it was less difficult to write the equation:

$$x + 2x + 3x + 15 = 465$$

We then took 15 away from each side:

$$x + 2x + 3x = 450$$

Then we combined the terms:

$$6x = 450$$

And we divided by six:

$$x = 75$$

Many wanted to stop there, but I insisted, to the accompaniment of several groans, that they also write down the full answer:

First flock = 75 sheep
Second flock = 150 sheep
Third flock = 240 sheep
Proof: 75 + 150 + 240 = 465

Why is it that children so often just want "the answer"? Why is it so hard to take the time to do a math problem carefully, and in sequence? I do not have answers to these questions, at least not answers that satisfy me. I have a feeling that the issue is connected with our consumer-oriented, instant-gratification, fast-food mentality. This has weakened what I referred to in earlier chapters as the "will forces" of children, or their ability to enter into an activity out of their own sense of purpose and search for meaning. Had I done all those morning-circle exercises in vain? Or perhaps I had not done *enough*? These were real questions for me as I looked at the lethargy that pervaded my seventh-graders. Fortunately, I taught eighth grade as well, a year in which much came together in a positive way.

In the meantime, I approached the seventh-graders' molasses-like lack of enthusiasm regarding word problems by asking them to invent their own. They were free to choose a subject and context, but it had to work out mathematically. Yes! One of them started off with a burst of energy on the theme of space rockets. Another used the construction of a house, while many used sports situations. They soon found that it was not as easy as they had anticipated, but with coaching from the sidelines, they kept at it. The acid test of success for their word problems was whether a friend could solve it. In many cases, after an unsuspecting friend had tried to do so with considerable consternation, the original composer had to make some "minor adjustments" so that the whole thing made sense. The exercise was successful in that the students became much more respectful of algebraic word problems and of my humble efforts—in future lessons. Algebraic equations offered excellent opportunities for practical applications to daily living.

As mentioned at the beginning of this chapter, my seventh-graders had grown very conscious of themselves and were mainly interested in personal matters. On the playground and at lunchtime they would converse in small groups for hours about all sorts of weighty subjects. Hair was a popular topic for both boys and girls. Food (especially their occasional overindulgences) and of course clothes were hot as well. When November arrived I decided to begin the physiology/health block with four main themes: air, food, clothes, and home.

It was fitting that we focused on the human being at this point in the twelve-year Waldorf science curriculum. Grades one through three had included activities and stories intended to awaken the child's sense of appreciation for and integration with the natural environment. In fourth grade we had studied animals (this study appears again in the twelfth grade as zoology). In fifth grade we examined plants, a subject that is recapitulated on a high-school level in the eleventh and twelfth grades. The mineralogy of sixth grade reappears as geology in ninth and tenth grades. In grades seven, eight, nine, and ten, Waldorf teachers focus on the human being, first in terms of general health, and then through anatomy and physiology. Rather than beginning with abstract theories and facts about various parts of the body, we began with issues relating to the everyday care of the house we call our body.

At first we talked about nutrition, the solid and liquid nourishment that is essential for life. I asked the class to keep records of what they consumed during a typical day, and then we used these to discuss proteins, carbohydrates, fats, oils, minerals, and vitamins. Wherever possible, I helped the students make connections, such as vitamin-C deficiency and the outbreak of scurvy on sea voyages during the early explorations. We spent considerable time on sugars and sweeteners in relation to health, focusing on the difference between honey, fructose, beet sugar, refined sugar, and saccharin. I told them of a boy in my first seventh-grade class who had had diabetes. The children were extremely interested in his lifestyle, and in the overall effects of sugar on the body. From this point it seemed natural to progress to a description of the digestive system. Our journey moved in this order: the mouth, tongue, saliva, teeth, pharynx, esophagus, stomach, small intestine, and large intestine. "But Mr. Finser, aren't you leaving something out?" So we covered the liver, the gall bladder, and solid and liquid elimination. We ended this first week with two controversial, yet vitally important, subjects: obesity and anorexia. Much of our work in this block was done in seminar format, through question and answer and round-table discussion.

During the second week we moved to the respiratory system and ended by discussing air pollution in general and smoking in particular.[8] I wanted the students to take individual responsibility on this theme, in addition to becoming familiar with all the graphic statistics now available, so I asked them to write letters and articles on passive smoke and smoking in public places.

In the third week we looked at the circulatory system and were treated to having a distinguished doctor give a presentation and answer questions for us on the heart.

Not to evade anything, we spent time on alcoholism and discussed addictions and peer pressure in general.

In an unusual, yet moving, finale, we visited a local home for children with special needs. My rowdy, athletic, overachieving students were awed and remarkably silent as they walked through rooms of children with multiple handicaps. We had prepared songs to play on our recorders, and my students found it quite a challenge to perform their soprano, alto, and tenor parts while some of the audience were stamping, continually clapping, or calling obscenities across the room. The compositions the children wrote afterwards showed that the experience had stirred them deeply in a way that was an excellent preparation for our next block, which followed immediately.

It was now December, and we began an English block that focused on the theme "wish, wonder, and surprise." Through poetry and expressive writing assignments, we worked at finding ways to share feelings. The visit to the special needs home had helped my students prepare the ground—they began to open up in ways I had never expected.

Every once in a while, an experience is so moving that it is hard to write about—and this was the case with our December block, which took place during the three weeks of Advent, in the darkest days of the year. Through poetry and dialogue, we shared experiences in a way that defies recall—even though my students did struggle with some of their poems. I have chosen a few examples of their poetry:

> A tear of pain
> A broken heart
> All that was won
> Shall never return.
>   (*Michael*)

Peace
Love, quiet
End of violence
Disarmament—no more weapons
   Wonderful.
   (*Abbie*)

Now see the darkness close in
In moonlight the shadows come out
Go and walk slowly about
How can I sleep with this tramping of shadowy feet?
The soul can join in with this beat.
   (*Tara*)

MISSING YOU
When I heard my dad was leaving
I thought of course he's teasing.
Then I looked at his face
There was no sign of sarcasm, not a trace.
Emporia, Kansas, he had said,
but by this time I had turned bright red.
I was about to cry but I held it in.
Then a tear rolled off my chin.

This was no ordinary tear,
it was filled with magic, it knew no fear.
Then it descended into my heart, and then,
right there and then,
I experienced a feeling
I will never be able to explain again.

For that most unusual tear
was made in heaven.
   (*Marc*)

Wild with excitement
In winter, spring, summer, and fall
Not knowing what it does, not caring at all
Deadly sometimes and then at times barely a whisper.
  The wind.
  (*Jacob*)

Chocolate
Rich brown
Endless blissful bites
Chunky chips of fudge
Joy.
  (*Samuel*)

  Alive
and kicking
Wondrously excited to be alive
I'm so
  happy.
  (*Susan*)

  Football
Running, catching
Tumbling, wrestling, grabbing
  Fun and high intensity
  Action.
  (*Doug*)

  Blindness
Quietly terrorized
Fear and anxiety
Unaware of happenings around
  Blackness.
  (*Margaret*)

Hate
Despise, loathe
very evil intentions
reborn again in generations
Fear.
   (*Joseph*)

I ski, I ski so quick and fast
I'm always the first and never the last.
(*Zachary, a week before he broke his leg*)

If I had my wishes
I'd never dry dishes,
Nor sweep the floor
it's such a bore.
I'd sit in bed
and scratch my head
and wonder why I had
such trouble writing poems.
   (*Kirsten*)

   Woods
Wild, dark
Growing, rustling, creaking
Sad yet strangely happy
   Free.
   (*Mary*)

Standing alone
Thoughtfully musing.
On one leg only.
Rippling the water around it.
King of the cliffs.
   (*Jonathan*)

As I sit upon this chair
Gazing up into the air
I listen to the wind whip round,
This house like a howling hound.
I think of those who have no home,
And on the street their days
    must roam,
Forever seeking a crust of bread,
Or somewhere to lay a weary head.
    (*Torrey*)

    Friends
Talking, laughing
Confiding and understanding
Everywhere having fun together
    Lucy.
    (*Torrey*)

A single rose
with petals
white as snow.

A single rose
with stem
as long as life.

A single rose
with leaves
as green as grass.

A single rose
with thorns
as sharp as a knife.

A single rose
that motivates
a lasting joy.

A single rose
that influences
a flood of tears.

A single rose
that inspires
romantic bliss.

A single rose
that banishes
away your fears.

A single rose.
        (*Donna*)

These are a small sampling of pages and pages of poems and writing submitted over the course of the three weeks. We published some of our work in a special volume, and the total project involved a history lesson on Johann Gutenberg and the invention of type, drawing lessons, and sessions in the school office to work with the office staff on typing and layout. The final volume was ready in time to present to parents as Christmas gifts. On the cover was an exquisite black-and-white drawing by Mary. The simple title was *Expressions*.

It may seem simplistic to say so, but in the months that followed, my class seemed to have an entirely new relationship to the printed word, and to anything that they read thereafter.[9]

When my students returned in January, after days of glorious downhill skiing during the Christmas holidays, we returned to our theme of "exploration." Instead of exploring the earth (as in geography and the lives of the explorers), or the human body (as in physiology), or the feeling life of soul (as in poetry), we began a more conscious exploration of *time*. The class had been studying history for several years, but it was at this point in our eight-year journey that I chose to help them develop a more conscious relationship to historical time.

I began by asking for their birth dates, which I listed on the blackboard. I asked them to think about all the things that had happened in their lives and in the world, during their thirteen years on the earth. I then asked for their parents' ages, and we estimated their birth dates—and looked back another thirty years or so. We did the same for grandparents and were now looking at three generations (around seventy-five years). The exercise was already becoming abstract enough to numb their minds. So I borrowed one of Francis Edmunds's exercises and asked a student to come to the front of the room. I called for another volunteer to represent her mother, another her grandmother, then her great-grandmother, and so on, until we had covered fifteen generations! The fifteen generations were standing in a row at the front of the room. "History tells the stories of all these generations and more," I said. "It lives in time." Before they sat down again, I mentioned that we were about to study the history of astronomy, and that one of the first people we would meet died in 1543, approximately fifteen generations ago. As I said this, I pointed to the last child in line: her expression clearly indicated that she grasped just how long ago that was.

When the students had returned to their chairs, I began describing Ptolemy's view of the universe, with the earth at its center. I reminded them of our extensive block on medieval history during the spring of sixth grade. Rather than "putting down" the geocentric *Weltanschauung*, I pointed out that the Ptolemaic world view is still the one that we experience in our everyday lives, through our senses—the sun "moves" around the earth, as do the moon and planets. And, this is the picture that is useful for what we do on the earth: telling time, plotting a position in navigation, and so on. I then tried to describe something of what life had been like in an agrarian society in which the church played the dominant role. If one were living in a medieval village, never leaving one's own valley, always staying within the protective reach of the local castle and the spiritual embrace of the church, living with a picture of earth and heaven, and seeing the sun rise and set daily and the moon and stars at night, all appearing to move around the earth, there would be no doubt that the earth was the center of the universe. This doctrine was taught by the church and reinforced from generation to generation. It was simply the way it was.[10]

Then something happened that changed the world forever. Rather than beginning with the birth of Copernicus in Turin, Poland, in 1473, I picked a symptom, an event from his early life, that most vividly demonstrated the change in human consciousness:

> Copernicus stood at the railing of a ship that was sailing across the Adriatic Sea. As countless people had done before him, he gazed out across the water at the shore of Italy, which seemed to be moving as he stood there on deck. But although many, many people had likewise seen the apparent movement of the shore from the deck of a ship, something arose within the soul of Copernicus that caused him to ask a question that changed his life and the course of modern science: Could it be, he asked himself, that just as the shore *seems* to be moving by—although I know it is the ship that is moving—could it be that likewise the sun only *appears* to move around the earth, while in fact it is the vessel we call the earth that moves around the sun?[11]

With this question, I unveiled two charts on the blackboard, one showing Ptolomey's universe and the other showing the Copernican sun-centered universe. Who was Copernicus, this man who asked a question that so radically changed the world? I described the life of Copernicus and in the days that followed introduced Giordano Bruno, Tycho Brahe, Johannes Kepler, Galileo, and Newton—the series of remarkable individuals who seemed to build on each other's work despite the separations of geography and time.[12]

In the sixteenth and seventeenth centuries, humanity was beginning to experience a new sense of freedom through a budding *sense-free thinking*—a new kind of thinking that could step outside a sense experience and relate it to other phenomena (as Copernicus did on his Adriatic voyage). In so doing, answers might be revealed that challenged existing beliefs and doctrines; thus these thinkers courageously challenged, questioned, and charted new territory. The price of this new freedom in terms of repercussions from the authorities representing established tradition—is vividly demonstrated by the reluctance of Copernicus to publish his book: he is said to have received the first printed copy of his life work, *De revolutionibus orbium coelestium,* only on his deathbed in 1543. The dramatic death at the stake of Giordano Bruno in 1600 is a further example of the price of freedom, as is the forced "recanting" of Galileo in 1633. My seventh-graders appeared to identify inwardly with these shakers of tradition, who were nevertheless staunch in their own piety:

"Let him not, therefore, be a slave, nor evil, nor in chains, nor idle, nor blind, nor imprisoned. For the body has no power over him. . . . Thus he will be strong against fortune, magnanimous in injury, undaunted in poverty, sickness and persecution. . . . Touch me, O God, and I shall be as it were a flame of fire." (Giordano Bruno)

"To look up at the sky and behold the wondrous works of God must make a man bow his head and heart in silence." (Copernicus)[13]

After meeting the likes of Giordano Bruno and Nicolaus Copernicus, the children seemed inwardly changed—not through my teaching but through these "meetings" with real personalities. The biographies stirred their feelings, an effect that was immediately evident in the coloration of their faces and the tone of their remarks as they sat in the classroom. But the more significant results of the meetings with these historical personalities only emerged over a period of days. The group seemed to change just as it did when a new child joined the class or someone was absent for a while. I had long recognized that a group is changed when just one person is added or subtracted, but now something else was dawning in my consciousness—the biographies were working in the same way! As soon as I took in this picture, the classroom seemed to be simply bursting with all the "people" who had visited us over the years. This flash of insight, coming in the middle of seventh grade when I was experiencing a physical isolation similar to that of my adolescent students, gave the force needed to steer me through the rest of the year. The students could avoid my handshake or act as if I didn't matter, but now I saw the big picture, populated by all the people, places, and things we had experienced together. This inner landscape could be called upon whenever the outer landscape became unbearable, and of the two, the inner landscape proved the stronger.[14]

Like the alternating flow of inbreathing and outbreathing, one main-lesson block took us into the cosmos and the next brought us back to earth again: we now moved from astronomy to physics and mechanics. In the world of everyday life, work has to be done, and we were intent on finding the most efficient way to do it. We attempted to lift a heavy wooden log from the ground, first by hand and then with the help of a lever. By hand, it took the whole class lifting at the same time to move the log a few inches. With a sufficiently long lever and a stable fulcrum, one student was able to do the work that had taken the entire class. Now this possibility had a definite appeal for seventh-graders!

Next, with the help of a spring scale, we were able to measure how helpful an inclined plane can be. Then we saw how wheels could make life even more enjoyable and efficient. After a brief foray into the various types of motive force in the natural world (such as water and wind), we spent quite some time exploring the uses that wheels have been put to throughout history—from Stone-Age rollers to wagons with a solid wheel and axle carved from a single log. We briefly revisited Egypt and Mesopotamia as we examined solid wheels with separate axles. The illustrations in our main-lesson books continued the story with spoked wheels, early waterwheels, horse-powered millstones, the hand-cranked windlass, early bicycles, ships' wheels, the tiller bar, and the use of levers that turn wheels, as in trains.[15]

We experimented with pulleys, not only by performing practical tasks but also through the mathematics of mechanical advantage. By adding one length of rope to our pulley system at a time, we increased mechanical advantage and lifted weights with less and less effort. True to Waldorf principles, we did not arrive at the abstract formulation "effort equals weight divided by mechanical advantage" until after the phenomenon had been fully explored and the children had "lived" the concept. In the end, this route was efficient and advantageous for me because the formula stuck, and I was free to move on to the screw and other mechanical phenomena. Again I found that breadth and depth were not mutually exclusive.

After a glorious three-week block of studying Renaissance artists, in which we visited the Metropolitan Museum of Art in New York City and did extensive perspective drawing in class, we returned to science and focused on electricity. I tried to follow the process of discovery as it had unfolded historically in the field of electricity, from the rubbing of amber to the Leyden jar and the Wimshurst Machine, to Galvani's work with frogs' legs and Volta's "pile," then on to Faraday, Maxwell, and Marconi. The most intriguing aspect of this study for me as a teacher, and also for the class, was that almost all of these now-famous discoveries in electricity had occurred as if by accident:

> This new method of producing continuous electrical effects had far-reaching results, one of which was the discovery of the magnetic properties of the electric current by the Dane Oersted—once again a purely accidental discovery, and directly counter to the assumptions of the discoverer himself. About to leave the lecture room where he had just been trying to prove the nonexistence of such magnetic properties in the direction of the current (an event seemingly crowned with success), Oersted happened to glance once more at his demonstration bench. To his astonishment, he noticed that one of the magnetic needles was out of alignment; it was evidently attracted by a magnetic field that had been created by a current running through a wire he had just been using, which was still in circuit. Thus what had escaped Oersted throughout his planned researches— namely, that the magnetic force which accompanies an electric current must be sought in a direction at right angles to the current—a fortuitous event enabled him to detect.[16]

The accidental discovery described above represents just one in a whole sequence of similar events. (The class especially loved the one in which frogs' legs began twitching inexplicably on the railing outside Galvani's laboratory window.) Even more so than for the early explorers, who had to venture into unknown seas, the path of discovery involving electricity was a kind of groping in the dark. It was as if people were working with phenomena that were not only unfamiliar, but for which they had not yet developed the forms of thought required to deal with them. There are those who feel that this is still the case today.[17] I felt it would be irresponsible of me just to present a series of "neat" experiments that would convey the capabilities of electricity; I wanted my students to apprehend, at least on an intuitive level, that something more than technical razzle-dazzle was the issue. I tried to do this by asking them to *observe* carefully. Impartial observations have led scientists forward in a way that continually disproves currently accepted conclusions. There were electrical phenomena that when actually seen through careful observing could more easily be understood. However, I sensed that it was the unexpected phenomena, those that crept up on us with an element of surprise, that really conveyed something of the inner nature of electricity—what stood behind it. The two types of observations—those that were predictable and those that were unexpected—are clearly represented in Lucy's account of the experiment with the Wimshurst Electrostatic Machine:

EQUIPMENT
Wimshurst machine, pith ball, cylinder, small bell on hook, the class.

PROCEDURE
We turned the crank, first with the pith ball between the terminals, then with the bell, and finally, with a circle of seventh-graders connecting the two ends.

OBSERVATIONS
1. The pith ball bounced back and forth in the cylinder.
2. The bell did likewise, thereby ringing.
3. The class felt a spark pass from hand to hand.
In all three instances, we observed how static electricity passed between the spark-gap electrodes.

Lucy, the child who had been given the story "The Blossoms of the Heather" in second grade, was now one of my best observers. She always seemed to see the essential aspects of the exercise yet was modest in sharing her achievements. Her account captured the tone that I was striving for, a sort of scientific understatement that did not run away with the subject with a lot of "technical explanation" but stayed true to the observations, to what was actually seen. I felt that such a conscious "limit-setting" could serve to counteract the rampant materialistic assertions and assumptions often expounded in the name of science.

The unexpected element in the above experiment was the use of the class as part of the demonstration. They formed a circle with all the usual seventh-grade skittishness about holding hands. A student touched the left-hand electrode, and when all were holding hands, I touched the right electrode. When they felt the spark pass swiftly from hand to hand, many literally jumped with surprise. They wanted to do this part of the demonstration again and again. It gave them a taste of the elemental quality of electricity and brought it close to home, through their own sensations—the experience jolted them. Later on, when we did more complicated work with electrical currents and the wiring of such simple electrical appliances as the bell, I was glad that first jolt had given them a healthy respect for the force of electricity. Respectful understanding can lead to responsible use. Steering the students in this direction was one of my primary goals as a teacher of science.

In the early spring, as the snow began to melt and the class became restless, we took part in a week-long outdoor adventure experience at the Hulbert Center in Fairlee, Vermont. The class had been looking forward to this trip for some time and, thanks to our energetic physical education teacher, had been well prepared.

In northern Vermont the weather was still "brisk" when the early morning breakfast team had to turn out for its walk across the field to the main dining hall. My class was divided into smaller teams of four to six children, and each team participated

in chores and all the adventure problem-solving exercises as a
social unit. The staff was exceptionally gifted in coaching the
teams, both in the practical tasks and in the outdoor experiences. Everyone was challenged: some needed to hold back and
listen to the ideas of other team members before leaping into the
problem-solving exercises. Others needed to help *everyone* climb
the wall and plan ahead. Some adventures involved physical
exertion, others were mind teasers. A high point was our day on
the high ropes course. It was marvelous to participate as a team
member rather than as class teacher and not have to initiate the
activities. Even sleeping in the boys' cabin for a week with ten
of my students was enlightening. Their playful qualities came
forward much more than in the usual school context. The children revealed themselves in new ways, astonished themselves
at times, and learned new skills of cooperation.

Instead of choosing something from main-lesson work for
our seventh-grade dramatic production, I decided to encourage
and support the rehearsals and performance of a play that the
class was working on in their German classes. Thanks to the
enthusiasm and talent of our German teacher, the class took up
the challenge and presented "Rumpelstilzchen" for the younger
grades.

In light of all that was described at the beginning of the chapter, this fairy tale might at first seem inappropriate for seventh-
graders. Yet as the children worked to learn their lines in German, and as the gestures and movements of the play began to
bring them out of their shells, the archetypal pictures and
deeper meanings of the story began to stir. Because the medium
used was a foreign language, the class did not mind the simplic-
ity of the production and were able to concentrate on what
would be best for the younger children. We had three casts for
most of the rehearsals, so every member of the class was challenged. The final performance included Abbie as our charming
narrator, Zachary as the king, Marc as the miller, Eben as the

fiery Rumpelstilzchen, Maria as the princess, and Lucy as the messenger.

While all this was happening during the German periods, the main-lesson focus turned toward chemistry. The class approached this subject with visions of multiple test tubes, strange-smelling gases, and a variety of equipment that would appear to dazzle and amaze them. Well, we did meet these expectations to some degree, but on the first day of the block they were surprised to find only one small item on the lab table: a common candle. I asked the students to list on a piece of paper everything they knew about candle flame. They soon completed the assignment.

We then embarked on a series of experiments that began with closer observation of the flame and the process of combustion:

1. We isolated and collected vapor and demonstrated by relighting the vapor that it is the vapor, not the wick, that burns.
2. We examined the physical properties of the candle flame with the help of a projector and screen, and by the nature of the shadow found which parts produced the greatest light and thus had the greatest density.
3. We demonstrated the area of greatest heat in the cross-section of the flame, observed the consumption of air in burning, and worked with various instances of incomplete combustion.[18]

After about a dozen experiments with the candle, I asked the class to write down again, this time as a homework assignment, all they knew about the candle flame. Before entering this second version in their main-lesson books, with appropriate color illustrations, I passed out the first pages they had written, and we spent a few minutes talking about the path of scientific inquiry. They were mature enough to see that what they had initially dismissed as too simple, childlike, and uninteresting was in fact full of hidden secrets. One can discover astonishing things by attending to the phenomena carefully and by not fearing to ask questions.

With this opening exercise behind us, we were ready to meet a variety of chemical phenomena, including combustion in a general sense—but illustrated by the burning of many specific substances. The class really enjoyed the experiments with coal, sulfur, and phosphorous. We also made fire extinguishers, did many experiments with acids and bases, and learned to use litmus paper. We got a little carried away with an experiment using hydrochloric acid, brown egg shells, and chalk and had to briefly evacuate the classroom.

Our final block of the year brought us back to history, which included a bird's-eye view of the Reformation, Tudor England, and the events leading to the colonization of America. Once again, I tried to find just the right biographies for my particular class so that the events of history would speak through the personal experiences and achievements of leading figures such as Martin Luther and Queen Elizabeth.

In order to show the changes that were taking place in organized religion at this period, I began with the remarkable story of Joan of Arc. It is with Joan that I would like to conclude this chapter, for she showed us hope, faith, and courage, qualities that particularly speak to the seventh-grader:

> The situation in France in 1412 was dire—the country lay under English occupation. Burgundy held all the east, Bedford the north; the Dauphin was considered weak and timid. His counselors were either foolish or false, and his money was spent. The Church, the time-honored bulwark of the French throne, was divided, with two popes claiming supremacy. Bedford was advancing on Orleans, the fortress that protected further passage up the Loire.

Shut in his closet, all alone, the Dauphin was in despair. He doubted himself and his lineage: were his detractors correct in saying that he was not of kingly blood? Away from the rest of the world, in his private chamber, the Dauphin uttered a heartfelt prayer: If he were indeed a bastard, then let God remove from his heart the desire for sovereignty. He asked not to be captured, and he asked for a sign. But how could such a sign be given? He told no living person of his prayer that day.

At this same time, a daughter was born to James and Isabel D'Arc of Domremy. She was born on January 6th, the day of the Epiphany, in 1412, and they named her Joan.

She grew up tall and sturdy, strong of body and clear of mind. One summer morning when she was thirteen years of age, she had gone out to the meadows to gather flowers, when she heard a voice saying: "Your mother needs you." Joan ran back to the house, but her mother said she had not called. So she returned to the fields. It was now noon. Suddenly, she was surrounded by a dazzling light, supplanting the day, and she was filled with terror. She heard a voice that spoke of faith and its observance, and asked her to seek the uncrowned king of France, depose his foes, and crown him at Rheims. These summonses persisted for several years, during which time Joan turned to a new piety and tended the poor.

Late one summer, when she was seventeen, and the siege of Orleans had begun, her voices became more insistent, and she decided she could delay no longer. Joan set out for Chinon and turned her back on her childhood home, which she would never see again.

Her passage to the Dauphin was not easy, but when she at last gained admittance to the royal chambers, the counselors tried to trick her. They asked the Dauphin to stand aside, clad in clothes like a noble's, to see if Joan would, as predicted, recognize him. They brought her in and said,

"Look! There is the king!" and tried to mislead her, but she walked straight up to the Dauphin and knelt before him saying: "God give you long life, noble king." Then he took her aside, and she told him she had brought a sign so that he should know she was from God. And she told him of his secret prayer in every detail, the prayer which he had told to no one.

At this point I went into some detail in describing the Dauphin's advisors, characterizing the pure Alencon and the fat, evil Tremoille. I contrasted Joan's surety of purpose with the cunning and scheming of the court and described all the delays that prevented the relief of Orleans.

After many trials and hours of questioning, Joan was finally granted permission to lead the French toward the besieged city. Along the way she asked her attendants to dig beneath the altar of a certain church and bring her the sword they would find there. Much to their amazement, they found—buried in the earth behind the altar of that shrine—an old sword with five crosses on it. When burnished, it shone brilliantly as it had of old.[19]

In reviewing this portion the next day, I asked the class if they had any idea about the origins of that sword. Some remembered the marvelous Excalibur, from an Arthurian tale told in the medieval history block in sixth grade; others recalled the sword in the story of Charlemagne and Roland. This started a spontaneous exercise in retrospect, with students remembering swords that had figured in our lessons, right back to fairy tales in first grade. By putting these images together, they were able to come up with such a remarkable characterization of "sword qualities" that at the end I added only one more reflection to summarize the day: These special swords, given to human beings with a kind of divine blessing, were seldom used to slay or wound but instead served to inspire and encourage the best in human striving. In a similar way, our thoughts can also become clear and incisive. If wielded by a person with a good heart, the sword of thought can inspire and lead others just as Joan's radiant sword rallied the French nation.

In telling the next portion of the story, I spent considerable time describing the geographical position of Orleans, the importance of the river Loire, and the various strategies that were considered in order to lift the siege. With wind and weather cooperating, just as Joan had predicted, the final assault was made:

> In the first hours of the morning of that great morrow, Saturday of the seventh of May, she heard Mass and, going out in harness, she said to her chaplain: "This day shall I be wounded, above the left breast. Yet shall I return; and by the bridge." At which last words he wondered the more, for the bridge was broken.
>
> So she rode out and crossed by water to the farther shore. ... Hour upon hour of that morning the stone walls of the rampart swarmed with the scaling ladders full of men hurled down, and assault upon assault repelled, and the Maid in the midst with her banner; when, at noon, a shaft struck right through the white shoulder plate over her left breast and she fell.
>
> They dressed the wound with oil; before the reddening of the day she had returned. But though the struggle still raged, the sun set upon the place unconquered ... and Talbot beyond the river heard the Bastard's trumpets sounding the recall.
>
> But Joan went into a field apart to pray; and having prayed, she urged the commander. ... Though the darkness was falling, he gave counter-orders and called for a last surge against that stone. In the ditch of the moat, Joan handed her standard to a Basque to hold. As this went

down the slope and the rampart hid it she thought it lost, and coming forward she went into the ditch and grasped it, and struggled on with the others toward the wall. They could see the white of that standard in the gloom, and she cried loudly: "When the flag touches the stone, all is yours!" And as the white of it touched the wall in the half-light, the defense crashed and the assault poured in.... Beyond the Tourelles a narrow plank way had been thrust over the gap of broken arches and the towers were surrounded. They fell as it was night, and all within were taken or slain. So Joan, wounded, came by the bridge in the darkness to Orleans freed, and Talbot heard the bells ringing through the night and knew what had befallen, and that Orleans was lost to him.[20]

Once again, instead of moving forward, the Dauphin's advisors plotted and schemed, and the move to Rheims was delayed again and again. But finally the coronation did occur, and the seventh-graders listened to the ritual and the high idealism of Joan:

> "High-born King, now is the will of God accomplished. For He it was who ordained that I should free Orleans and bring you here to this city of Rheims for your sacring, to blazon it forth that you are Rightful Lord. And now the Realm of France is yours."[21]

We now arrive at the crucial juncture for seventh-graders, the point in Joan's biography when her voices left her. They had given her spiritual guidance, but now they fell silent, and all that she did from here on had to be guided by her own judgment. She was now alone, uncertain. What should she do next? Was her task completed? Should the army go to relieve Paris? Which way should she turn? Now she had to make every decision out of herself, through her own insight.

In view of the characterization of seventh-graders given at the beginning of this chapter, this moment in the life of Joan becomes an opportunity to grow, to take a further step in self-development and independence. The seventh-grader stands at a similar point in life: with the story of Joan before us, I did not have to verbalize it, but this was the time to say farewell to early childhood and to many of the "safe" structures that had carried them up to this point. The path of individualization calls for a stepping beyond the protective arms of family and teachers. The students needed to begin the process of letting go—including letting go of *me*—in order to discover *self*-guidance.

The final scenes from Joan's life speak strongly to the student: the faith that had sustained her is now transformed into the courage to continue. Joan is captured, imprisoned, questioned, and tried. George Bernard Shaw's *Saint Joan* does an excellent job of dramatizing the trial and the personal and public torment that Joan suffers. Her voices have left her. Should she now agree to deny them, to say they were evil, in order to save herself? With my seventh-graders before me, I described the final scenes from her life:

And stones were thrown, and there was a tumult, and Joan was led away. But as for Couchon, he broke his word and had them take her, not to the Church prison, unchained, with women to tend her, but to the castle dungeon, chained, and to the company of those grooms through horror of whom she had signed. And they gave her woman's clothes, and she wore them, being now at the mercy of those grooms.

Now on the Sunday morning she would rise, and she said to those grooms, "Loose my chains, for I have need to rise." Then one of them took away her woman's dress that lay on the bed and brought, in a bag, the man's dress she had worn before her abjuration.... Then she would not rise, seeing that she had only this to wear; for she said: "It is forbidden me." But, when it was already midday, she could hold out no longer, and she put on her man's dress as before.

And when it was known the next day that she was so dressed, eight of her judges came and asked her why she had again taken on men's clothes; and they told her that this was relapse.... On the next day...Couchon gathered his tribe about him and they condemned her for a renegade relapse, to be handed over early upon the morrow to the secular arm and the fire....

Then Peter Couchon, that evil bishop, came into the dungeon and she said to him: "Bishop, it is by you that I die! Had you put me in the Church's prison with women to guard me as was of right, this would not have been. I summon you before God the great Judge...." They relented in the matter of the Communion, which she had been so long denied. The Mass, which she had longed for through all that dereliction, she might not hear; but she received the Body of the Lord.

Then they put on her a long white dress and set her in the tumbril with the Dominican who was to be with her till the end.... They set a guard about her of two hundred men with staves and pikes, who went before her through a press of people in the streets on either side.... And when they had come into the market square, there was a great concourse of many thousands awaiting them, and in the midst...was a heap of mortar very high, hardened into stone, and a tall stake standing in it, and faggots piled around it. These, after one deputed had preached to her, she mounted without faltering, and was chained to the stake. But being there, above the people, and seen by all, she forgave her enemies and begged each priest in that multitude to say one Mass for her soul.

Then she asked for a cross, and an English soldier bound two sticks together and held it up for her to take, which she kissed and put into the bosom of her white robe.... English lords clamored at the delay, the torch was set to the faggots, and in the midst of the smoke they heard her proclaiming firmly that indeed her mission was of God, and they heard her praying to the saints; till in a very little while, a loud voice came from the midst of the burning, the Holy Name Jesus, called so loudly that every man heard it to the very ends of the square. And after that there was silence, and no sound but the crackling of the fire.

Order was given for the embers to be pulled apart so that all might see she was dead, But, lest her relics should be worshipped, men were bidden bear her ashes to the River Seine which ran nearby. So they threw into the river the ashes of that Maiden—and her heart, which the fire had not consumed.[22]

This story of faith, courage, love, and hope still speaks to us, six hundred years later.

8. Rounding the Corners

My eight-year journey would not have been possible without the daily support—and frequent inspirations—that I received from my colleagues. They loaned me materials, took time to discuss particular children, and by example, gave me something to work toward. When people ask me what suggestions I have for school reform, my reply is often quite simple: let teachers do more together. When teachers collaborate on a regular basis, on a personal and institutional level, change occurs as inevitably as when yeast is used in baking. From one colleague I learned how to do blackboard drawings, from another colleague I gleaned insights on dramatic work, and from yet another I added to my repertoire of circle activities for the younger grades. It was not unusual to see a teacher dashing into a neighboring classroom ten minutes before classes began to receive last-minute assistance with the apparatus for a scientific experiment. Once, when I was teaching an eighth-grade history lesson, a colleague knocked on my door; she needed help with a chemistry experiment that had not quite succeeded. Making a virtue out of necessity, I took my whole class in, and we all helped set things to rights. As teachers, most of us felt quite comfortable with modeling the learning process for the children. None of us could possibly know everything that was needed for teaching, and rather than cover up our inadequacies under false bravado, we acknowledged the as-sistance from our colleagues, which lessened the pressure on both teachers and students. The assistance rendered was not always just on a practical level, for with the intimacy that comes from many years of working together, we were often able to be there for one another when life crises intervened. Seldom have I seen people "carry" one another as they do in a Waldorf school faculty.

In keeping with these thoughts, I would like to set the theme for the last chapter of my journey by recalling something that a colleague, then entering the eighth grade with his class, did on opening day some years before. He went to the front of the room and, without a word, calmly played a scale on the piano: C D E F G A B.... After a considerable pause, he played the final high C. If the reader has a piano, or any other instrument for that matter, please try the sequence. By pausing at the seventh note, you can gain a sense for the seventh-grade challenges mentioned in the last chapter. But of course, the scale is not complete without the "return," the completion of the octave. The last note brings a sigh of relief to the listener. It is a welcome resolution of the conflict expressed by the preceding interval—the process is rounded out. Thus, thanks to the inspiration received from my colleague many years ago, I would like to consider this chapter not as a conclusion, for no journey is ever over, but rather as a rounding of corners, a return.

The children in my eighth grade had now come full circle. They retained the intellectual astuteness they had displayed as seventh-graders but were now able to see the big picture, one in which I once again seemed to have a role to play. They were still very much involved with each other, but with an eye toward high school, they were eager to glean every last bit of preparation they could from their teachers. They spoke more respectfully, acted with amazing responsibility at times, and showed an appreciation for the "fairy-tale element" in biography, the often inexplicable meaning behind the story line. Whereas in sixth and seventh grades everything had to make rational sense in order to be true, my eighth-graders were at times willing to live with ambiguity. They could become passionately involved in causes, such as saving rain forests, yet at the same time they were also able to stand back and objectively examine issues with a sense of perspective. The "last lap" brought an intensity, a poignancy, that seemed to make each student awake to the small, magical things that life brings, and to the social ramifications of classroom events. They were able to live fully in the present. They had truly rounded a corner.

Fortunately, the curriculum spoke to these qualities. In history we focused on the human struggle for freedom and equality, and examined various revolutions: the American, French, Russian, and Industrial revolutions and, at the end of the year, the remarkable opening up of Eastern Europe. Geography was considered from a worldwide perspective: we compared the deserts, jungles, and grasslands of the world, hopping from continent to continent in pursuit of common themes. Meteorology and world weather patterns complemented this work in yet another block. We worked with organic chemistry and solid geometry and completely reviewed mathematics. We looked at the relationship of the Industrial Revolution to the events of the Civil War, of World War I, and of World War II. The computer was introduced in the context of the Information Revolution, and we recreated an early mainframe computer before working with personal computers. We focused on themes that brought several disciplines together—for example, mechanics, ecology, organic chemistry, and history (see the Dust Bowl story at the end of this chapter). We tried to see the relationship between things: between the actions of people and the environment, between science and history. During the summer when I was doing my planning, I had decided to frame the year with Shakespeare, beginning with a review of Elizabethan England through telling the story of Shakespeare's life and a dramatic reading of *Twelfth Night*, and ending our eighth-grade year with a full production of the same play. This allowed many months for the language of Shakespeare to sink in and be experienced over time, so that its meaning would be enhanced. We played Shakespearean songs on our soprano, alto, and tenor recorders, learned about Elizabethan costumes, made props, and took the time to try out many different parts before settling on definite roles in January. A three-day mini-Shakespeare week in September provided a historical backdrop for Elizabeth's successors on the throne, Charles I and Oliver Cromwell, the battles between royalty and the Church, the Civil War, and the persecution of individuals because of their religious preferences. This set the stage for the emigration to America by Europeans searching for spiritual freedom.

In covering the colonization of America and the events leading up to the American Revolution, I tried to teach with an eye toward later events in our history. Therefore, I spent considerable time characterizing and contrasting the geography and the lifestyles of the people who settled in Virginia, Massachusetts, and Pennsylvania.

The discovery of tobacco in Jamestown led to the development of plantations to exploit this lucrative crop, and to the early importation of slaves to work for the English aristocrats who settled in Virginia. Their style of leadership, as seen through the eyes of Pocahontas, was autocratic and erratic. Relations with Native Americans suffered as the lure of tobacco profits brought increasing human costs in its wake.

The early Puritans brought with them a zeal for freedom and individualism to the rocky, colder coastline of Massachusetts. Cod fishing, shipbuilding, and trading became the livelihoods of these early settlers. Their strict laws mandated prison terms for small crimes such as petty theft and drunkenness, the stocks for speaking against the Church, and death for adultery. When presented with the biography of Anne Hutchinson, the students realized that for the Puritans, tolerance was restricted to those of their own faith and lifestyle.

Between these two, in the middle, we found the likes of William Penn, a man who helped us bridge the Old World and the New in the search for freedom of religion and tolerance for all people, including Native Americans. No statement showed more strongly Penn's character than the letter sent to the English king by six native chieftains:

> We the Kings and Sachems of the Ancient Nations of the Susquehanna and Savannah Indians, understanding that our loving and good friend Brother William Penn is to our great grief and the trouble of all the Indians of these parts obliged to go back to England . . . acknowledge that he has been not only just but always kind to us . . . not suffering us to receive any wrong from any of the people under his government. Giving us, as is well known, his house for our home at all times. . . . Besides that he has paid us for our lands, which no Governor ever did before him, and we hope that the Great King of the English will be good and kind to him and his children. Then we shall have confidence that we and our children and people will be well used and be encouraged to live among the Christians according to the agreement that he and we have solemnly made, for as long as the Sun and the Moon shall endure, one head, one mouth, and one heart.[1]

In this letter, and in the biography of William Penn, one experiences the path of the heart, the middle realm of the human constitution. On either side were two extremes—the willful landowners of the South and the headstrong individualists of the North. Thus the seeds for civil war were sown during the colonial period. To bring these contrasts into consciousness, I asked each student in the class to write a letter "home" to England, as though from a settler in Virginia, Massachusetts, or Pennsylvania. The letters were to include mention of the climate, the daily routine, the occupation, and the lifestyle of the writer. In writing home to the Old World, many also found ways to describe the hardships of their passage across the Atlantic and of their early years in the colonies. After reading the letters the next day, I asked the class to consider what might have happened had the

Mayflower landed in Virginia, as was intended. The class was able to step back from the actual historical events and examine some of the themes that had been presented.

In the biography of Thomas Jefferson we were able to relive many of the major events of the time. Jefferson was the architect and builder of Monticello. He was living in Richmond when it was attacked by Benedict Arnold and had to be evacuated. Jefferson developed a friendship with Lafayette and supported French assistance for the colonies, which brought him into debate with Hamilton. While a member of the Virginia House of Representatives Jefferson defied the governor; later, he participated in the Continental Congress, drafted the Declaration of Independence, and served as Governor of Virginia during the Revolutionary War. A member of the Virginia Legislature after the war, he served as a diplomat in Europe, then as first Secretary of State, then Vice-President, and finally, as President of the United States for two terms. The class was astounded that even after this long career the fullness of his life continued, including his cultivation of the arts, his financial generosity, and his correspondence with his old political nemesis, Adams, who died just hours before Jefferson did on July 4, 1826.

During this block we took a day to bike along a section of the Knox Trail, which follows the route taken by General Henry Knox, the man who managed to transport heavy artillery over backcountry trails from Fort Ticonderoga to Boston where George Washington awaited him, during the depths of winter in 1775–76. We traced the path of his journey along a dirt road called the Dugway, past several markers along Route 71 into New York State (now part of the town of Hillsdale), then followed another dirt road, and finally headed back for a picnic lunch in the village of Green River, which apparently contained at least one stone house when Knox passed through it. The class handled this expedition so well that I began planning a week-long bike trip with them on Cape Cod for the end of the year. We held bake sales, pizza days, and other fund raisers to make this possible.

Early in October we took a break from American history and returned to our study of physiology, which we had begun the year before. The first lesson began with unexpected instructions. "Please draw a sketch of the house you live in." The students set to work drawing freehand sketches of their houses—some colonials, some saltboxes, and some ranch styles. After I had collected their efforts, they were confounded to hear that these were not the houses I had meant. I recited the lines from a brief poem by Frederick Lawrence Knowles:

> This body is my house—it is not I.
> Triumphant in this faith I live and die.[2]

I continued by saying that the whole world is reflected in this house, "body." On a bright October day, for instance, one can see the clear dome of the heavens. Where can we find this in our body's house? Within seconds someone had pointed out the dome of the head, which then led us into the etymology of *domus,* or house: domain, domestic, domicile, dominate, dominant, dominion. We briefly reviewed the previous year's work on physiology and the environment: air and respiration, fluids and circulation, plants, animals, and nutrition.

In the earlier grades this introduction would have been enough, but I had been finding that with each succeeding year—and now especially in eighth grade—the students were eager for more content. So I plunged ahead with our first topic: the muscles. Again, we began with an experiential exercise. They were asked to sit quietly with their limbs absolutely still. I asked them to notice whatever was NOT still—the heart, the breath, their thoughts. Then I asked them to guess how many muscles they had used during the minute of stillness. Some suggested five, others a dozen. Few were prepared for my estimate that they had been using over three hundred. That woke them up. Now that their interest was aroused, I described a person with good muscular control—a musician or gymnast. Without embarrassing anyone, I also described someone with poor muscular control. In everything we do, muscles are needed—even for a smile or a frown, and especially for good posture.

With a timely visit from Jaimen McMillan, we were able to carry forward the next day with specific exercises to enhance and improve posture. At this age, an emphasis on good posture is essential to establish its importance for good health. Jaimen worked with individual children, answered their questions in a refreshing, candid way, and then took us onto the playing field for some related exercises and games.[3]

Our study of the muscles included the smooth or involuntary muscles, the cardiac muscles, and the skeletal or voluntary muscles. We also studied the role of oxygen and glucose in muscular activity. My athletes were especially interested in discussing muscle cramping and the production of lactic acid. Many had thoughts about balanced exercise. They could sound wonderfully philosophical until the afternoon sports period began.

Part of the process of "rounding the corners" in the eighth grade involved mentioning something to the class, when the opportunity arose, that had been carried in my consciousness and my intentions over the whole eight years but had not been expressed to them until now. For example, I had worked with the concept of *will* since the early grades, especially in the morning circle, as I tried to balance the reflective aspects of the lesson with enthusiastic activity. Now in eighth grade, in the context of discussing muscles, I was able to draw the following connection:

In a healthy human being, the muscles do not move by themselves.

We move them. Conscious will is unique to the human being. Animals do not make decisions and carry them out, as we do. They are subject to instinct and desire. Yet the will—this precious human capacity—is very mysterious. The will can transform a thought into an action; it can move a muscle; but it is not the will alone that determines how the muscles work. We decide to take a step, and our will does it. Luckily! If we had to be conscious of everything involved in that process, our progress would be slow—in fact, we would probably stay rooted to the spot. Our will carries things out for us. But we can choose whether to be awake or not in our activities in life. The will of the human being is itself like an invisible muscle. It too needs exercise to become strong.[4]

Next we discovered the wonders of the skeletal system. With an actual skeleton before us, we examined it as a whole and in its parts. We observed the strikingly small skull and its rounded, concentrated shape. The dome of the skull had openings for sense organs, and except for the jaw, little movement was possible since the parts (the cranial bones) were joined by sutures. We observed the thorax and the rhythmic repetition of the ribs. We examined the spine and noted the differences between the cervical, thoracic, lumbar, and sacral vertebrae. We discussed the polarities found in the forms—the rounded parts that echoed the dome of the skull and the radial bones of the limbs. We spent more time on particular aspects, such as the thighbone (femur), and looked for metamorphoses in form and function. A forensic expert visited our class and was able to identify the age, sex, and occupation of our skeleton. We did masses of drawings, even attempting a black-and-white sketch of the entire skeleton. The window sills were soon littered with clay models of the humerus, femur, tibia, and fibula. It was a glorious three weeks.[5] We ended with a special examination of the senses, focusing on the eye and ear.[6] Again, the connectedness of the curriculum became apparent as I taught. These last days of physiology prepared the way for a history lesson that would come at the end of the year, in which the children would meet an individual, Jacques Lusseyran, who had been blinded as a child. This man developed a special "vision"—an extraordinary capacity of inner observation (see end of chapter). The entire lesson on the eye was especially poignant because the class had so intimately experienced my son's accident when they were in third grade.

From physiology we moved on to comparative geography. We looked at the world as a whole, comparing the poles, the northern forests, the grasslands, the deserts, and the rain forests. We touched down at particular places in the world to sample cultures and terrains not covered in earlier grades. Students did individual research projects and gave presentations on topics such as the fresh-water lakes of the world, the sky above, or the margins of the land known as beaches.[7]

I was able to put myself into preparation and teaching one hundred percent, thanks to having relinquished my duties as faculty chair at the end of seventh grade. My successor occasionally sought my advice, but for the most part I was free to concentrate on finishing the eighth grade. Faculty meetings now became pedagogically stimulating and refreshing, since the agenda was no longer my responsibility. It was also at this time that my colleagues and the board nominated me for Massachusetts Teacher of the Year and for a Christa McAuliffe Fellowship. Even though I was not a finalist, their recommendations were a source of personal satisfaction.

In November the class took a whirlwind tour of the French Revolution: the absolute rulership of Louis XVI, the gathering discontent, the storming of the Bastille. We read *A Tale of Two Cities* by Charles Dickens, studied the rise of Mirabeau, Danton, and Robespierre; then turned to Marie Antoinette, the rule of the guillotine, chaos, and the life of Napoleon Bonaparte.

Instead of returning to the narrative form used in the younger grades when describing a figure such as Napoleon, I tried to present different aspects of the picture in a parallel manner so that the thinking and inner activity of the students were stimulated through putting things together for themselves. I described Napoleon's physical appearance. He was

5'5" yet looked taller in his general's hat. He had a deep pallor with furrowed rings under his eyes, was untidy and sickly, and had yellow skin, but his eyes sparkled with keenness and will power. He seemed to have an expression for every thought. He often gazed upon his beautiful hands.

Then I described Napoleon's mental and emotional characteristics. He had an incredible memory: he knew the names of all the officers in his regiments, as well as the places where they had been recruited. He was concise in his speech. As a boy he loved to organize snowball fights at school, and he dabbled in literature, philosophy, and medicine. He was exceptionally brave in battle, yet timid when facing the unknown. He was passionate in love, ambitious, impetuous, and at times, ruthless. He remained loyal to his officers. Above all, he had an amazing ability to inspire devotion in his followers, even when they lay dying in the snow in Russia.

I then went into Napoleon's career, a veritable roller-coaster ride of glorious successes and abject failures. Having visited Waterloo myself, I was able to describe the scene of his famous last battle in detail. But I devoted extra time to the Russian campaign, as it granted me an opportunity to describe the vastness of the land, the nature of the people, and the conditions that were to lead to the revolution 105 years later.[8] As a fitting finish, my students learned to perform a four-part adaptation of "La Réjouissance" from the Fireworks music on their recorders, and in chorus we sang the "Ode to Joy" from Beethoven's *Ninth Symphony.* Departing from customary Waldorf practices, I even brought in my cassette tape player so that we could listen to excerpts from the *Ninth Symphony* in between the episodes of Napoleon's story. Blackboard illustrations depicted Russia in winter, making his Russian campaign a multimedia event.

While the class was experiencing all these subjects in the fall main lessons, our extra main-lesson time (the forty-minute periods during the day when the students were not working on foreign languages, eurythmy, or singing) was devoted to an intensive math review. In sixth grade I adopted *Math 76* in the Saxon series, and by eighth grade we were working with *Algebra 1/2*.[9] Although I generally refrained from using texts, I found the Saxon series to be especially well done. The concepts are reviewed in a regular fashion, building confidence and skill through constant practice. The text is clear and the problem sets just the right length. Instead of spending my time writing problems on the board, correcting students' copying mistakes, and running off dittos, I was able to spend my time coaching. I still introduced new concepts myself, but the text was invaluable in supplementing my efforts. Thanks to this continual practice in math and a similar effort in English, most of my students found themselves well prepared for high school, in some cases entering advanced-level courses in ninth grade. The basic skills did not have to come at the expense of the capacities spoken of in earlier chapters—imagination, a sense for truth, and flexible thinking.[10]

In December we continued with geometry, with special emphasis on constructing the Platonic solids. In January we continued our work in physics, focusing on the mechanics of liquids and gases. It was after this block that I presented the whole sweep of inventors and pioneers who were instrumental in bringing about what is called the Industrial Revolution and the technological advances that followed, including Robert Fulton, James Watt, George Stephenson, Alexander Graham Bell, George Westinghouse, Thomas Edison, George Washington Carver, and Amelia Earhart. Each student researched one inventor, and I presented a combined sequence on the Industrial Revolution and the American Civil War, beginning with the life of John Ericsson: [11]

Born on July 31, 1803, in the province of Varmland, Sweden, John showed remarkable abilities even as a child. When his mother began to teach him to read and write, he became absorbed in creating "better letters" and had to be persuaded that the ones in print were commonly accepted, that all the books in Sweden used them, and that the authors were unlikely to change their letters because a small boy had invented a new alphabet. At the age of six, having accompanied his father to the family iron mine, John constructed a model of the entire mining operation, including wooden replicas of the shops, miniature ladders, a shaft, and a small winch to haul up the imaginary ore. When his father's mine was closed and the family endured bankruptcy, John continued his projects with scraps of materials discarded by others. To his delight, his father was then employed by the Gota Canal project under the supervision of the Mechanical Corps of the Navy, and John received free lessons from many of the engineers. He soon astonished them by building a working model of a sawmill, using scraps such as a watch spring to make the saw, and a tin spoon welded and shaped into a crank. When placed in a stream, the miniature sawmill actually worked!

John's drawings and models attracted the attention of Count van Platen, head of the canal project. With his patronage, John and his brother Nils were accepted as cadets in the Mechanical Corps of the Navy, even though neither was yet in his teens. John demonstrated an uncanny ability for finding the people he needed for each stage of his learning, including those who taught him drafting skills, painting, and French and English. He learned surveying (a stool had to be carried along so he could use the equipment), and at age fourteen he was put in command of six hundred workers.

Much to the dismay of his patron, John was inspired by dinner time talk of Napoleon and recent battles on the continent. In a rush of enthusiasm he volunteered for the 23rd Rifle Corps, where he soon became an expert shot but, because of his unusual abilities, was quickly put to work making maps. He worked so hard that the commanding officer requested that Ericsson be listed as two men so that his superiors would not be perplexed. Wanting to illustrate a book with engravings, Ericsson asked for a three-day leave to visit Stockholm. Knocking on the door of a respected engraver, John politely asked to examine his tools. When asked why, John replied that he wanted to inspect the tools so that he could teach himself how to do engraving. One can well imagine the reaction of the skilled craftsman, who declared that it had taken him many years to learn his craft and that he was not about to show his tools to someone off the street so that he could "learn" engraving. The door slammed in his face, Ericsson stormed through the streets in a rage, but then, characteristically, he decided to invent the tools himself. Not surprisingly, his final product was a success.

Having stumbled across an idea for a more efficient use of steam in engines, Ericsson traveled to England where he went to work in a manufacturing house as the resident inventor. He designed steam engines and a steam-operated pump for putting out the notorious London fires and built the famous *Novelty*, a steam locomotive that successfully competed (until the last round) against the *Rocket* designed by the famous George Stephenson. Yet his inventions rarely met with financial success.

"By this time John Ericsson was beginning to comprehend the trials and uncertainties that shadow the path of an inventor: Four barriers had to be surmounted with every project. First came the initial problem of persuading someone to invest faith and money in his idea. Second were the blunders of the mechanics who carried out his designs. Third was the crushing resistance of the public to any change in general, along with the hatred of those who might be put out of business by a new machine. Finally, there was the claim of prior rights to an idea by other inventors as soon as an invention seemed likely to be profitable....

"To someone who once remarked what a pity it was that he had not graduated from a technological institute, Ericsson replied: 'No, it was very fortunate. If I had taken a course at an institute I should have acquired such a belief in authorities that I should never have been able to develop originality.'"[12]

By describing Ericsson's early childhood and ending this first lesson with the above quotes on the process of invention and originality, I felt I was once again using the Tuchman model described in the last chapter. Many themes were found in one specific biography: the stubborn genius, the process of gaining acceptance, the rejection of accepted practices, and, in the next installment of the story, emigration to the United States.

Without dwelling on the many events in Ericsson's life after his arrival in New York City, I focused on the invention of the *Monitor*, the first ironclad vessel, which helped turn the tide in the Civil War. At the age of sixty, Ericsson was asked by the government to meet the challenge of the *Merrimac*, which was being developed by the Confederate army. The story, told in detail, contained all the excitement of any war project, complete with last-minute glitches, operators that did not fully understand the equipment, and the famous battle on March 8, 1862, in Chesapeake Bay, in which the *Monitor* prevailed against the *Merrimac*, saved the nation's capitol, and cut off a vital harbor that the Confederacy had been using. Despite congratulatory resolutions from the city of New York and the U.S. Congress, Ericsson never received the financial reimbursement he had been promised. Yet with incessant energy and perseverance, he continued working right up to the day of his death at the age of eighty-six.

Not adequately conveyed in the above paragraphs is the temperament of the man—his choleric nature and will to succeed. My students were able to appreciate the fiery, impossible personality of John Ericsson—and still respect his genius. By telling his biography, I had hoped to put a human face on the process of invention and on the many mechanical marvels we encountered in our study of the Industrial Revolution.

During the next two months I faced a double assignment: to teach two consecutive main-lesson blocks (algebra and meteorology), while at the same time rehearsing what would become our largest production ever, *Twelfth Night*. Fortunately, I was able to devote most of my energy to Shakespeare, thanks to the timely arrival of a student teacher from the Waldorf Program at Antioch New England. With her help, we were able to share the tasks at hand. She taught the first hour of each main lesson, while I prepared the rehearsal that followed. Her cheerful manner, meticulous preparation, and constant encouragement really made the difference for me and the class during those challenging weeks.

How can I begin to describe the flurry of activity surrounding the play? So much happened all at once that even those who took part were not always aware, until afterwards, of how many people had contributed and how much the students had achieved. One crew made sets, another group composed large veil paintings for our backdrops, others made costumes and borrowed props from nearby theater groups. Parents came in to help rehearse small scenes, and we often had two or three rehearsals going on simultaneously. Still another group practiced their recorders, for one of my reasons in selecting *Twelfth Night* was the musicality of the play—"If music be the food of love, play on!"[13] Eben, Tim, and I spent hours working up the best system of lighting we had ever enjoyed. Then there were dress rehearsals, the last-minute panic, and the crush of people filling the auditorium. We did two performances, one for the children at school during the day and one for parents and friends in the evening. So many of the children returned in the evening that there was standing room only.

One parent, well versed in literature and Shakespeare, said to me afterwards that he had never seen such a performance, even in professional settings. I guessed and felt that we had touched him deeply. His view was that the eighth-graders, at their particular age, were able to portray the essence of Shakespeare—the humor, entanglements, and feelings—without their own personalities getting in the way. Adults have the task of overcoming their own personalities in order to enter into Shakespeare. This parent felt that we had chosen the right play and captured it with just the right age group.

Even now, some years later, my feelings are still full when I recall this production. After so many years of working with these children, it was a great joy to see them transformed into Shakespearean players. I had always tried to imagine the best in each student, and now on this occasion I saw it in each one. The language of Shakespeare ennobled their thoughts and brought out the higher self of each student. I remember feeling, with tears in my eyes, "I will never forget them in this moment."

Those who are familiar with *Twelfth Night* and have followed the development of the class through the preceding chapters may appreciate the significance of the part for the each student.

ORSINO, *Duke of Illyria*: Marc
SEBASTIAN, *brother to Viola*: Lee
ANTONIO, *a sea captain and friend to Sebastian*: Doug
A SEA CAPTAIN, *friend to Viola*: Michael, Tim
VALENTINE AND CURIO, *attendants*: Sally, Anthony
SIR TOBY BELCH, *uncle to Olivia*: Samuel
SIR ANDREW AGUECHEEK: Jonathan F.A.
MALVOLIO, *steward to Olivia*: Jonathan B.
FABIAN, *servant to Olivia*: Maria, Lucy
FESTE, *a clown*: Donna
OLIVIA, *a rich countess*: Susan, Scott
VIOLA: Abbie, Margaret
MARIA, *Olivia's woman*: Torrey, Mary

What could a teacher possibly do after this high point in the year? Any main lesson block, no matter how interesting, would pale in the aftermath of the play. So we revisited the Hulbert Outdoor Education Center in Vermont for another week of adventure and high ropes challenges. Then it was time for spring vacation.

In late April and early May we came back to the classroom for organic chemistry. I began with a reading of *The Man Who Planted Trees* by Jean Giono in order to connect organic chemistry to the world of growing, living things. We then studied the process of photosynthesis. We experimented with sugars, making the Fehling's solution tests on cane sugar, fructose, honey, and maple syrup; on strawberry, mint, and apple jellies, and on butter cookies, vanilla flavoring, caramels, marshmallows, pink lemonade, jello, and V8 juice. We surveyed the use of sugar through the ages, from the patriarchs of old who prized honey, to Alexander the Great who brought cane sugar back to Greece, to the search for new sugars and spices during the Age of Exploration, to the development of beet sugar during the continental blockade of Europe during the time of Napoleon, to the use of sugar for the manufacture of explosives during World War I, and to the use of artificial sweeteners today. In addition to performing many more experiments with organic substances, we looked at the modern-day exploitation of workers on sugar plantations in the Dominican Republic. As someone remarked afterwards, "I always knew sugar wasn't so good for you, but I had no idea how much suffering has happened in the production and harvest of sugar cane."

Then, to make a bridge between organic chemistry and our last block on modern history, I told the story of the Dust Bowl:[14]

> The first farmer was impressed by the wind. It was intimidating, yet at the same time exhilarating. It played with the tall grass, a flat green carpet stretching as far as

the eye could see. Nothing disturbed the peaceful blowing of the wind, not even the occasional rabbit or the grazing buffalo.

The Indians often roamed the plains of the midwest on horseback. They would hunt what they needed and then move on. Not so with the first buffalo hunters from the east. As soon as J. Wright Mooar shipped his first fifty buffalo hides east, the likes of Billy Dixon, Antelope Jack, Blue Billie, Dirty Face Jones, and others arrived for the quick kill. Whole trainloads of sportsmen then followed. Soon the buffalo were gone, the Indians defeated and rounded up on reservations.

Then the cattlemen arrived, and with Glidden's timely invention of barbed wire, more ranchers staked claims to the ample grazing lands. Yet 1885 brought a drought, and in December of that year, a blizzard struck. Eighty percent of all the cattle perished. For a brief time, the grasslands returned to their natural beauty:

"I can remember nothing more beautiful than my first sight of the Plains," Arthur Duncan's wife wrote. "It was the time of year when nature was at its best. The grass and trees were green, and wild flowers made beautiful bouquets of color everywhere. The tall mesquite grass cast lacy shadows across our pathway, birds sang, and even the tall grasses seemed to wave a welcome as we passed. There was a primitive peace and beauty in the stillness of the twilight. It seemed an ideal place to build a home."[15]

The first crops were plentiful, thanks to the rich soil beneath the sod. There were no weeds. Yet in 1891 there was another drought, and then came the grasshoppers ... The trains of wagons heading back home had signs that summed it all up:[16]

"In Kansas we trusted, in Kansas we busted."

"Potatoes they grow small in Kansas
They plant them in the fall
And eat them skins and all
In Kansas."

Only one prophet spoke out against one-crop farming ("monoculture") in the plains. Payne's bulletins advised balanced farming, with "crops" that could walk to the market: livestock, grass, and feed-grain crops were three legs to the stool, without which there would be no balance. But no one listened.

Then came the great land boom. W. P. Soash fitted out a luxury train and offered free trips from New York to the Plains, with no obligation to buy. He advertised a few success stories of enormous profits, and soon one train after another was rumbling through Iowa to Texas. The 1910 census showed a population increase of 350%, while the acreage under cultivation in the plains increased by 600%. Only Payne's voice spoke in opposition to this boom. But few heard, and some even asserted that plowing fields brought on the rain.

Nature gave her own brief warning signal when in 1913 a fifteen-mile dust storm blew through Thomas County, Kansas. But then World War I arrived and the slogan was: "Plant more wheat! Wheat will win the war!"[17]The closing of the Dardanelles by the German blockade of Russia cut off a vital supply of wheat to the Allies, and prices went up. Farmers received 87 cents per bushel in 1914, $1.61 in 1916. The next year the United States went to war. It now became the patriotic duty of the farmers to plow up more land and plant more wheat. At $2.10 per bushel, few needed persuasion. Again, just at a crucial moment in history, an invention came along that changed everything. The tractor arrived on the plains. The Indians used to say that plowing turned good country upside down. Now with the tractor, both good and bad acreage was plowed up as the quotas for production were increased in the final days of the war. Between 1914 and 1917 wheat production expanded by 27,000,000 acres.

When prices fell after the war, farmers were compelled to plow up more land just to stay even. They searched for ways to lower their production costs. Salesmen streamed across the plains states offering yet another new invention, the combine, a factory on wheels. Now that the harvesting could be done in less time, more acres could be cultivated. Farming was now a business.

Yet conditions were dry. Rainfall decreased each year. April 14, 1933, brought a phenomenon no one would ever forget:

"It seemed every field in western Kansas began to move. Great air currents rushing down from the north, running close to the earth, whipped up the topsoil and sent it skimming along in a fine cloud—to choke and cut and beat at every living thing. For a while the dust hugged the surface; it whipped from one field to another, cutting away at the topsoil. Soon the surface of both fields was moving. As the storm increased, the dust rose higher above the ground. Visibility shrank from miles to yards. A strange bluish-green light, like the tip of a welder's torch, played round about automobiles on the highway.

"Toward noon in Kansas the wind suddenly seemed to roll, picking up great chunks of earth and humus, throwing it into the air. Soon a great, tumbling cloud of dust—ebony black at its base and muddy tan toward the top—was rolling southward toward Texas.... As it approached, there was a great rush of wind. Then darkness—total, utter darkness—as it struck. The darkness was dust. The windows turned solid pitch; even flower boxes six inches beyond the pane were shut from view. As the front of the storm roared on, the people quickly became aware of an awful, oppressive silence. They were frightened.... Food on tables freshly set for dinner was ruined. Milk turned black. Beds, rugs, furniture... were covered with a film of dust....

"People began to wonder if this was not the way deserts start. The whole nation was frightened and worried."[18]

Why did this happen? If people had only understood the life cycle of grass, this tragedy could have been avoided. Grass grows almost anywhere, matures, dies, and then returns organic material to the soil. This organic material gradually builds up a spongy substance called humus, which soaks up moisture and stores it in a kind of savings account for times of drought. The farmers had skimmed back the protective covering of grass and mined the soil of its richness—they had taken without restoring, unaware of the need to keep rebuilding the humus. An organic chemist would have known better. But no one listened to the warnings. Without the protective anchoring grass, drought turned the soil into dust. The land was tired—the soil, which had taken thousands of years to build up, was blown away in minutes.

This story seemed to connect many threads of environmental education that had been touched upon over the course of eight years. There were the nature stories in first and second grades—such as "The Blossoms of the Heather"—when the child's natural sense of beauty and oneness with nature told more than my stories could. In third grade the farming block gave us an opportunity to make our own garden and study crop rotation. The "Man and Animal" study came in fourth grade, the botany blocks in fifth. Geography was taught through the upper grades, and organic chemistry in eighth. If nothing else, my task in these lessons had been to draw my students' attention to the world around them, a world that can be destroyed in minutes if we are not constantly wakeful and attentive. *How we care for nature ultimately depends on what sort of people we are.*

As I prepared for my final block with the class, this last thought was uppermost in my mind. In the vast array of events and dates connected with this century, could I find specific symptoms of our time that would help my students find kindred souls—people whose lives could provide inspiration—on their paths in life? In an age of atomic energy, chemical weapons, world wars, and individual alienation and disenchantment, could I find a few biographies that would really count? My search was for what I call transformative individuals, those who had crossed the divides of nationality and race to speak to our common humanity. My last block was populated with individuals such as Harriet Tubman, Martin Luther King, Mahatma Gandhi, Mother Teresa, and Jacques Lusseyran.

In this last block, and in fact throughout seventh and eighth grades, I often used the technique of "polarity" in teaching history. This involved finding scenes, events, and biographies that could be contrasted with one another in such a way as to create added meaning. The students would have to wrestle with the contrasting pictures presented and form concepts out of their own activity in reconciling these events or images. Thus, for example, I covered World War II through the contrasting biographies of Adolf Hitler and Jacques Lusseyran, telling one segment of each life story at a time. At first I did not mention either name so that in the review session the following day I could ask, "What sort of person was the first individual described yesterday? What does his life story to date tell us about how he saw the world? What can you tell us about the character of the second person?" My students were encouraged to develop their own interpretations out of the phenomena presented in class rather than through the media or through popular mythology. The underlying theme during the week that we studied World War II was *What is blindness, what is vision?*

Below are two biographies. To contribute to the experience of contrast, I stood on one side of the room while telling the first and on the opposite side while telling the second.

BIOGRAPHY A: Born at half past six on the evening of April 20, 1889, at an inn located in the small town of Braunau on the frontier between Austria and Bavaria, this child was the third child in the family and was born to his father's third wife. His siblings, however, all died before the age of six. At school, he was a poor student and left in 1905 without the usual certificate. He spent two years dreaming of becoming an artist, did not work, and tried twice to enter the Academy in Vienna.

Those who knew him in his youth spoke of someone who showed extreme mood changes, one moment brooding and the next bursting out into wild, excited talk. He seemed incapable of sustained work: he slept in the streets during the summer and in a doss house during the winter. One person described him as having long hair (with lice) and a feverish look in his eyes, and wearing old, torn trousers and a long coat. His only income came from painting postcards on the street. He spent hours in the coffeehouses reading newspapers and debating the issues of the day with anyone who would listen. He had strong opinions, which were prejudiced. His speech was laced with anti-semitism.[19]

BIOGRAPHY B: This child was born in a modest Paris house at noon on September 19, 1924. He later described his parents as being ideal, in that they were intelligent, devoted, and kind in all things. This child loved to run and explore. One of his favorite early childhood games was to chase sunbeams in the yard. When introduced to crayoning, this child said it was like holding light in your hands. His favorite color was green, which he later learned is the color of hope.

One day, as his parents waited for him to join them on the journey back to Paris from their countryside vacation home, this child stood in the garden and began to weep. He knew he was looking at the garden—the trees, the green, the light—for the last time. He could not explain, but he know he would never see the garden again.

Back at school three weeks later, he was rushing out to recess with his friends when he was pushed from behind and fell against the corner of the teacher's desk. His glasses were shatterproof and did not break, but one arm of the spectacles went deep into the tissues of the right eye and tore it away. When he came to, he remembered asking, "My eyes, where are my eyes?"[20] They rushed him to the hospital and operated immediately. When he awoke again, he was completely and permanently blind.

The accident occurred on May 3, but by the end of the month he was up and walking, holding the hand of his mother or father. In June he began to learn braille. In July he played on the beach and learned to use a trapeze. But more remarkable than his recovery was the way in which he learned to live with blindness. At first his head followed every sound, and he would be filled with a terrible void and would despair. Then he began to look within, and he discovered an inner light of confidence and joy. When this happened he was able to walk about the room, sensing objects, and standing tall. Fear caused him to stumble and strike things, but feelings of harmony and friendship brought back the experience of lightness, and he could walk with confidence. Back at school, he found he had an inner screen upon which he could picture what was said and record it for later use. His memory became so keen that he was soon able, with the help of his braille typewriter, to do all his schoolwork and then some. His friendships deepened, and during vacations one could often see him with Jean, walking the high mountain trails with one arm on the shoulder of his friend. Yet when they got lost, it was always the blind one who knew the way home, for it was he who had noticed the change in the path from sand to gravel, the direction of the sun from the warmth on his face, and the smell of the flowers along the way. The blind one often led the way home.[21]

Comparing the two stories, we identified the individuals by name, and I described Hitler's rise to power:

BIOGRAPHY A—SECOND DAY: He was rejected for military service on grounds of poor health, then served as a messenger. He was gassed in 1918 and collapsed with an eye injury, which resulted in the award of an Iron Cross for service to his country. He built up his party after World War I through the use of propaganda (a kind of lie perpetrated on a large scale) to move the masses, held mass meetings to build his own power, formed the SA, and brought off the Munich Putsch. The rest of the story was then the story of Europe, Hitler's imprisonment, the publication of *Mein Kampf*, the elections, the depression, and Hitler's ever increasing fanaticism and power. [22]

The class was especially impressed (negatively) with the descriptions of Hitler's daily lifestyle, as portrayed by Albert Speer: the late-night movies, the idle conversations, the lack of concentrated work, the shallowness of his thoughts.[23]

BIOGRAPHY B—THIRD DAY: When Jacques first heard the news of Hitler's *Anschluss* on the radio, he was filled with foreboding and began to study German with intensity—two hours every day for the next five years. Then Paris was occupied, and the spirit of the people was smothered, as though a heavy blanket had been placed over a flame. How could they survive?

The most precious commodity was information—reliable, factual information not filtered by the SS. To this end, Lusseyran began to organize an underground resistance movement and newspaper. The movement helped fallen airmen, recruited new members, and distributed news; in the end, the newspaper achieved a circulation of 250,000 throughout France.[24]

Most important for my class of soon-to-graduate students was the way in which Lusseyran interviewed potential members of the underground:

> Picture the city of Paris under the long shadow of occupation: deserted streets and intimidating patrols. Imagine someone knocking at the door of an apartment, entering, walking down a long corridor to find a sparsely lit room at the end. The visitor would be surprised to find that the occupant of this apartment was a young high-school student; that the books on the shelves were all in braille; that this young man was blind. The conversation would begin with a few random topics—the weather, literature, and the like—and if the visitor's replies were hesitant, or if the handshake or tread of feet on the stairs had been amiss, the conversation would end after a few moments. But if the blind one sensed that the person in front of him could be trusted, they would proceed, and the visitor might even be invited upstairs to meet the executive committee of the resistance movement
>
> Lusseyran used his inner sight—his remarkable intuition—to determine if the person interviewed could be trusted with the lives of the entire organization. Over the years he interviewed hundreds of people and memorized their names, addresses, and telephone numbers so that nothing had to be committed to paper: he never made a mistake.
>
> Only once was he overruled by the executive committee. While interviewing a man named Elio, a "black bar" descended over his consciousness, and he felt uncertain. The

committee desperately needed someone with Elio's credentials, so he was accepted. Over a year later Elio betrayed them all.

Lusseyran was arrested, interrogated, and sent to prison. He listened to the officer, who spoke with his secretary during the questioning: at first, Lusseyran did not let on that he understood German. When he suddenly revealed this fact, the officer was so astonished that he inadvertently shared valuable information, which enabled Lusseyran to piece together the puzzle of what "they" knew and thereby ascertain that Elio had been the one who betrayed them. In this way Lusseyran was also able to protect those who had not come into contact with Elio.

At this point in the story I described the ordeal that followed for Lusseyran in more detail than space here permits: his horrible ride in cattle cars across Europe, the psychological as well as physical abuse that he suffered, his internment in Buchenwald. Yet the remarkable theme that runs through this epic is that at all times—especially in the concentration camp—it was the blind one who assisted the weak, shared valuable information, translated, and gave others hope. As the Americans advanced across the continent, the Nazis offered freedom to those who wanted it, and 80,000 prisoners leapt at the chance. Lusseyran counseled against it, and because of his advice many remained behind. Later, it was learned that those who had been thus released were gunned down by SS troops sixty miles from Buchenwald. Only ten survived.[25]

Lusseyran was still alive when the camp was liberated. When he got back home in France, he found some of his old comrades; others had died. Once he had regained his health, he devoted the rest of his life to teaching. He died in a car crash in 1971.

The themes we developed in class after hearing these biographies centered around several questions:

How does one know when someone can be trusted?

Which man was really blind?

What was it that allowed Lusseyran to help so many people?

How can it be that Hitler was elected by thousands of voters and is known to millions today because of the atrocities he perpetrated, while Lusseyran was elected to nothing and today is still relatively unknown?

What is true leadership?

In a democracy where majority rules, which type of leader is most likely to be elected? Why?

Looking ahead to high school and beyond, do you feel you have the strength to be different?

I have forgotten the precise responses to these questions, but I remember feeling afterwards that the class had managed to validate their entire Waldorf education. They spoke persuasively, with clear thoughts and opinions, and with depth of feeling. They knew we were talking about more than just a history lesson. The wisdom and perspective shared in the classroom that day made me feel that my efforts over eight long years had been worthwhile.

We were now ready for our week-long bicycling trip on Cape Cod. What an expedition! We hired a large U-Haul truck to carry our thirty-some bikes, brought clothing for all weathers, food for the road, and lots of enthusiasm. We stayed at the youth hostel in Orleans, prepared our own meals, and took several long beach breaks in between our cycling trips. Our first day on the trail, we lost six people (they were so far behind that they didn't see us turn off into Brewster State Park). The lost cyclists acted with great responsibility, however. They stayed together and phoned our home base when they realized they were lost. Once together again, we refined our travel procedures and continued exploring the coastline. Each evening we had dinner together at a restaurant. Our hosts often remarked that this was one of the most respectful, polite groups they had ever entertained. We went on a whale watch and played on the National Seashore beaches. The whole week was a celebration.

Back home, we had one more week of school left, which we used for finishing up our work and for an extensive review of the eight years. At first I was hesitant to review very much because I did not want to spoil anything by rehashing things in a superficial way. Fortunately, the class was eager to do the exercise I gave them, which was to travel backwards through the years. Different children took up the narrative at various points, helping one another relive experiences that had different levels of meaning. It was wonderful to see their faces light up as they remembered special moments. Some focused on anecdotes—"when so-and-so did such-and-such." Others mentioned projects, plays, things Mr. Finser had once done or said. The review became easier as we went backwards. They had more to say and were more passionate about the earlier grades. The abstractions and math problem sets were not mentioned much, but anything that had engaged their will, their inner and outer activity, remained a vivid memory. Aspects of the curriculum that had contained a strong imaginative quality—such as mythology, painting, drawing, speech—seemed to have matured into a form of knowing with the heart. Often, when a myth or biography came up, they used only a few words but spoke with thoughtful wisdom.

As I was deciding what to include in this text, I used the children's review as my guide. I included the stories they selected, the subjects that seemed to have lasted in their memories. In this sense, they wrote this book.

Finally, it was Graduation Day, the end of the journey. Can words ever express the intense feelings of such a day?

The class and I graduated together, as we had done everything else. It was not my show—they participated actively in conceptualizing, developing, and carrying out the program:

* Emily played the piano as people entered the beautifully decorated room.

* When everyone was seated, I welcomed the large audience and formally introduced the class of 1990. As my students filed in, wearing jackets and ties and long dresses, they were welcomed by a standing ovation.

* The class then stood and spoke for the last time the morning verse they had recited since the fifth grade :

> I look into the world,
> in which the sun is shining,
> in which the stars are sparkling,
> where stones in stillness lie,
> where living plants are growing,
> where animals live in feeling,
> where human beings within their souls
> give dwelling to the spirit.

> I look into the soul
> that lives within my being.
> The World Creator weaves
> in sunlight and in soul light,
> in world space there without,
> in soul depths here within.
> To Thee, Creator Spirit,
> I turn my heart to ask
> that blessing and pure strength
> for learning and for work
> may ever grow within me.

* The first speaker was a member of my earlier class, a student who had graduated eight years before and had now

finished high school and college. An African-American, he spoke about his personal journey and the continuing impact of his Waldorf years upon his life.

* Jonathan then played his silver flute.

* I shared memories of the eight years we had spent together, including the home visits, Herr Finser and Eben, Maria's foot races. I read "The Blossoms of the Heather." I spoke of teachers who had worked with the class, inner and outer weather, a rainy-day barbecue in sixth grade, moments of temper, from certain students, and wonderful sense-of-humor incidents. For instance, at lunch one day Marc had asked, "Does anyone have anything I could borrow?" We all knew Marc's love of good food. I thanked the students for being who they were: "I've enjoyed the sociability of this class, your sense of belonging together, your commitment to working things out, your growing sense of responsibility year by year, and your ability to share."

* Abbie read a poem she had composed for the occasion:

Off in the distance
I see a plant with a bud
Not at all aware of the dangers that await it in life...

Whatever path that destiny has chosen, I must follow
Whatever law my soul has written, I must obey.
Behind me I see a bud
Before me, a flower.
I see a flower in the distance.

* Tim shared a poem, and Marc read part of an essay.

* Marc's mom spoke of her experiences as a parent over our eight years.

* The class recited "To Wonder at Beauty," a verse given to the first Waldorf school in Stuttgart by Rudolf Steiner, and one that appeared inside the cover of each diploma that my students received:

> To wonder at beauty,
> Stand guard over truth,
> Look up to the noble,
> Decide for the good,
> Leads man on his journey
> To goals for his life,
> To right in his doing,
> To peace in his feeling,
> To light in his thought,
> And teaches him trust
> In the guidance of God,
> In all that there is,
> In the world-wide All,
> In the soul's deep soil.[26]

* The class then gathered around the piano, and to Emily's skillful accompaniment, we sang Bach's *Jesu Joy of Man's Desiring*.

* The time of farewell was drawing near, and I then shared my wish for the class, expressed in the familiar Irish prayer:

> May the road rise up to meet you
> May the wind be always at your back.
> May the sun shine warm upon your face
> And the rain fall soft upon your fields
> And until we meet again
> May God hold you
> In the palm of his hand.

* With a full heart, I called each student's name, and each stepped forward to receive his or her diploma from the faculty chair and a last handshake from me. In return each gave me a hug.

* The entire faculty of the Rudolf Steiner School, twenty-some strong, rose and stood along one side of the room so that they could give each student a farewell handshake, or a hug, as the class filed out of the room to the reception. Very few eyes were still dry by the end of the ceremony.

Almost four years passed before I could write about my journey with this class. The experience was so full that I needed time to process it, time to sort things out, time to find concepts for the experiences. Once I began writing, the words gushed forth. I came to trust the process of process. Writing this book has completed my journey. In telling this narrative, I can now give it to my readers, knowing that it is a personal statement about one teacher's attempt to understand what happened over the course of eight years.

One thing has remained with me above all—how little I did as a person, and how much came about through the children in my care, and through their efforts. The more I learned to know them, the more I realized that they were constantly teaching me. They were not encumbered by the heavy baggage of material knowledge that adults possess. They seemed to have resources that were fresh, inspired, and full of star wisdom. My best moments were those in which I was truly open to what the children had to teach me. For that, I am deeply grateful.

Educating for Creative Thinking:
The Waldorf Approach

Joan Almon

Old solutions are not adequate for modern problems. Their solution requires a renewal of thinking, and there is no better starting point for that renewal than with the education of children, especially young children. Educators generally agree that the quality of thinking among American students has been deteriorating at the very time when modern life needs more creativity and liveliness in human thought. In this article, I will explore some aspects of the development of creative thinking and some of the ways in which Waldorf education works to cultivate it among its students.

THINKING AND THE GOALS OF WALDORF EDUCATION

Although Waldorf education originated over seventy years ago, many people believe it will show its full promise in the twenty-first century rather than in the twentieth. The fact that it has been undergoing rapid growth all around the world since 1970, and that the growth rate is accelerating in the 1990s, indicates that it may well be an education now coming into its own because it fosters a thinking appropriate for our age.

At the same time, many other forms of education are under increasing attack. American public schools, for example, are facing a crisis in thinking, and educators everywhere are trying to understand why. There are three key manifestations of the crisis, as has been reported in the media and discussed at educational conferences. At the preschool level, many children are showing signs of stress and are not doing well in academically oriented kindergartens. Educators are now recommending a return to a play-oriented curriculum in the kindergarten, rather than the academic one that has prevailed for the past twenty years. At the elementary school level, one frequently hears about burnout among third- and fourth-grade pupils. After age nine, many children simply do not want to learn any more. In the high school, educators say that many students seem unable to think. Ask them a defined question that requires a true/ false answer or a multiple choice, and they do all right. But ask them to think through a problem and explain their solutions, and many are at a loss. Few educators seem to see a relationship between these three crises, but, from a Waldorf point of view, the problems of the elementary school and high school follow on the heels of early academics in the kindergartens as surely as night follows day.

The high school situation is of particular concern to American society, which is looking for an acceleration in thinking but is finding instead a decay. The educational community is deeply concerned over how to "teach thinking" to its students. The crisis in thinking is well described by Jane Healy, an educator whose interest is brain research and the development of the mind. In her book *Endangered Minds* (1990), she writes:

> "Teaching thinking skills," another "movement" currently passing through the education system, is a response to a growing concern that Johnny can't think any better than he can read. Programs attempting to teach thinking skills are selling like hotcakes at teachers' conferences and workshops. Yet critics scornfully point out it is a contradiction in terms to rely on packets, workbooks, computer drills, and worksheets to engage students' higher cognitive abilities. (308)

Healy goes on to point out the need for two types of mental activity in the students if they are to be well-developed thinkers: the analytic and the creative.

> Good thinking requires good analytic skills, but it also depends on imagination. Both halves of the brain, not simply the linear, analytic-verbal left hemisphere, contribute to it. The more visual, intuitive right hemisphere probably provides much of the inspiration, while the left marches along in its dutiful role as timekeeper and realist.... Some observers, concerned about declines in creative thinking, as well as in imagination, have advocated teaching methods and classroom experiences to stimulate the right hemisphere ... [but] it is increasingly clear that genuine creative imagination springs from much deeper developmental roots which can easily get short-changed in homes and in schools. (315–16)

It is these deeper developmental roots of creative thinking that have interested me greatly as a Waldorf educator of young children. Analytic thinking is a very important aspect of thought in modern life and needs to be cultivated, along with the creative side of thinking. But because it is already so valued by modern society, I will only touch on it lightly in this article, although much could be said about how to integrate it into a creative curriculum. The focus will be on the other half of thinking, the creative, imaginative side. Under present social circumstances, there is a great danger that the creative aspect of the mind will atrophy under the onslaught of the media, of the hours spent in dry academic studies, and of the pressure produced by standardized exams. If we can help children to grow up with both sides of the brain actively maturing, then new forms of thought are possible, forms that are much needed now and in the future. It is clear that creative, multidisciplinary approaches to learning will be necessary if we are to solve major problems such as environmental issues. There is much talk about divergent thinking as an appropriate form for the future. Such thinking is defined as "creative, imaginative and flexible thinking that results in a variety and abundance of ideas or answers to a problem" (Houston 1990, 72). Parents and educators remark that they commonly find such thinking in Waldorf graduates.

As a young teacher in the early 1970s, I was committed to being very eclectic in my approach to education. Some friends and I started a nursery school whose primary goal was to keep the spirit of the child lively and growing. We had all experienced the deadening effects of our own education and were convinced that there must be a better way to keep the inner spark of the child alive. When we first discovered Waldorf education, we liked the ideas and the methods, but it was really the children who convinced me that this education brought them more deep-seated satisfaction than any of the other approaches that we offered them. As we brought more Waldorf ideas into the classroom, the children turned to them and drank them in deeply. They opened to them like flowers opening to the sun. Their responses went well beyond their enjoyment of other educational practices that we offered them. The children convinced me that they loved Waldorf education, but I had many questions concerning whether this form of education worked over the long run. What sort of thinking did the students display in high school? How did they do in college? How did they do in life? For years, I plagued the more experienced Waldorf teachers with my questions.

One Waldorf high school teacher told a story that made a deep impression on me. When her high school was new, it encouraged its twelfth graders to apply to less-pressured colleges, steering them toward small liberal arts schools. Gradually, the school's confidence grew, and it began to encourage students to apply to Ivy League schools. A number were accepted and, in their first year there, letters from the colleges began to arrive at the school, saying, "Send us more of your students. They are not necessarily the most intellectual students we have had, but they are by far the most well rounded."

These thoughts are echoed by other educators who have worked with Waldorf graduates. For example, Dr. Warren Eickelberg (1991), professor of biology and director of the premedical curriculum at Adelphi University, has worked with a number of Waldorf graduates. He has this to say about them:

> Without any doubt my past three decades (in the teaching profession) have been marked by change, change, and ever more change. Throughout this dynamism of activity, where values were under attack and standards of behavior were challenged, from time to time there would be a unique stabilizing influence in my classes: a Waldorf School graduate. And they were different from others. Without exception they were, at the same time, caring people, creative students, individuals of identifiable values, and students who, when they spoke, made a difference. Waldorf School graduates see behind the facts that often must be repeated or explained on examination. They are keenly interested in the macrocosm of the universe and microcosm of the cell's ultrastructure, but they know that Chemistry, Biology and Physics can't tell them much about the nature of love. I feel certain that all Waldorf School graduates believe in the orderliness of our universe, and they believe the human mind can discern this order and appreciate its beauty. (2)

Another quotation indicates that it is not only at the college level that the Waldorf students' thinking capacities shine forth. In Marin County, California, the Waldorf school goes only to eighth grade, and students transfer to local high schools, private and public, for the remainder of their schooling. A number have attended the Marin Academy, and its history teacher, James Shipman (1991) describes them in this way:

What I find most remarkable about Waldorf kids [is that] they have been taught to think; thinking is an "okay" activity for them to engage in. I think they intrinsically understand the difference between thinking about an issue and merely memorizing "the right answer" for the test.... It is as if somewhere in their early years of schooling they somehow got the idea that learning is a lifelong enterprise. (1)

These anecdotal remarks describe some of the qualities of Waldorf students. There are not yet many quantitative studies about Waldorf education, but one major study in Germany compared Waldorf graduates with those graduating from college preparatory high schools called *Gymnasia*. Professors at the University of Bonn studied the test scores of 1,460 Waldorf students on the very rigorous state college entrance exam, the *Abitur*. The study compared their scores with those of students attending *Gymnasia*. The expectation was that *Gymnasia* students would score higher than the Waldorf students because the whole of the state school curriculum is geared toward the *Abitur*, but the opposite was found. Not only did the Waldorf school students score better than *Gymnasia* students, but the longer the students had been in a Waldorf school, the higher they scored (*Der Spiegel*). While the *Abitur* is hardly a test of creative thinking, these results do show that Waldorf education, far from handicapping students who prepare for such tests, actually seems to help them do well.

A THREEFOLD VIEW OF THE HUMAN BEING

What is it about Waldorf education that cultivates such all-around human qualities, including a strong capacity for thinking? When Rudolf Steiner founded the first Waldorf School, he placed much emphasis on three activities of the human soul—thinking, feeling, and willing. Steiner related these three aspects with the major parts of the physical body. He associated thinking with the brain and nervous system, feeling with the heart and lungs, which he called the rhythmic system, and will activity with the limbs and metabolic system.

The three areas are distinct but also highly interconnected. One cannot function without the other two, yet each brings its unique qualities to the individual. When we speak of a well-balanced person, we usually mean that all three aspects are active and working together harmoniously. If one aspect predominates so strongly that others are suppressed, we find one-sided people. From this condition there arise stereotypes and caricatures. The caricature professor, for example, lives in an ivory tower, a picture of living solely in the activity of thinking, isolated from feelings and will. In contrast, the oversized jock, all brawn and no brain, lives in the will, in the limbs and in the huge amounts of food he consumes. In between, the artist is wrapped up in the feeling life, a bohemian existence teeming with human relationships and with little connection to the practical or intellectual. These are extremes, of course, but the pictures are helpful in understanding how one-sided we become if we do not cultivate all three aspects of our nature.

Rudolf Steiner not only described the three aspects in rich detail but spoke of how to educate children in order to develop all three capacities. Thinking, feeling, and willing do not develop at identical rates, but rather the focus is first on one, then on another. In the first seven years of life, the child is primarily living in the *will*, learning nearly everything through physical activity. During these years, learning takes place mostly in an unconscious manner through the child's imitation of the activities of adults and older children. Between the approximate ages of seven and fourteen, the child's *feeling* life is the strongest, and all that is taught through imagination and the arts penetrates deeply. Human relationships are also of great importance at this age. In a Waldorf school, they are fostered through the relationship with the class teacher, who ideally remains with the class for eight grades, teaching all the main lesson subjects and developing a deep connection with the children and their families. It is also very important that, in addition to creativity and imagination, the teacher foster an orderliness and healthy respect for boundaries in the classroom. These qualities will emerge later in the students' thinking, as well.

In the high school, cognitive and intellectual *thinking* awakens strongly, and students now work with teachers who are specialists in their own subjects. The students are helped to observe phenomena, especially in the sciences, so that they can formulate their own conclusions and learn to explain and defend them. The thrust is toward developing independent judgment in the students, rather than feeding them finished statements. By working with diverse points of view in their studies, the students become skilled in looking at questions from a number of sides and appreciating the differences that are uncovered.

When the *thinking* in the high school years builds upon the *feeling* in the grade-school years and upon the *will* fostered in the preschool age, the result is a mind characterized by creative imagination (thinking plus feeling), coupled with a strong wish to bring ideas down into practical reality (thinking plus will). It is a mind that sees relationships between the sciences or the world of nature on the one side and the humanities or the world of humankind on the other. It enjoys the interpenetration of the two. Such a mind also sees human activity, including thinking, as a harmonious art of a greater universal picture. The cultivation of such a worldview is an essential element of Waldorf education.

From early childhood on, a sense of wonder, gratitude, and reverence is cultivated in the children. They see themselves as part of a greater universe in which the hand of the creator plays a mighty role. Waldorf education is not a religious education in the sense of teaching a religion, but Rudolf Steiner spoke often of the sense of wonder in childhood and the importance of cultivating it as a precursor to thinking. He described it in this way (1979, 14) : "It is absolutely essential that before we begin to think, before we so much as begin to set our thinking in motion, we experience the condition of wonder." Although they are not affiliated with any religious institution, the Waldorf schools are filled with a deep reverence for the divine aspects of life. The human being is viewed as a bridge between the heavenly and earthly realms of life, and Waldorf education makes room for both realms.

LAYING A FOUNDATION FOR CREATIVE THINKING

The development of thinking is a rich and complex story, and one can give only a brief introduction to it in an article of this length. I have chosen to focus primarily on the first seven years of childhood for two reasons. One is that early childhood has been the focus of my own work for the past twenty years, and the other is that it is during these first six or seven years of life that a lifelong foundation for thinking is laid. Absorbing academic content can wait until first grade begins, but the early years are full of experiences that affect the way the mind works and whether it will be rich or poor in creative forces.

The First Three Years

One can say that the most fundamental steps in thinking are taken during the first three years of life when the child has traditionally been at home. During the first year, the child focuses on physical movement, gradually gaining control over his head, trunk, and limbs. Controlling the head, turning over, sitting upright, standing, and walking are the high points that every parent eagerly awaits. Once the child is able to walk erect, around age one, he or she leaves the horizontal realm and enters the vertical. A new perspective of the world enters the child's being.

During the second year, the child works actively on the acquisition of language. Words begin to come, at first usually nouns for naming objects. The child begins to group and sort the surrounding world through the naming process. Little Hannah, for example, was fascinated by the dog across the street. Her first word was "dog," and for some time "dog" meant any creature that moved, be it on four feet or on two. Gradually she learned that Mommy, Daddy, and other humans were not "dogs" but had their own names. Then she began to realize that not all four-footed creatures were called "dogs" as she distinguished them from cats, squirrels, and other animals. In Hannah, one could see that the development of language is more than the mere acquisition of words. It is a whole process of sorting out the world and relating to it.

Out of speech, the rudiments of thinking begin to emerge. The more able the child is to describe the world with words, the more the child begins to ponder the world and tries to understand it. Now comes the series of "Why?" questions, as the child seeks to understand the world. Why is the sky blue, the sun yellow? Answers about atmospheric conditions and burning gases have no real meaning to the young child, but answers about the qualities of nature and how they make us feel satisfy deeply. The child's mind understands that the blue sky is like a great blue blanket that stretches over us and makes us feel safe, whereas a yellow sun fills us with warmth. The three-year-olds challenge us to return to a place of imagination and wonder in our own thinking as we ponder their questions.

During the third year, as the child enters the realm of fantasy-filled thinking, several other major changes take place. At first glance, they do not seem related to thinking, but actually they are an integral part of it and show us much about the true nature of human thought. A most noticeable development is the use of the word "no" as the child enters the terrible twos. To the beleaguered parent, it seems as if a monster has entered the home, but all the child really wants to say is, "Step back and give me space. Something new is about to be born." What is new is an emerging sense of self, the beginning of a sense of "I." The word "I" is a most personal word that cannot be taught from without; it must arise from within. Prior to using this word, the child usually speaks of himself or herself as "(Johnny or Jane) wants milk" or "Me wants milk." By now saying "I want milk," a new phase of self-awareness enters the child.

When this new sense of self enters, it often comes so strongly that one feels there is no room left in the child for a sense of "we." The child's social sense is pushed aside for the moment. It may seem that there is no one on the face of the earth quite so egotistical as a strong-willed three-year-old who has just discovered his or her own I. Consideration for others seems to disappear for a time, and only I-ness exists. Fortunately, the next stage of development brings forth an interest in the world, and the child begins to feel part of a larger social body again. The initial awareness of self is a necessary step for thinking because to think requires drawing into oneself. We do not stand in the center of the marketplace to do our thinking. We retreat into the ivory tower of our own minds. Descartes said, "I think, therefore I am," but the three-year-old seems more to say, "I am, therefore I think." The experience of "I am" and the experience of thinking go hand in hand.

There is one other major development in the child that coincides with the development of thinking around age three, namely, the birth of fantasy in the child. Often beginning around two-and a half, the child's play becomes less reality based and more filled with fantasy. Banging on the pots and pans no longer suffices. Now the pot may become a house, and the spoon a person who lives in it. Offer a two-year-old—who is still engaged in sorting out reality—a bowl of sand and say that it is a birthday cake, and she is very apt to put it in her mouth. Offer it to a three-year-old, and she or he may look quizzically at you and ask, "It's make-believe, right?" Offer it to a four-year-old, and he or she knows it is a play cake and proceeds to decorate it with sticks and leaves and calls friends together for a birthday party. Fantasy, once born, allows children to play with the simplest objects and transform them into all that is needed for their play. Born around the same time as thinking, fantasy is a powerful partner to it. If fantasy is allowed to ripen side by side with thinking, these two faculties mature into creative thinking, a capacity to visualize not only how things are but also how they might be.

Regrettably, a great deal of modern education has misunderstood the importance of fantasy in the development of thinking. For the past twenty years or more, the cultivation of healthy fantasy in young children has been largely ignored in American early childhood centers. Emphasis instead has been placed on the development of rational, intellectual thought. From a Waldorf point of view, the absence of fantasy in the early years leads directly to the problems of stress, burnout, and the inability to think that now plague so many American students. One of the great scientific minds of the twentieth century, Albert Einstein (in Stimpson 1988), understood the importance of fantasy as a critical part of modern human thought. "When I examine myself and my methods of thought," he said, "I come to the conclusion that the gift of fantasy has meant more to me than any talent for abstract, positive thinking." (139)

The Kindergarten

If the child enters a mixed-age Waldorf kindergarten around age three-and-a-half, then the "I" of the child is usually well established, and interest in life outside the self and home is beginning. The child enters the kindergarten at a time when his or her fantasy forces have been awakened and have begun to manifest in a lively way. Fantasy will go through several steps of development during the kindergarten years. At first, fantasy, young and fertile, bubbles up like the sweet porridge in the Grimms's fairy tale of that name. Like sweet porridge, it flows out everywhere. The child's fantasy is so full of activity and change that the three-year-old is more or less in perpetual motion. Gradually, the child becomes more focused in play, and the four-year-old can set up a play situation and remain with it for half an hour or more. The threes and fours, however, still have much in common in their play, for both are dependent on creating play situations out of what is at hand. They typically enter the kindergarten without an idea of what they want to play and wait for inspiration. This or that object captures their fancy, and their fantasy transforms it into what is needed. It is a great help to the growing fantasy if very simple natural objects are given as play materials. From these simple logs, stones, cloths, and other building materials, the child can create anything he or she needs, and the fantasy is not limited by defined objects. A fire engine that clearly looks like a fire engine is of no use to a child who wants a space ship, or vice versa. But a handful of chairs, some cloths, and ropes can become any vehicle that the child desires.

A new stage of play consciousness begins with the five-year-olds, who often enter the kindergarten with an "idea" in mind. They do not wait for inspiration to arise from the objects at hand, but start with an idea for play and then seek to create the objects that they need. They can easily stay with a play situation for an hour or longer and may play out the same idea for days on end. With the six-year-olds, this process goes one step further. They have an idea but often need few materials, if any, to carry out their idea. They will go through a period of time during which they take great pains to build a house or vehicle but take few props inside with them. Instead they "talk out" their play, expressing all the steps in play through conversation. What previously took place outwardly with objects and busy limbs now takes place inwardly as imagination is born.

This change from fantasy play to imaginative play was beautifully described to me by Bronja Zahlingen, a well-known Waldorf kindergarten teacher from Vienna. As a child, she loved to play with small objects on a deep window seat in her bedroom. She would create a scene with little dolls and houses, and play with them for long periods of time. She remembers that one day, when she was about six years old, she set up a scene as usual but then closed her eyes and played "inside." Imagination had been born, and she was able to participate in her play in a new way.

The development of imagination is an essential step in thinking, but where the development of fantasy has been curtailed, the development of imagination also suffers. Without imagination, one cannot picture an event in history, a verbal problem in mathematics, or the characters of a book. To approach academic subjects without imagination is a dull affair at best, and it is not surprising that children who are being educated without benefit of imagination at the elementary level find learning so uninteresting. Their newborn imagination is not being fed and nourished. Those who have been asked to master academics at the kindergarten level may suffer an even deeper problem, for in them imagination may be aborted before being born. There are indications that children who learn to read before age six or seven lose their early advantages, for they lose interest in reading and may eventually suffer burnout. This is not surprising when one thinks of how dull reading and learning are without benefit of imagination to bring them alive. In contrast, in my experience, the children who are the best players in the kindergarten and have the most active fantasy tend to become the most imaginative elementary pupils with the greatest interest in reading. They also tend to be the best-adjusted emotionally, both as children and even as adolescents and adults.

The relationship between success in fantasy play during the kindergarten years and later gains in mental development, as well as in social and emotional development, has been explored extensively by Sara Smilansky (1990) and others. They found that children who scored highest in what they called socio-dramatic play also showed the greatest gains in a number of cognitive areas such as higher intellectual competence, longer attention span, and more innovation and imaginativeness. The good players also showed more empathy toward others, less aggression, and in general more social and emotional adjustment. In addition, children who played well showed better ability to take on the perspective of others and showed fewer signs of fear, sadness, and fatigue. Smilansky's findings also point to simple, open-ended play materials as contributing more toward these developments than identifiable "toys" or learning materials. Her work is a strong confirmation of the relationship between fantasy play in young children and the development of capacities for strong thinking and a healthy emotional life. (Smilansky 1990, 18–42)

Grades One to Eight

Between the approximate years of seven and fourteen, the intense physical activity of early childhood gives way to the feeling life of the child. Learning through imitation diminishes, and the child turns to the teacher in a new way, looking to her or him as a loving authority who knows the world. The preschool child feels, "I can do whatever you can do through imitation." The elementary child feels, "There is so much I do not know, but you are my teacher and you know and will teach me." The path to knowledge for the school child is through the relationship with the teacher as a loving authority.

The Waldorf class teacher is faced with a number of challenges in working with the child. The curriculum is particularly rich and diverse, and the teacher is expected to offer creative presentations on a vast array of subjects over an eight-year period. The intellectual challenge to the teachers is enormous. Their own thinking is constantly stimulated, as well as their own creativity and love of learning. Moreover, they have to find the living relationship that they form with their class over the eight-year period. Relationships with the children and their families are worked on and deepened over these years, and the children benefit tremendously from the continuity of relationship. At the same time, they learn to relate to a variety of teachers, for they have specialty classes in subjects as varied as foreign languages, arts, handwork, gymnastics, and gardening.

Another aspect new to the school child is the freeing of the memory forces. Preschool children often amaze us with the details that they remember of past events, but they can rarely call up memory at will. Rather, something is needed—a sound, smell, or sight—to trigger their memory, which then flows forth in abundance. By contrast, the school children are able to go into their minds and find the memory that they seek, an essential quality needed for mastering academic subjects.

An additional change in the elementary children is that they are very interested in rules. One sees this in play, where games with rules now predominate over the creative fantasy play of the younger child. In learning, too, the child is ready to be guided by rules. The rules of mathematics or writing make sense to the elementary child in a way that they cannot make sense to the younger child, for whom rules still have little inner meaning.

There are many other aspects of consciousness that awaken in the school child. Many are related to the maturation of the rhythmic system, for heart and lungs now settle into a regular rhythm, whereas in the younger child they are still quite irregular. With the development of the rhythmic system comes the love of rhythmic games such as jumping rope with verses, rhythmic hand clapping, and throwing balls to the accompaniment of long verses. Moving in a rhythmic way (for example, in counting and recitation) speaks deeply to the school child.

As the rhythmic system develops, the feeling life of the child comes more and more to the fore. Education can be cool and intellectual and bypass the feelings, or it can stir them deeply. The teacher approaches the curriculum in artistic ways, bringing to life a wide range of subjects. The love that the children develop in these years for the subjects that they study ripens into a deeper quest for knowledge in adolescence and beyond. One of the tasks of the Waldorf elementary teacher is to present the curriculum in such a way that it stirs the imagination and feelings of the students, creating a context in which they can experience sympathy and antipathy, joy and sorrow, anger and tranquility, and much more. Through mythologies, great stories, and stirring biographies, the children's own moral impulses are awakened, and an idealism begins to grow in them that will flower in adolescence.

High School

Around age fourteen, the more formed cognitive and intellectual thinking life of the teenager begins to develop strongly. Now the student works with teachers who are specialists in their fields. They guide the student through the phase of critical thinking so characteristic of the young teenager and help the older adolescent develop independent judgment. In the Waldorf high school, students are taught to observe and reflect so that they may arrive at their own conclusions about life.

They are encouraged to examine problems from many points of view, so that their thinking can be well rounded rather than narrow. From deep within adolescents, there awakens a quest for truth, and this pursuit of truth takes them on journeys as profound as those of King Arthur's knights seeking the Holy Grail. Indeed, an idealism enters their being at this time not unlike that found in the Grail seekers of old. The Waldorf high school teacher recognizes that profound questions are stirring in thc students, such as "Who am I? What am I doing here? What is it I am seeking in life?" The academic subjects, both in the humanities and in the sciences, open doors to those deeper answers that students are seeking at this age.

High school students experience so many changes in the physical body, emotional life, and mental realms that it is very easy for them to become unbalanced in their development. Many teenagers devote themselves so fully to the cultivation of social life that they have little energy left for the development of thinking. Others turn their energies so avidly toward sports that the development of thinking again suffers. Whereas a balanced interest in social life and sports aids thinking, an excessive interest in them diverts energy from thought. There are no foolproof ways for guiding young people through adolescence, but there is a much greater chance that their minds will be able to blossom in a well-balanced manner if their physical nature has had a healthy chance to develop in early childhood and if their emotional life has had the opportunity to deepen during the elementary school years.

THINKING IN ADULTHOOD

All that has taken place in the first two decades lays a foundation for the coming of age at twenty-one, when young persons experience a more profound birth of the "I" or individuality than that which took place at age three. Now they are ready to take on much more inner responsibility for their own life's direction. Their "I" works through their thinking, feeling, and willing, and where these aspects of the self have been allowed to develop in a healthy and harmonious way, the "I" has a strong, clear instrument for its future use. If the instrument is damaged, then young adults will have to work extra hard to bring about a healing so that the individuality can sound forth in a clear and wholesome way.

If the mind is fertile and well related to the feelings and the will activity, then there are tremendous possibilities for growth and development throughout a whole life. Our self-education may then lead us into the new realms of thinking spoken of by Rudolf Steiner. He described the modern human being as standing on a threshold New capacities for higher forms of thinking can now be developed that were not possible before. In the opening sentence to his book, *How To KNow Higher Worlds* (1994, 13), he writes, "The capacities by which we can gain insights into higher worlds lie dormant within each one of us." The challenge for the modern human being is to awaken these faculties.

This awakening is not an easy process, but Steiner gives exercises and indications for helping to bring it about in a healthy manner. The path is made easier if the faculties of thinking have been allowed to mature in such a way that fantasy and imagination ripen in their own time, and independent thinking filled with idealism grows in the adolescent. All of this, when coupled with a sense of wonder, opens doors to new ways of thinking. A renewal in thinking becomes possible and, through it, a renewal of all other spheres of life.

REFERENCES

Der Spiegel. 14 December 1981.

Eickelberg, W. 1991. In *The Results of Waldorf Education* (brochure). Kimberton, Penn.: Kimberton Waldorf School.

Healy, J. M. 1990. *Endangered Minds.* New York: Simon and Schuster.

Houston, J.E., ed. 1990. *Thesaurus of ERIC Descriptors.* Phoenix, Ariz.: Oryx Press.

Shipman, J. 1991. *The Results of Waldorf Education* (brochure). Kimberton, Penn.: Kimberton Waldorf School.

Smilansky, S. 1990. "Sociodramatic Play: Its Relevance to Behavior and Achievement in School." In *Children's Play and Learning,* ed. Edgar Klugman and Sara Smilansky. New York: Teachers College Press.

Steiner, R. 1994. *How To Know Higher Worlds.* Hudson, N. Y.: Anthroposophic Press.

—— 1979. *The World of the Senses and the World of the Spirit.* N. Vancouver, Canada: Steiner Books, Inc.

Stimpson, J. 1988. *Contemporary Quotations.* New York: Houghton-Mifflin.

CHAPTER 1

1. Rudolf Steiner, *Soul Economy and Waldorf Education* (Spring Valley, New York: Anthroposophic Press), 124.

2. Rudolf Steiner, *Balance in Teaching* (Spring Valley, New York: Mercury Press, 1982), 18. In these concentrated lectures, Rudolf Steiner develops the theme of reverence as an essential ingredient for successful teaching. The following quotation (slightly adapted) is one of my favorites (and also expands upon the points made at the start of this chapter): "The child is the mediator, and the teacher is actually working with forces sent down from the spiritual world. When reverence for the divine-spiritual permeates the instruction, it truly works miracles. And if you have this reverence, if you have this feeling that by means of the connection with the forces developed in the spiritual world during the time before birth—if you have this feeling which engenders a deep reverence—then you will see that through the presence of such a feeling you can accomplish more than through any amount of intellectual theorizing about what should be done.

    The teacher's feelings are the most important means of education, and the feeling of reverence can have an immeasurable formative influence upon the child."

3. Rudolf Steiner, *The Kingdom of Childhood* (Spring Valley, New York: Anthroposophic Press, 1982), 23–27. The importance of the change of teeth is mentioned in many of Rudolf Steiner's pedagogical lectures. Stated briefly, the child spends the first six to seven years of life building up the physical body, working with what has been inherited, and gradually transforming the physical nature to correspond with the intent of his or her spiritual heritage. The change of teeth indicates that these growth forces are now freed for learning and the development of new capacities. Rudolf Steiner often refers to four "births": the physical birth, the birth of the etheric body at the change of teeth, the birth of the astral body at age 14, and the birth of the ego at age 21.

4. Steiner, *The Kingdom of Childhood*, 35. The emphasis on creating a beautiful environment for the young child is based upon the reality that the child "is wholly sense-organ" and reacts to all the impressions aroused in it by the people in its surroundings. The statement that immediately follows puts the essence of this book in the context of the child's health: "The child's health for the whole of its life to come depends on how the people in its environment conduct themselves in the child's presence.

The inclinations that the child develops depend on how one behaves in its presence" [translation adapted, ed.]. In other words, the child's health is directly affected not only by what we bring as teachers, but by how we bring it, and by what is living in us at the time. This means that it is important for teachers to continually grow and renew themselves—through the arts, through nature, through study and through travel—and that this is not a selfish, personal matter, to be pursued only when "time allows." On the contrary, it is essential for health-giving teaching.

5. Rudolf Steiner, *Discussions with Teachers* (London: Rudolf Steiner Press, 1967), 38.

6. These deeper, latent issues are connected with karma; see Rudolf Steiner, *Karmic Relationships*, vols. 1–8 (London: Rudolf Steiner Press).

7. Rudolf Steiner, *Deeper Insights into Education* (Hudson, New York: Anthroposophic Press, 1983), 42. The role of the Waldorf teacher as an authority figure is developed in much more detail in the context of the age seven to fourteen year period of child development. Steiner writes in this volume: "A great deal of what is taught to a child in his eighth or ninth year will be accepted only if the child feels himself in the presence of a beloved teacher, confronted by an obvious authority. The teacher should represent for the child the whole world of truth, beauty, and goodness. What the teacher holds to be beautiful or true or good should also be so for the pupil. This obvious authority, during the period between the change of teeth and puberty, must be the basis for all the teaching. A child does not always understand the things that he accepts under the influence of this authority, but he accepts them because he loves the teacher. What he has accepted will then emerge in later life, say in his thirty-fifth year, as an essential enlivening of his whole inner being. Anyone who says that one should merely teach children trivial mental conceptions has no real insight into human nature, nor does he know what a vital force it is when in his thirty-fifth year a person can call up something he once accepted simply through love for his teacher" [translation adapted, ed.].

8. In anthroposophical terms, these vital forces or life forces are the etheric forces, or etheric body—see footnote 12, chapter six.

9. Rudolf Steiner, *The Inner Nature of Music* (Hudson, New York: Anthroposophic Press, 1983). In this book Steiner describes, as he does elsewhere, the importance of working with the mood of the fifth, or the pentatonic scale, with young children, as it corresponds, in the development of humanity, to the stage of consciousness that the young child experiences today. As a class teacher, I used a wooden pentatonic recorder made by Choroi.

10. Verse by Rudolf Steiner, in Rudolf Steiner, *The Deepening of Waldorf Education* (Forest Row, Sussex, England: The Steiner Schools Fellowship Publications, 1980). Other teachers use other translations. The following version was translated by Arvia Ege:

> The sun, with loving light,
> Makes bright for me the day.
> The soul, with spirit power,
> Gives strength unto my limbs.
> In sunlight's radiant glance
> I reverence, O God,
> The human power that you
> So lovingly have planted
> For me within my soul,
> That I with all my might
> May love to work and learn.
> From you come love and strength,
> To you stream love and thanks.

11. Margaret Rowe, Elizabeth Gmeyner, and Joyce Russell, *The Key of the Kingdom: A Book of Stories and Poems for Children* (New York: Anthroposophical Publishing Co., 1951), 3.

12. Steiner, *Kingdom of Childhood*, 40–44.

13. Steiner, *Deeper Insights into Education*, op. cit. p.42.

13. From Grimm's *Fairy Tales*.

14. Rudolf Steiner suggested using verses for the various letters. In my experience, most Waldorf teachers make up their own, based upon the stories they select and the needs of their particular class.

15. Molly de Havas, *Singing Words* (Chichester, Great Britain: Chichester Press, 1951), 28.

16. Walter Braithwaite, "Snow White and the Seven Dwarfs," (1939), 35–40.

17. This reference to "living material" may seem obscure to some readers. It refers to a content that contains wisdom rather than information and calls upon the deeper, imaginative capacities of the child in such a way that it can continue to live in the child's consciousness for years to come. Waldorf education is not strictly skills-oriented but rather concerns itself with what is long-term and outcome-based. That is, the lesson's pictorial content should nourish the individual for many years but will probably not be fully understood conceptually until later in life; in fact, new levels and nuances of the meaning will probably continue to be discovered throughout adult life.

CHAPTER 2

1. Dorothy Harrer, *Math Lessons for Elementary Grades* (Spring Valley, New York: Mercury Press, 1985), 1–34.

2. Steiner, *Balance in Teaching*, 31–38.

3. Steiner, *Deeper Insights into Education*, 38.

4. This process of gradually taking hold of the physical organism and becoming "present" in it is called, in anthroposophical terms, the "incarnation process."

5. In *The Kingdom of Childhood* (p. 38), Steiner relates a child's walking to his or her previous life on earth, which gives an even greater dimension to the "big picture" work of the class teacher. Also, in *Balance in Teaching* (p. 45) he describes the incarnation process in more detail, mentioning that the ego "entrenches" itself in the physical organism mainly in the years 0–7, in the etheric organism from 7–14, and in the astral organism from 14–21; it does not fully become itself until after age 21. All along the way, the ego can either entrench itself too much or too little. Helping to balance this process is one of the tasks of curative eurythmy, a form of movement therapy that is based on the artistic eurythmy experienced by all the children in Waldorf eurythmy classes. Curative eurythmy uses intensified, therapeutic exercises that strengthen the organism to compensate for its imbalances; this process is always carried out in collaboration with an anthroposophical physician.

6. See notes 3 and 8, Chapter 1.

7. The habits and inclinations that are inherited, or brought over from a former existence, are seated in the etheric body. Changing or breaking burdensome habits is very difficult as an adult, but an alert teacher can do much to help transform them when the child is still young.

8. Rowe, *Key of the Kingdom*, 27.

9. Steiner, *Kingdom of Childhood*, 49.

10. From *Aesop's Fables*.

11. Margaret also experienced incontinence at night until April 1984. Steiner indicates in *Curative Education* (London: Rudolf Steiner Press, 1972) that nocturnal enuresis is a sign that the astral body "is overflowing" (77 ff.). The indication is that the teacher should avoid all shocks, sudden events, and noises in the child's environment. In view of Margaret's poor eyesight, I was even careful not to throw a bean bag to her without a verbal warning. Steiner further indicates in the curative lectures that consciously altering the tempo of one's teaching can help consolidate and strengthen the astral organism in relation to the ego.

12. Jacques Lusseyran, *And There Was Light: The Heroic Experiences of a Blind Fighter for Freedom* (Worcester, Great Britain: Billing & Sons, 1963), 11.

13. In his 1992 book, *Care of the Soul* (HarperCollinsPublishers), Thomas Moore relates that Renaissance doctors said that "the essence of each person originates as a star in the heavens. How different this is from the modern view that a person is [only] what he makes himself to be" (p.1).

14. Ursula Synge, *The Giant at the Ford and Other Legends of the Saints* (Athenaeum, New York: Margaret K. McEldery, 1980), 106.

15. Rudolf Steiner, *Study of Man* (London: Rudolf Steiner Press, 1966), 15.

16. Rudolf Steiner, *The Four Temperaments* (New York: Anthroposophic Press, 1980). This pamphlet describes the temperaments in relation to the incarnation of the child, and the ways in which to meet these differences in the classroom. I recommend that teachers also work with the Jungian model of learning styles, particularly as developed by Briggs-Myers.

17. Steiner, *The Kingdom of Childhood*, 23. In Lecture One, Steiner actually compares using abstract ideas to trying to squeeze the child into the same pair of shoes over many years: "We give the child concepts that are intended to be permanent: we worry him with fixed concepts that are to remain unchanged, whereas we should be giving him concepts capable of expansion. We are constantly squeezing the soul into the ideas we give the child." I feel it is very helpful for a teacher to ask the question before each lesson: What am I giving the children that will stand the test of time?

18. Steiner, *Balance in Teaching*, 8–9. These pages describe in some detail how the feeling of continual discovery—and not knowing until afterwards how things should really be taught—is essential for developing the inner attitude needed for teaching.

CHAPTER 3

1. Rudolf Steiner, *A Modern Art of Education* (London: Rudolf Steiner Press, 1972), 206.

2. Steiner, *Modern Art of Education*, 196.

3. Steiner, *Modern Art of Education*, 173–74.

4. Steiner, *Modern Art of Education*, 174.

5. Hermann Koepke, *Encountering the Self: Transformation and Destiny in the Ninth Year* (Hudson, New York: Anthroposophic Press, 1989), 4.

6. *The Complete Grimm's Fairy Tales*, (New York: Panthean Books, 1972).

7. Adapted from *Aesop's Fables*.

8. Genesis, my adaptation.

9. Koepke, *Encountering the Self*, 37.

10. Koepke, *Encountering the Self*, 36.

11. I have no published source for this poem.

12. Jeanne Zay, the most experienced teacher at the Great Barrington School at the time, wrote this skit and passed it on to me.

13. Pelham Moffat, *21 Plays for Children* (Edinburgh: Rudolf Steiner School Press, 1967) 13–28.

14. Exodus 37.

15. In the very first pages of Rudolf Steiner's *How To Know Higher Worlds*, trans. Christopher Bamford (Hudson, New York: Anthroposophic Press, 1994), his basic book on self-development, Steiner describes the path of veneration with particular reference to children, and a fundamental attitude of soul: "Spiritual researchers call this basic attitude *the path of reverence*, of devotion to truth and knowledge. Only those who have acquired this fundamental mood or attitude can become pupils in an esoteric school. Anyone with any experience in this area knows that those who later become students of esoteric knowledge demonstrate this gift for reverence in childhood. Some children look up to those whom they revere with a holy awe. Their profound respect for these people works into the deepest recesses of their hearts and forbids any thoughts of criticism or opposition to arise. Such children grow up into young people who enjoy looking up to something that fills them with reverence. Many of these young people become students of esoteric knowledge.... We should not fear that such feelings of reverence lead to subservience and slavery; on the contrary, a child's reverence for others develops into a reverence for truth and knowledge. Experience teaches that we know best how to hold our heads high in freedom if we have learned to feel reverence when it is appropriate—and it is appropriate whenever it flows from the depths of the heart. " (16–17)

CHAPTER 4

1. During the summer and fall of 1992, I conducted a survey of sixty Waldorf and sixty public-school teachers and found that the issue of balancing home versus school responsibilities was indeed of deep concern. The results of the survey of this and other questions are available in my program summary (Union Institute, Cincinnati, Ohio, 1992).

2. In *The Child's Changing Consciousness and Waldorf Education* (Hudson, New York: Anthroposophic Press, 1988), 30–32, Rudolf Steiner describes the importance of learning to walk, speak, and think during the first three years of childhood. In regard to walking, which Max did not learn during his first six years, Steiner writes: "To learn to walk is to learn to experience the principles of statics and dynamics in one's own inner being and to relate these to the entire universe.... The activities of the legs, in a certain way, have the effect of producing in the physical and

soul life a stronger connection with what is of the nature of beat, of what cuts into life. In the attunement of the movements of the right and left legs, we learn to relate ourselves to what lies below our feet. Through the emancipation of the movements of our arms from those of our legs, a new musical and melodious element is introduced into the beat and rhythm, provided by the activities of our legs. The content of our lives, or one might say, the theme of our lives, comes to the fore in the movement of our arms."

3. There are many Camphill communities worldwide, which work with children and adults in need of special care. More information can be obtained by writing to Camphill Special Schools, Inc., Beaver Run, RD 1, Box 240, Glenmoore, PA 19343.

4. Readers wishing to study further aspects of faculty-directed Waldorf schools are invited to read my chapter in *The Art of Administration*, published by the Association of Waldorf Schools of North America, 3911 Bannister Road, Fair Oaks, CA 95628.

5. The Weleda Pharmacy publishes a newsletter and has both a retail and a wholesale outlet on Route 45, Chestnut Ridge, New York.

6. Thomas's grandmother is Ruth E. Finser; she lives in Orleans, Massachusetts, on Cape Cod.

7. Steiner often refers to the importance of self-development in Waldorf teaching. The most basic book for the beginning reader is *How To Know Higher Worlds*.

8. Steiner, *The Deepening of Waldorf Education*.

9. Steiner, *Study of Man*, 31.

10. Steiner, *Balance in Teaching*, 35–38. Steiner describes how true comprehension, true understanding, occurs only when the rhythmic system is engaged: "Through those activities that involve rhythmic movement and breathing, children are able to experience true comprehension."

11. Molly Von Heider, *And Then Take Hands* (Millbrae, CA: Dawne-Leigh Books, 1981), 35.

12. Meta Roller, *Fremdsprachunterricht als Sprechunterricht*.

13. Tongue twisters were taken from a variety of sources; I have no published references.

14. Kevin Crossley-Holland, *The Norse Myths* (New York: Pantheon Books, 1980), 3.

15. Regarding homework, my main goal was to encourage good *work habits*. This meant that we used special homework folders, had an assignment on a certain day each week in fourth grade, and emphasized promptness and completion rather than quantity. I alerted parents to my expectations

for homework at the first class night of each school year so that they could plan to be "on hand" for coaching if needed. I felt that once an assignment was given, it was essential for the child's moral development to insist that it be completed. Thus, in the spirit of building good habits, I found a geode that was placed on my desk as a "homework stone." On the morning after an assignment, each child, upon entering the room, was required to place his or her homework under the stone and shake my hand. If the assignment was forgotten or left behind, the child was expected to sit down at a desk just outside the room and do it before beginning the day. This was rarely necessary, as the class soon realized that the few assignments given were to be taken seriously. Besides, in fourth grade at least, they loved the very idea of homework! In later grades, when the enthusiasm had waned somewhat, the work habits that had been established earlier (also habits of accuracy and neatness) helped carry them through. Each year we added to our expectations, so that by eighth grade, three to four nights of homework per week were not unusual. However, these assignments were not always academic: we had nights for recorder practice, learning lines for a play, or finishing a crafts project. Generally though, homework was for skill building and finishing work that could not be completed at school. I saved new learning for the school day, when the children were most alert and energetic.

16. Crossley-Holland, *Norse Myths*, 38–43.

17. Eileen Hutchins, "Iduna and the Golden Apples" in *And Then Take Hands*, 115–25.

18. Crossley-Holland, *Norse Myths*, 194.

19. Rudolf Steiner, *The Cycle of the Year* (Spring Valley, New York: Anthroposophic Press, 1984), 22.

20. Harrer, *Math Lessons*, 99.

21. Rudolf Steiner, *Education as a Social Problem* (Spring Valley, New York: Anthroposophic Press, 1969), 65–72.

22. I had used these verses in teaching German and simply translated them for the fourth-grade punctuation block.

23. In preparing this book, it was brought to my attention that the dash and the hyphen have different functions. The hyphen is a connector: it holds two elements together that function as one, like "City-State," or "a right-handed person." The dash is used to denote a sudden break in thought that causes an abrupt change in sentence structure. Perhaps another verse needs to be written to sort out dash and hyphen.

24. Willi Aeppli, *Rudolf Steiner Education and the Developing Child* (Hudson, New York: Anthroposophic Press, 1986), 134. In this section, Aeppli, a retired Waldorf teacher living in Switzerland, describes the fables as

follows: "Their message is that every soul quality, when subjected to inner observation, can appear as a specific animal. The entire animal kingdom lies within one and the same human being as soul capacity. The table 'teaches' us how these forces can be brought into internal harmony."

25. Rudolf Steiner, *The Spiritual Ground of Education* (Blauvelt, New York: Spiritual Science Library, 1989), 71. "Each capacity or group of faculties in the human being is expressed in a one-sided form in some animal species."

26. Rudolf Steiner, *Man as a Being of Sense and Perception* (London: Anthroposophical Publishing Company, 1958), 9. Unlike many contemporary scientists, Steiner spoke of twelve senses: "First the ego-sense, which as I have said is to be distinguished from the consciousness of our own ego. By the ego-sense we mean nothing more than the capacity to perceive the ego of another human being. The second sense is the sense of thought, the third the word-sense, the fourth the sense of hearing, the fifth the sense of warmth, the sixth the sense of sight, the seventh the sense of taste, the eighth the sense of smell, the ninth the sense of balance. Anyone who is able to make distinctions in the realm of the senses knows that, just as there is a clearly defined realm of sight, so there is a clearly defined realm from which we receive simply a sensation of standing as human being in a certain state of balance. Without a sense to convey this state of standing balanced, or of being poised, or of dancing in balance, we should be entirely unable to develop full consciousness. Next comes the sense of movement. This is the perception of whether we are at rest or in movement. We must experience this within ourselves, just as we experience the sense of sight. The eleventh sense is the sense of life, and the twelfth the sense of touch" [translation slightly adapted, ed.].

27. See note 10, above.

28. An excellent source for zoology teaching in a Waldorf school (at least for mammals) is Wolfgang Schad, *Man and Mammal: Toward a Biology of Form*, trans. Carroll Scherer (Garden City, New York: Waldorf Press, 1977). Although this source is more appropriate for high school work, I did find much inspiration in it for my teaching, which I then adapted for fourth grade.

29. Rudolf Steiner, *Man as Symphony of the Creative Word* (Worcestershire, England: 1978), 21, 24.

CHAPTER 5

1. For more on May Day celebrations, I highly recommend an article by Christopher Belski in the Summer 1993 issue of *Windows*, the Great Bar-

rington Rudolf Steiner School newsletter, 6–8. Address: West Plain Road, Great Barrington, MA 01230.

2. It was a tradition at the Great Barrington school to celebrate Halloween with an assembly; some Waldorf schools celebrate All Soul's Day on November 2 instead, putting the ghosts and goblins of Halloween to rest.

3. My treatment of the festivals in this paragraph is ridiculously inadequate. The festivals play a vital role in Waldorf education and in the anthroposophical experience of the year. I recommend *The Festivals and Their Meaning*, as well as *The Cycle of the Year*, both by Rudolf Steiner and available from the Anthroposophic Press, Hudson, NY.

4. Rudolf Steiner, *Human Values in Education* (London: Rudolf Steiner Press, 1971), 111. On the next page he states, "We need the support of that social element in which the children are growing up. We need the inner support of the parents in connection with all the questions that continually crop up when the child comes to school... a support that is social in its nature and is at the same time both free and living."

5. Rudolf Steiner, *Awakening to Community* (Spring Valley, New York: Anthroposophic Press, 1974), 26–29.

6. Rudolf Steiner, *From Symptom to Reality in Modern History* (London: Rudolf Steiner Press, 1976), 92. Steiner describes symptomatology as "showing that what are usually called historical facts are not the essential elements in history but are symbols of the true reality that lies behind them."

7. Marjorie Spock, "The Ten-Year-Old," unpublished manuscript, 1.

8. Dorothy Harrer, *Ancient History* (Garden City, New York: Waldorf School of Garden City, 1960), 5.

9. Harrer, *Ancient History*, 23.

10. Rudolf Steiner, *An Outline of Occult Science* (Spring Valley, New York: Anthroposophic Press, 1972), 230.

11. The eightfold path appears in a transformed way in Steiner's *How To Know Higher Worlds*.

12. Hermann Koepke, *Das Leben des Zarathustra* (Dornach, Switzerland: Rudolf Geering Verlag, 1986), 3. I found this little book while on my fourth-grade trip to Dornach and was initially extremely frustrated that it was in German. I began a rough translation, a project only recently completed. The page numbers given here and in the following notes refer to the original.

13. Koepke, *Zarathustra*, 5.

14. Koepke, *Zarathustra*, 7.

15. Koepke, *Zarathustra*, 8–9.

16, Torin Finser, "An Examination of Adolf Hitler and Nazi Germany" (undergraduate thesis, Bowdoin College, 1977).

17. Koepke, *Zarathustra*, 11.

18. Koepke, *Zarathustra*, 14.

19. Koepke, *Zarathustra*, 14.

20. Ehrenfried Pfeiffer, *The Zarathustrian Way* (Spring Valley, New York: Mercury Press, 1982) 14. Some time after I had taught the Persian history block, I came across this pamphlet, which contained the insights of Pfeiffer, a leading biodynamic farmer, on the importance of Zarathustra: "Zarathustra shows how far behind even our modern age is with its abstract moral-less science. It is shown that the dangers of the atomic age, the terrors of scientific inventions during the last war have (lightly as yet) awakened the consciousness of man to the realization that modern 'civilization' had advanced but little philosophically, morally, and humanely, and only progressed in deadly destructive and abstract science.... To Zarathustra it was revealed and he practiced accordingly that to know about nature's secrets, to handle and to apply nature's forces, involves also the guarding of the proper use of matter and forces, to keep the fires sacred, to apply only the healing process...."

In *The Gospel of St. Matthew*, Rudolf Steiner speaks of how evil comes into being when something good fails to change over time, remaining stagnant and at the mercy of the nature forces and Ahriman, or Angru Mainyu. "It was realized [in Persia] that the new must come into being and that the old must not be swept away; the goal of the Universe—above all, the good of the Earth—will be achieved through the creating of balance, of harmony, between the old and the new. This conception... lies at the basis of all forms of higher development originating in Zoroastrianism" (p 38).

21. Steiner, *How To Know Higher Worlds*, 81.

22. Rudolf Steiner, *Ancient Myths: Their Meaning and Connection with Evolution* (North Vancouver, Canada: Steiner Book Centre, 1971), 36. Steiner states: "The time in which Typhon slew Osiris was indicated to be in the November days of autumn when the sun sets in the seventeenth degree of Scorpio" (translation adapted, ed.).

23. Steiner, *Occult Science*, 239.

24. Steiner, *Ancient Myths*, 19.

25. Rudolf Steiner describes how, over the course of history, the human being moved from a pictorial consciousness to a new, pictureless mode that was accessible only to the human ego, a principle that gradually manifested in most of humanity in the centuries after Christ. The

possibility for this new, abstract thinking took centuries to develop: it brought a new clarity and sense of self with it. However, it also brought a danger because this kind of thinking can operate in a way that is completely detached from human feelings. Steiner describes that in our age, humanity's task is to take the clarity of thinking that has been developed and now regain the pictorial mode of consciousness, enabling clarity to unite with warmth of soul and feeling: this is an artistic path and holds tremendous potential for every realm of human activity and achievement.

26. Edouard Schuré, *The Great Initiates* (Blauvelt, New York: Multimedia Publishing Company, Steiner Books, 1961), 144.

27. Schuré, *Great Initiates*, 145.

28. Bernhard Lievegoed, *Man on the Threshold* (Stroud, England: Hawthorn Press, 1985), 23.

29. Gottfried Richter, *Art and Human Consciousness* (Edinburgh: Floris Books, 1982), 84–88.

30. Torin Finser, "Perseus," Great Barrington Rudolf Steiner School Newsletter (Spring 1987).

31. Kenneth Thomasma, *Naya Nuki—Girl Who Ran* (Grand Rapids, Michigan: Baker Book House Company, 1983).

32. In *The Developing Child* (131), Aeppli writes about the relationship to botany and the development of thinking: "Tracing the transformations of the archetypal plant develops the objective faculty of thinking. The thinking of children is trained on the plant. On it they can form their thoughts. The plant, however, is not a dead object but the expression of a very real, living, and creative world. From this life, which lives and creates outside of him, the child develops his own living concepts and ideas. The thoughts that the child develops by following the metamorphosis of the plant are capable of growth and are alive enough to be as creative as the archetypal plant itself.

"Between the ages of nine and ten the child's need for causality comes strongly into play for the first time. Botany satisfies this need in the most natural and healthy way. We may, for example, draw the children's attention to the soil...."

33. *Weleda News*, 2 (1980).

34. Robert Bly, *Iron John* (Reading, Massachusetts: Addison-Wesley Publishing Company, 1990), 130.

35. Bly, *Iron John*, 134.

36. "Meno," in *Plato*, trans. G.M.A. Grube (Indianapolis: Hackett Publishing Company, 1976), 14.

CHAPTER 6

1. In *Soul Economy and Waldorf Education*, Rudolf Steiner describes the change in the muscular system from ages ten through twelve: "At that time of life [age ten], the muscular system always responds to and cooperates with the soul nature of the child, especially where the more intimate forces of growth are at work. The interior swelling or stretching of the muscles mainly depends upon the development of the child's soul forces. And the characteristic feature of the age between ten and twelve consists in the muscles having an especially intimate relationship with respiration and blood circulation. They are attuned to the middle system of breathing and blood circulation. And as Waldorf education appeals so strongly to this very part of the child's being, we indirectly promote the growth and development of the child's muscles.

   "Towards the twelfth year a new situation arises. The muscles no longer remain so intimately connected with the child's respiration and blood circulation; they now incline more towards the bony system, adapting themselves to the dynamics of the skeleton.... The muscles, previously closely allied to the rhythmic system, now become entirely oriented towards the bony system. In this way the child adapts itself more strongly to the external world than was the case before the twelfth year" (190). In *Practical Advice to Teachers* (London: Rudolf Steiner Press, 1976), Steiner approaches the twelve-year change from a different perspective: "What we are accustomed to calling in spiritual science the astral body permeates the etheric body and unites with it. Of course the astral body as an independent being is not born until puberty, but it manifests itself in a peculiar manner through the etheric body by permeating and invigorating it between the twelfth and thirteenth years.... It expresses itself in the way the child ... begins to develop an understanding for the impulses of spirit and soul such as those at work in the external world as the forces of history.... At this point the children begin to take an inner interest in great historical connections" (116–17).

2. Marjorie Spock, "Grade Six," unpublished ms., 1: "The imaginative thinking characteristic of early childhood disappears. It has undergone a metamorphosis from which the thought powers emerge as the ability to form abstract concepts.... Thought, then, is literally imagination's child."

3. Richard Moeschl, *Children at Risk: Understanding and Educating Young Adolescents* (San Raphael, California: Marin Waldorf School, 1986), 29.

4. In "Twelve Years Old," Hans Engel describes the student at this age as awakening in his soul to himself as a being of will (26).

5. A. Renwick Sheen, *Geometry and the Imagination* (Wilton, New Hampshire: Association of Waldorf Schools of North America, 1991), 18–19.

6. In *A Modern Art of Education*, Steiner shows that different subjects work on the various aspects of the human being, while geometry is more universal: "The remarkable thing is that arithmetic and geometry affect both the physical-etheric and the astral-ego. Arithmetic and geometry are really like a chameleon; by their very nature they harmonize with every part of man's being. Whereas lessons on the plant and animal kingdoms should be given at a definite age, arithmetic and geometry must be taught through the whole period of childhood—though naturally in a form suited to the changing characteristics of the different life-periods" (154).

   In the next paragraph Steiner describes how, during sleep, the etheric body continues to calculate and process the work of the day in arithmetic and geometry. "If we are aware of this fact and plan our teaching accordingly, great vitality can be generated in the being of the child" (154).

7. In *Discussions with Teachers*, Steiner indicates that plane geometry should be taught before solid geometry because children experience surfaces before they experience three dimensions (47).

8. Much of the narrative on the early history of Rome comes from my unpublished manuscript on the relationship of the seven kings to the essential nature of the human being as described by Rudolf Steiner. The historical source I used most was Livy's *Early History of Rome* (Middlesex, England: Penguin Books, 1960).

9. Karl Heyer, *Beitrage zur Geschichte des Abendlandes: Von der Atlantis bis Rom*.

10. Livy, *The Early History of Rome*.

11. Steiner speaks of the "rights life" as part of a "Threefold Social Order" in *Towards Social Renewal* (Bristol, England: Rudolf Steiner Press, 1992), which is mentioned again at the end of this section on Roman history.

12. In *Theosophy* (Hudson, New York: Anthroposophic Press, 1994), Steiner describes the essential nature of the human being as consisting of several aspects or "bodies": the physical, the etheric, the astral, and the ego. As these terms are crucial for an understanding of Anthroposophy, I would like to describe them briefly:

   In his introduction to Steiner's *The Origins of Natural Science* (Spring Valley, New York: Anthroposophic Press, 1985), Owen Barfield states: "It is unfortunate that the word 'body' has become, for most people, almost synonymous with 'lump of solid matter'; particularly unfortunate, where it is the human body that is at issue, since nine-tenths of that is composed of fluids, and of fluids that are for the most part in motion. In Steiner's terminology, 'body' signifies something more like 'systematically organized unit or entity', as distinct from the matter or substance of which it is composed. Thus, the fact that the frame of a living human being contains, and not at random, fluid and air, as well as solid substance, entails the existence of other 'bodies' besides the physically organized one. These are especially relevant when the discourse turns from knowledge of quantity (measurement and mathematics) to knowledge of quality, an aspect of nature that is virtually a closed book to the science of today" .

The Physical: Steiner refers to the physical body of the human being as consisting of physical substance that can be perceived by the physical senses. The corpse—the part of us left on the earth after death—represents the physical body without the other members.

The Etheric: This body, also called the "life force," consists of that which promotes growth and gives structure to the physical body of the human being. The etheric body preserves the physical and prevents it from dissolving during earth life. The human being is connected to the mineral kingdom through the physical body and to the plant world through the etheric body.

The Astral: Through the astral body the human being becomes aware of sensations, instincts, impulses, and passions. The astral body helps us become conscious of our inner life, as well as of the meaning behind the sense impressions gleaned from the world around us. Animals also experience the world with the help of the astral body.

The Ego: According to Rudolf Steiner, the human being alone has an independent ego—that inner kernel of self to which we refer when we say "I." This ego is a "drop of the divine"—that part of us that finds an earthly home in the other bodies.

As I taught the early history of Rome, I worked with these aspects of the human being, described in the first chapter of *Theosophy*. Romulus, the founder of Rome, represents the physical body in all its strength, while Numa stands for the etheric, the life-engendering aspects of nature, religion, culture, and community. He received his inspirations from the nymph Egeria, and he often wandered for hours along the shores of the lakes and streams. Tullus Hostilius is a personification of the astral body, with all its passion and feeling, as well as its tendency to run wild unless checked by the rulership of the ego. It was the fourth king, Ancus, who brought organization and order to Rome, as does the ego for the human being.

The task of self-development, as described in Anthroposophy, is to enable the ego to gradually transform the "lower members" into higher capacities (see *Theosophy, How To Know Higher Worlds, Occult Science*). Part of the tragedy of Rome was that this upward movement did not occur; instead Rome descended into the self-centered pride of the last king.

13. Livy, *Early History of Rome*, 60.

14. See the above reference to the ego and to *Theosophy,* note 12.

15. Livy, *Early History of Rome*, 60.

16. Siegfried E. Finser, "The Last King," unpublished manuscript, 9. Also, Rudolf Steiner's *Christ and the Spiritual World* (London: Rudolf Steiner Press, 1963) has a marvelous section on the Sybils (36–42).

17. Finser, "The Last King," 15.

18. Finser, "The Last King," 18.

19. Steiner, See note 11 on the Three Fold Social Order.

20. Steiner, *Practical Advice to Teachers*, 120–21.

21. Manfred von Mackensen, *A Phenomena-Based Physics*, trans. John Petering (Boulder, Colorado: Denver Waldorf School, 1987), 8; Hermann Baravalle, *Introduction to Physics in the Waldorf Schools* (Englewood, New Jersey: Waldorf School Monographs, 1967), 5.

22. Steiner, *Balance in Teaching*, 35.

23. John Benians, *Insights into Child Development* (Spring Valley, New York: Mercury Press, 1990), 116.

24. In *From Symptom to Reality in Modern History*, and in numerous other places, Steiner makes repeated references to the age of the consciousness soul.

25. Betty and Franklin Kane, "Earth, Who Gives to Us...," *Education as an Art* 28:3 (Summer 1970):10. They describe teaching mineralogy in a more comprehensive way than mentioned in my text: "In sixth grade the mineral kingdom is taken up in the context of the earth as a living organism. The great forces, such as mountain building, erosion, volcanic action, and earthquakes, are studied. The change of rock from mountain top to sand on the beach, of limestone to marble, of thundering waterfalls to a heavily used, polluted river, of ancient fern forests to diamond—all of these are examples of the powerful forces working in this living earth. The kinds of soil that emerge where there is a predominance of one mineral, too much or too little water, good or poor aeration, and the quality of heat absorbed, bring in the importance of the elements. Here, as in the study of all the kingdoms, time is important. The time and conditions needed for a perfect crystal to form can be millions of years. The children learn to respect the time needed for a forest to grow or a valley to form of sediment.... In these middle-school years the feelings are stirred by dramatic presentations. Joy, sorrow, anxiety, relief are all experienced. If the feelings are not engaged, ecology is just an intellectual study."

26. Walter Johannes Stein, *Gold in History and in Modern Times and Labor in History and in Modern Times* (Spring Valley, New York: St. George Publications, 1986), 27.

CHAPTER 7

1. In his book *Educating the Adolescent: Discipline or Freedom* (Hudson, New York: Anthroposophic Press, 1988), Erich Gabert describes some further aspects of the developmental changes occurring in the early teens: "Every teenager becomes unpleasant at times, even impossible! Often he will break through the wall that sets him apart and will attach himself passionately to another person as he once used to, but he knows that this is only a temporary thing, that the essence of his childhood can never return. The agonizing detachment is truly final. And the young person has no way of knowing why he struggles so hard to be alone, struggles to stay apart, and struggles to prevent anything from disturbing his solitude....

    "A particular element of this inner life is the feeling that it is closed away in itself, so that anyone who tries to peer in must be repulsed. This produces the very delicate, subtle experience of shame that is characteristic of this age. Something like a protective shell holds and conceals what is beginning to grow within like a tender plant. This is the process Rudolf Steiner calls the 'birth of the astral soul-nature of the human being', it is the process of becoming an independent personality. It means the severing of the bonds that held the younger child in an unconscious relationship with his environment and with the people around him....

    "The forces of antipathy in adolescence, besides isolating his inner life in a kind of shell, have another highly significant effect on the young person. When he looks out over the newly built wall around his dwelling place—his 'self'—he sees the outside world in an entirely new light. Not only has he stepped back from the objects and persons outside, but he also finds that in doing this he can see them much more clearly than before... and is able to acquire the capacity of judgment. A future creative thinking is in preparation. This is its foundation" (9–11).

2. In one of his earliest essays on education, *The Education of the Child in the Light of Anthroposophy* (New York: Anthroposophic Press, 1965), Rudolf Steiner addresses these same themes: "With puberty the time has arrived when the human being is ripe for the formation of his own judgments about the things he has already learned" (45).

3. Fontaine Maury Belford, *The Uses of the Heart—Meditations on the Book of Common Prayer* (Union Institute, 1993), 48.

4. Barbara Tuchman, *Practicing History: Selected Essays* (New York: Knopf, 1981).

    In an article that appears in *Waldorf Schools: Upper Grades and High School*, William Bryant makes the connection between the use of biography and adolescence: "The path of isolation continues and deepens as they contract more and more into centric beings within their own self-awareness. Thus, the role of biography becomes ever more vital, to unite them with their humankind.... As the earthly physical development has reached a particular point, so the age of idealism and hero worship arises. The young people are deeply concerned with the nature of life and human values. Here then is the gift of the biography.

Men and women worthy of their esteem can speak to them from the past.... Biography possesses remedial qualities, too, for we can bring a great life to bear on the particular problems of a child. This can be related to and guided by the temperaments" (177–79).

5. In Volume One of *Conferences with the Teachers of the Waldorf School*, Rudolf Steiner made the following statements about avoiding dogma: "We do not want the Waldorf School to be a denominational school. The Waldorf School is not meant to be a denominational school for cramming the children with as many anthroposophical dogmas as possible.

We do not intend teaching anthroposophical dogmas but want to strive to put Anthroposophy into practice.

We want to transform what can be acquired anthroposophically and turn it into a real and proper method of education....

We must be conscious of the great tasks involved. We cannot be merely teachers, we shall have to be carriers of civilization to the greatest degree and in the best sense of the word. We must cultivate a living interest in everything that is going on at the present time. Otherwise we shall be bad teachers for this kind of school.... Interest for the world must be what gives us the enthusiasm we need both for school work and for our work. We shall need to have elasticity of spirit and devotion for our work" (35).

6. Ian Cameron, *Magellan* (New York: Saturday Review Press, 1973), 8–9.

7. Steiner, *Practical Advice to Teachers*, 154.

8. In lectures that Rudolf Steiner gave to the workmen at the Goetheanum in 1922 and 1923, currently published in two volumes under the title *Health and Illness* (Spring Valley, New York: Anthroposophic Press, 1983), he spoke at length about the effects of nicotine and alcohol on the body, as well as about health issues in general. In teaching the physiology block in seventh grade, in addition to conventional texts on nutrition, I used Rudolf Hauschka's *The Nature of Substance* (London: Rudolf Steiner Press, 1983) and Gerhard Schmidt's *The Dynamics of Nutrition* (Wyoming, Rhode Island: Biodynamic Literature, 1980) for an anthroposophical orientation to these issues.

9. In a lecture [given towards the end of World War I and currently published in *Aspects of Human Evolution* (Hudson, New York: Anthroposophic Press, 1987)] that focuses on the differences between Eastern

and Western Europe, Rudolf Steiner spoke about printing in a way that provoked my thoughts as I taught Wish, Wonder, and Surprise: "In the West we cling to what can be pinned down and put into print. We place the greatest store on what we can objectify by detaching it from the human being. To do so is regarded so highly that our libraries grow into gigantic monstrosities, immensely appreciated more particularly by those working on some branch of science. However, there is another reason why libraries are so appreciated: they keep in storage thoughts which have become divorced from their human source" (162–63).

10. Later in the block I mentioned that, because Arabic and Greek scientific books had been translated, beginning in the eleventh century, the change in thinking represented by Copernicus had already been penetrating European thought before 1543.

11. For this picture of Copernicus, I am indebted to Henry Barnes, of Hillsdale, New York, who tells this story far better than I.

12. Rudolf Steiner refers to the early astronomers many times. The sources I used included both the lecture of December 31, 1912, which appears in *Occult History* (London: Rudolf Steiner Press, 1957), and Chapter Five of *The Riddles of Philosophy* (Spring Valley, New York: Anthroposophic Press, 1973), in which Steiner states: "A transformation takes place in the organization of the human soul. In the field of philosophical life, this transformation becomes manifest through the fact that thought cannot now be felt as a perception, but as a product of self-consciousness.... It becomes apparent in the renaissance of art and science.... Just compare the state of the form of thinking about nature as it develops in Copernicus, Galileo, and Kepler with what has preceded them. This natural-scientific conception corresponds to the mood of the human soul at the beginning of the modern age in the sixteenth century" (70).

13. Once again, I am indebted to Henry Barnes for these citations.

14. The reader wishing to go further than this general description of "inner landscape" may look to Steiner's indications on the role of sleep in education, such as the following in *Man: Hieroglyph of the Universe* (London: Rudolf Steiner Press, 1972): "But if we rightly observe life, we cannot exclude the sleeping condition from human life as a whole. We instruct our children during the day. Out of all we bring to the child, much of it is not his at once, but becomes so only the next day, after the ego and astral body have passed through the night-condition; only then does the child duly receive what we have given him by day. We must always have this in mind and regulate our teaching and education accordingly" 146).

Thus the content of the day, including the biographies told in class, becomes part of the child's spiritual constitution while sleeping, so that the child in fact returns to the classroom changed. The responsibility placed on the teacher in the whole process is, of course, enormous.

15. Harry Walton, *The How and Why of Mechanical Movements* (New York: E. P. Dutton & Co., Popular Science Publishing Co., 1968), 25–38.

16. Ernst Lehrs, *Man or Matter* (London: Rudolf Steiner Press, 1958), 54.

17. Lehrs, *Man or Matter*, 54.

18. Michael Faraday, *Faraday's Chemical History of a Candle* was my main source for these explorations with the candle flame. The back of this book contains the actual experiments mentioned.

19. Hilaire Belloc, *Joan of Arc* (New York: The Declan X. McMullen Co., 1949), 31. I used *Joan of Arc* for my teaching as well as for the text in this narrative.

20. Belloc, *Joan of Arc*, 44–46.

21. Belloc, *Joan of Arc*, 61.

22. Belloc, *Joan of Arc*, 82–84. Rudolf Steiner referred to Joan of Arc in numerous lectures, including this one from *Occult History*: "What would the development of modern Europe have been if at the beginning of the fifteenth century the Maid of Orleans had not entered the arena of events? . . . Without the working of higher, supersensible Powers through the Maid of Orleans, the whole of France, indeed the whole of Europe in the 15th century, would have taken on an altogether different form. . . . You also know from ordinary history that it was she who, under the unceasing impulse and urge of her intense faith . . . and in face of the greatest difficulties, led the armies to victory and the King to his crowning. Who intervened at that time in the course of history? None other than Beings of the higher Hierarchies! The Maid of Orleans was an outer instrument of these Beings, and it was they who guided the deeds of history" (27–28).

Another reference: "I will not repeat here what can be read in history books. We can see in what a gentle, tender form, imbued with the noblest qualities of the human soul, the Sybylline power of the Maid of Orleans is revealed" (*Christ and the Spiritual World*, 120).

And another: "In Joan of Arc it is particularly interesting to see how this happened. Her inner being was opened, as it were. But it was not that part of her inner life which was bound to the physical body. It was the perception of her ethereal and astral being that was spiritually opened, so much so that we find in her case a true analogy to the events of Initiation" (*Anthroposophical Movement*, 391).

And another: "The cosmic Spirit guiding evolution needed in the Maid of Orleans a human soul who passed the last thirteen days of pregnancy up to the 6th of January in the body of the mother and was then born. Here we see deeply into the condition lying behind the scenes of existence. . . . A soul was born there who was initiated, so to say, by the Cosmic Spirit itself up to the time of her birth" ("The Christ-Impulse as Bearer of the Union of the Spiritual and the Bodily," typescript only, available from the Rudolf Steiner Library, RD2, Box 215, Ghent, NY 12075).

Finally, I would like to refer the reader to a marvelous pamphlet that helps when living with the biography of Joan, namely Steiner's *Faith, Love, Hope* (North Vancouver, Canada: Steiner Book Centre, n.d.).

CHAPTER 8

1. Hildegarde Dolson, *William Penn, Quaker Hero* (New York: Random House, 1961).

2. This Knowles poem was taken from my own eighth-grade anatomy main-lesson book, made when I was a student at the Green Meadow Waldorf School in the 1960s.

3. Jaimen McMillan is co-director of the School for Bothmer Gymnastics in Stuttgart (Germany) and director of Spatial Studies Institute, Inc., which offers conferences and workshops on the movement and spatial development of the child; its five-year In-Service Training Program certifies movement-education teachers and movement therapists for Waldorf schools and related institutions. For information, contact SSI, 423 County Route 71, Hillsdale, NY 12529.

4. This passage on the muscles and the will was taken from the text I composed and dictated for the students' main lesson books in 1989.

5. See L.F.C. Mees, *Secrets of the Skeleton* (Spring Valley, N.Y.: Anthroposophic Press, 1984).

6. Those readers who would like to read more on the senses are encouraged to take up *The Twelve Senses,* by Albert Soesman (Stroud, Gloucester: Hawthorn Press, 1992). Pages 82-94 are devoted to the eye. I also recommend Walther Buhler's book, *Living With Your Body* (London: Rudolf Steiner Press, 1979).

7. David Attenborough, *The Living Planet* (Boston: Little Brown and Co., 1984).

8. Henry Barnes, "Napoleon Bonaparte" (unpublished manuscript prepared for his master's thesis).

9. John Saxon, *Algebra 1/2: An Incremental Development* (Norman, OK: Saxon Publications, 1983).

10. Readers interested in the opinions of high school and college teachers who have taught Waldorf school graduates are invited to read *The Results of Waldorf Education,* prepared by the Kimberton Waldorf School (West Seven Stars Road, Kimberton, PA 19442).

11. The section on Ericsson was taken from *Captain John Ericsson: Father of the Monitor*, by Constance Buel Burnett (New York: Vanguard Press, 1960).

12. Burnett, 118–119.

13. William Neilson and Charles Hill, eds., *The Complete Plays of William Shakespeare* (Cambridge, Mass: Houghton Mifflin Co., 1942), 281.

14. Vance Johnson, *Heavens Tableland* (New York: Farrar, Strauss and Co, 1947) was the source for the entire section on the dust bowl.

15. *Heaven's Tableland*, 48.

16. *Heaven's Tableland*, 62.

17. *Heaven's Tableland*, 109.

18. *Heaven's Tableland*, 155-59.

19. Alan Bullock, *Hitler: A Study in Tyranny* (New York: Harper & Row Publishers, Perennial Library, 1971), 1-30.

20. Jacques Lusseyran, *And There Was Light*, 7.

21. Lusseyran, *And There Was Light*, 62-68

22. Bullock, *Hitler*, 55-56.

23. Albert Speer, *Inside the Third Reich* (New York: Macmillan Co., 1970), 88–94.

24. Lusseyran, *And There Was Light*, 134.

25. Lusseyran, *And There Was Light*, 242.

26. Rowe, Gmeyner, and Russell, *The Key of the Kingdom*, 81. Verse by Rudolf Steiner, translation by Arvia MacKaye Ege.

School as a Journey